**FROM THE RIO GRANDE TO THE ARCTIC**
**The Story of the Richfield Oil Corporation**

**University of Oklahoma Press : Norman**

# FROM THE RIO GRANDE TO THE ARCTIC  The Story of the Richfield Oil Corporation

## by CHARLES S. JONES

Foreword by ROBERT O. ANDERSON

International Standard Book Number: 0–8061–0976–9

Library of Congress Catalog Card Number: 70–160504

*To my wife, Jenny,*
*who had the strength and good humor to live through these events*
*with me for more than half a century and the patience to bear*
*with me when I sat down to write about them*

## FOREWORD

As someone who has urged another to write, I feel a particular identity with this book. After the merger of Atlantic Refining Company and Richfield Oil Corporation, I encouraged my good friend and colleague, Charles S. Jones, to write about an era in American industry in which he held a unique and active position. This book is much more than a book about the oil industry; it is a book about our country, and more particularly California, spanning more than half of this century.

Charlie Jones was a unique and strong character with a master's grasp of the worldwide nature of the petroleum industry. He also had a great understanding of his fellow man and the problems of contemporary society. His book is an authoritative account of a great industry and modestly demeans the author's major role therein.

As a close personal friend and one who fully knew and understood his wisdom and judgment in business and civic matters, I regret that in these pages so little is revealed of the personal attributes of a friend that I loved and admired so much. The reader should know that Charlie combined kindness with a happy sense of humor. He was the essence of integrity. Vigorous and rugged, at all times he was a man among men. A commanding figure, standing well over six and a half feet tall, he moved with the dignity of a great Indian chief. He even had the great regal nose to go with it. Peering out of a duck blind, that great beak would quiver with anticipation and eagerness. His eyes would light up with excitement on seeing an approaching flight of birds, and he would quietly slip into his seat, murmuring, "Mark."

Charlie loved the outdoors and was never happier than at his home in Baja, California, or on the ranch in Idaho. A lifelong conservationist, he had a library filled with books on every conceivable subject dealing with flora and fauna. In conversation, it was readily apparent that he had done more than merely purchase them. He could quote chapter and verse and knew every new writer in the field, as well as his personal background.

Charlie's inquisitive search for knowledge was that of the true scholar and extended into nearly every field of human endeavor. He believed that life should be lived to the fullest possible degree. In a day when specialists have become commonplace, he moved ahead as a great and knowledgeable generalist, watchfully aware of everything about him.

His friends were legion, and his more than passing interest in politics provided a wide acquaintanceship with many in political life. Presidents, statesmen, and diplomats were among his close friends. Republicans and Democrats alike respected his advice, and while a Republican himself, he served in various public capacities under both Democratic and Republican administrations. One of the young political hopefuls that Charlie helped in his early career was a young congressman from California named

*Charles S. Jones, 1965*

Richard M. Nixon. Upon Charlie's death on December 9, 1970, President Nixon wrote as follows:

> The productive life of Charles Jones combined the finest traditions of American business with the highest ideals of public service and civic achievement.
>
> His profound beliefs and ready ability to translate principles into action won him admiration and respect, not only in California but throughout the nation. His strength of character and soundness of judgment made him sought out by Presidents and leaders in every walk of life. He showed courage in his convictions, discretion in disagreements and selflessness in service to his country.
>
> I had the great privilege of having the benefit of his personal friendship and his wise counsel for all the years I have been in public life, win or lose. He was one of those rare individuals who made his friendship known even more openly when I lost than when I won.
>
> His courage and indomitable spirit during his last difficult illness was an inspiration to me and all others who had the privilege of seeing him in those days.
>
> It is perhaps trite to put it this way but, however you measure a man, Charlie Jones has to be rated as one of the greatest.

I happen to know both men, and the President's characterization of Charlie could only have come from his own hand—a tribute to a friend with whom he had seen much and under difficult circumstances.

President Eisenhower was an old bridge-playing crony of Charlie's and fellow hunter. Together with a few friends, the two would play cards into the small hours of the morning, talking about shooting days long gone or long to come.

A few years ago, Charlie and I were hunting in Mexico, and in the evening after a pleasant day of hunting, he recalled a favorite bit of poetry. As he rolled it out in his stentorian voice, a guitar across his knee, I realized that he was the essence of what he spoke:

> "A fighter's life is short at best
>    No time to waste
>    No time to rest
> The spotlight shifts
> The clock ticks fast
>    All youth becomes old age at last.

All fighters weaken
All fighters crack
All fighters go
And they never come back
Well—
　　So it goes
　　　Time hits the hardest blows."
JOSEPH MONCURE MARCH[1]

And so it was with Charlie. He worked and played hard, he fought to the end for what he believed in. He left behind a huge pair of shoes, a great heritage, and a host of true friends.

ROBERT O. ANDERSON

*Roswell, New Mexico*
*August 25, 1971*

[1] *The Set Up*, New York, Covici, Friede, Inc., 1928. Reprinted by permission of Crown Publishers, Inc., New York.

## PREFACE

THIS history is not intended to be a scholarly treatise or a statistical tome on Richfield Oil Corporation and its predecessors but rather a chronological account of the decisions and events, good and bad, which from my vantage point had an important bearing on the destiny of the company.

I was born in Bonham, Texas, on November 14, 1895. I attended the public schools of Bonham, went to work at an early age, and continued my education in business school at night. After the usual youthful dabbling in different jobs, I married a pretty girl named Genevieve Farnum in 1915 and began a career in public accounting in El Paso, Texas. A few years later I was appointed by Governor Pat M. Neff to the Texas State Board of Certified Public Accountants.

My interest in the oil industry began through business association with the Lockhart brothers and the Rio Grande Oil Company at the time of the Pershing expedition into Mexico. In 1918 I was elected to the Rio Grande Board of Directors. I moved to Los Angeles in 1923 and arranged for some major financing for Rio Grande in California which enabled the company to build a refinery there and move its general offices to Los Angeles. Soon afterward I left public accounting to become vice-president and treasurer of Rio Grande. In 1932, I was elected president of Rio Grande.

In March, 1937, when Rio Grande was merged with Richfield, I was elected president of the new Richfield Oil Corporation and, upon the death of W. Alton Jones (no relation) in 1962, succeeded him as chairman of the board. As one who spent more than fifty years in a management position in the oil industry, I believed that my account of the history of Richfield from its beginning was worth recording, and I was encouraged by Robert O. Anderson, the present chairman of the board of Atlantic Richfield Company, to undertake this project.

Owing to the paucity of recorded data pertaining to the early days, some parts of the history are not as lively as others—the early story of the United Oil Company, for instance. But I believe that the reader will find a moral in the contrast between the conservative beginnings of United and the wheeling and dealing and the navigational errors which finally floundered that good ship on the rocks. During the 1920's I knew most of the United-Richfield personalities, did business with them—and competed with them.

This account is based on careful research of records—and on my memory, which has also been carefully researched. Wherever possible, footnotes have been avoided, but the story has been reviewed by those still living who participated in it. Arthur Mills Lockhart, the sole surviving Lockhart brother, read the portion of the book that deals with the Rio Grande Oil Company. He was the company's New Mexico manager at the time of Pancho Villa's raid on Columbus, New Mexico, in 1916 and vividly remembers the raid, as well as the Ravel brothers.

The appendices present the historical record of the Richfield Oil Corporation, changes in directors and officers, financial statements, and other data which researchers may find helpful.

My lifetime has spanned a remarkable era in American industrial history. I was born before the first automobile was driven across the country, and I have lived to see the dawn of the space age. If there has ever been a time in my life when exciting opportunities for constructive endeavor were not legion, I do not now remember it.

I am deeply grateful to have been able to play a role in the oil industry during a dynamic half-century in its history.

CHARLES S. JONES

# ACKNOWLEDGMENTS

IN writing this book I have had the help of many people and organizations. First and foremost is Joseph A. ("Tommy") Thompson, who retired from the Atlantic Richfield Company in 1966, after forty-one years in management and supervisory positions in the accounting departments of three Richfield companies, beginning with Richfield Oil Company in 1925. Tommy conducted most of the historical research to reinforce my memory and to illuminate certain episodes with which I had only passing familiarity. With an accountant's professionalism he checked dates, names, figures, and other data to assure maximum accuracy, both in the text and in the appendices. Tommy was always resourceful in finding, analyzing, and selecting material and illustrations for consideration.

I am also indebted to E. B. Downey, assistant secretary-treasurer for both Rio Grande and Richfield Oil Corporation, who retired after thirty-five years of service. His research on the history of Rio Grande Oil Company was invaluable.

Remi Nadeau, an author and a former Richfield employee, provided important editorial assistance in preparing the manuscript for publication.

Arthur M. Lockhart, former vice-president and director of Rio Grande Oil Company and now owner of the Envoy Petroleum Company, Long Beach, California, was most accommodating in providing material and photographs and in reading that part of the manuscript concerning Rio Grande Oil Company.

Russell R. Palmer, writer and publisher of the *California Petroleum Register*, for many years editor of the former *Petroleum World*, and always a friend of Richfield, gave his enthusiastic assistance and made available his private library containing many early copies of the *Petroleum World*.

Also very helpful was Leo M. Metzler, assistant secretary, Western Oil and Gas Association, who placed at my disposal the Western Oil and Gas Association Library, with its many historical photographs and publications.

Thomas J. O'Sullivan, supervisor of reproduction, Administration Department, Atlantic Richfield Company, was exceptionally cooperative in reproducing copies and photographs of much historical material and many photographs.

The late Dudley M. Steele, Richfield's first manager of aviation and for many years a leader prominent in aviation circles, provided information about the early aviation history of Richfield and other companies and generously gave permission to me to use it. After leaving Richfield, he showed unabated zeal in winning recognition for Richfield's pioneer efforts in promoting aviation.

Harrison Chandler, president of Chandis Securities Company and retired president of Times Mirror Press, recalled for me the story of the tankship *Charles S. Jones*'s encounter with Japanese submarines en route to Australia during World War II.

I am also grateful to the following for special assistance or accommodation:

Erich W. Zimmermann, for permission to quote from his book, *Conservation in the Production of Petroleum*, published by Yale University Press.

The Los Angeles Public Library, for courteous and willing services, especially the Business and Economics, Newspaper, and History departments.

The *Los Angeles Times*, for giving access to the many files and books in its library.

The Columbus Development Board, Inc., for the use of photographs relating to Pancho Villa's raid on Columbus, New Mexico, in 1916.

Lockheed Aircraft Corporation, for the use of the photograph relating to Sir Hubert Wilkins' polar flight.

*Life Magazine*, for the use of photographs relating to the Japanese submarine attack on the Elwood Oil Field in 1942.

I would also like to mention Haldeen Braddy, professor of English in the University of Texas, whose authoritative histories of Pancho Villa's raid into New Mexico and General Pershing's expedition into Mexico against Villa provided useful background information for the chapters on Rio Grande Oil Company's role in those episodes.

Throughout the writing of this book I enjoyed the interest and encouragement of Robert O. Anderson, chairman of the board of Atlantic Richfield Company and almost countless others within the corporation.

Finally, I wish to thank the many retired and former employees of Richfield who contributed information and pictures for consideration. They made the history that I have tried to recapture between these covers.

CHARLES S. JONES

# CONTENTS

Foreword, by Robert O. Anderson               *Page*   vii
Preface                                                    xiii
Acknowledgments                            xvii

Part One    *The Legacy of Rio Grande*

1.   Pancho Villa Brings a Customer           3
2.   Fuel for Pershing's Wheels            13
3.   The Kaiser Provides a Market          17
4.   The Lockharts Move West             27
5.   Foray into Mexico                     34
6.   Rio Grande Looks for Oil              37
7.   The Elwood Field                    40

| | | |
|---|---|---|
| 8. | Elwood's Boom and Bust—A Case History | 48 |
| 9. | The Throes of Sudden Wealth | 52 |
| 10. | Enter Harry F. Sinclair | 58 |

Part Two    *The Heritage of Richfield*

| | | |
|---|---|---|
| 11. | The United Oil Company | 67 |
| 12. | Richfield's Beginning | 81 |
| 13. | The Eagle Takes Flight | 90 |
| 14. | The "Gasoline of Power" | 95 |
| 15. | Exit Colon Whittier | 118 |
| 16. | The Eagle Flies High | 129 |
| 17. | The Mills of the Gods Grind a Little Faster | 132 |
| 18. | The Move Eastward | 139 |
| 19. | The Eagle Falters | 144 |
| 20. | The Desperate Months | 148 |
| 21. | The Eagle Falls | 153 |
| 22. | Enter Henry Doherty | 156 |
| 23. | Harry F. Sinclair Takes a Hand | 163 |
| 24. | Richfield Reborn | 167 |

Part Three    *A Team of Eagles*

| | | |
|---|---|---|
| 25. | The Eagle on Its Feet | 177 |
| 26. | North Coles Levee | 189 |
| 27. | Tension at the Top | 199 |
| 28. | Of Ports and Railroads | 204 |
| 29. | "We *Had* 100-Octane!" | 207 |
| 30. | Battling the Japanese Navy | 210 |
| 31. | Battling the United States Navy | 224 |
| 32. | Richfield and Smog Control | 229 |
| 33. | The Retreat From Texas | 233 |
| 34. | The Rush to Cuyama | 239 |
| 35. | The Labor Strike of 1948 | 251 |
| 36. | Taming the Cuyama | 256 |
| 37. | The Egyptian Affair | 267 |
| 38. | The Conservation Crusade | 273 |

Part Four    *Joining the Giants*

| | | |
|---|---|---|
| 39. | North to Alaska | 283 |

| | | |
|---|---|---|
| 40. | The Suez Crisis | 291 |
| 41. | The Promise of Nuclear Recovery | 294 |
| 42. | Doubling in Gas | 299 |
| 43. | Justice Rears Its Head | 302 |
| 44. | The Merger with Atlantic | 308 |
| 45. | To the North Slope | 316 |
| 46. | "The Perils of Richfield" | 323 |
| 47. | The Biggest Bonanza | 327 |

Appendices

| | | |
|---|---|---|
| A. | The Richfield Family Tree | 334 |
| B. | Chronological Record of Richfield Oil Corporation and Its Predecessors | 336 |
| C. | Directors and Officers, 1937 and 1965 | 338 |
| D. | Changes in Directors and Officers, 1937–65 | 340 |
| E. | Net Income and Dividends Paid, 1937–65 | 343 |
| F. | Gross Crude-Oil Production and Reserves | 345 |
| G. | Consolidated Balance Sheets, 1937 and 1965 | 347 |
| H. | Income Account by Years, 1937–65 | 348 |
| I. | Cities Service's Stock Offer, 1931 | 350 |
| J. | Newspaper Articles, 1933, on Government Suit | 352 |
| Index | | 355 |

# ILLUSTRATIONS

Charles S. Jones                                                *Page*   ix
Lloyd E. Lockhart                                                         5
The Van Horn Trading Company                                              6
An early Rio Grande Oil Company tank truck                                7
The Ravel general store, Columbus, New Mexico                             9
General Pershing's troops loading supplies at Columbus                   11
Pershing's cavalry assembling at the Rio Grande                          14
A United States Army border-patrol biplane, 1916                         15
The Lockhart family                                                      19
The Lockhart brothers                                                    20
The executives of Rio Grande Oil Company, 1923                           22
Desdemona, Texas, 1919                                                   24
Rio Grande's first refinery at El Paso                                   25

Rio Grande's refinery at Phoenix, Arizona     28
The Rio Grande refinery at Vinvale, California     31
Rio Grande tank cars at Vinvale     33
Luton-Bell No. 1, the Elwood Field discovery well     45
Wharves lining the shore at Elwood Field     46
Tankers in the Santa Barbara Channel     47
Tidelands drilling at Elwood Field     50
Matthew C. Brush visiting the Elwood Field     55
Harry F. Sinclair     59
The trimotor Fokker, one of Rio Grande's first company planes     61
An early photograph of the Midway-Sunset Field     68
Colon F. Whittier     69
United's twenty-acre parcel in the Midway-Sunset Field     71
Signal Hill Field     74
The Hass lease on Signal Hill     77
James A. Talbot     79
Frederick Ranney Kellogg     82
Wooden derricks at the Maricopa Field     83
The original Los Angeles Oil & Refining Company     84
Richfield Station (later Atwood Station)     86
Clarence Mark Fuller     87
The first Richfield tank wagon     88
Richfield's Phoenix refinery at Bakersfield     91
Richfield's fifth delivery truck     92
A Richfield railroad tank car, vintage 1928     92
Ascot Speedway, Los Angeles     96
Roscoe Sarles     99
Jimmy Murphy     100
The national auto racing champions, 1921–32     101
Fred Frame and Harry Hartz     102
Richfield's sculptured racing car     103
"The Scroll of Racing Fame," 1921–32     104
Ralph Snoddy and *Miss Rioco*     105
Arthur C. Goebel     106
Refueling President Truman's plane, *The Independence*     106
A 1930 Richfield advertisement     107
Dudley M. Steele and Colonel Charles A. Lindbergh     108
Fueling an airplane with a hand pump     109
George Hubert Wilkins and Carl B. Eielson, 1928     110
A 1928 Richfield advertisement of victories in air races     111

The *Angeleno* being refueled in the air, 1929                    112
Two of Richfield's thirty-four beacon towers                      113
Richfield's beacon towers and stations                            114
The Richfield Building in Los Angeles                             115
The launching of the Transcontinental Air
      Transport, July, 1929                                       116
Five Richfield stations, 1920's to 1960's                         120
Richfield's storage depot and warehouse, Oakland, California      123
Richfield's tankship *Richfield*                                  124
The *Richfield*, bound for Oakland, California                    125
The self-propelled barge *Richlube*                               125
Richfield's refinery at Hynes, California                         126
Chart of manipulations of Richfield common stock, 1928–32         134
Edward L. Doheny                                                  136
Henry L. Doherty                                                  158
W. Alton Jones                                                    161
The first meeting of the Board of Directors of Richfield
      Oil Corporation, March 13, 1937                             172
The personnel in charge of Richfield's refinery at
      Watson, California                                          181
Richfield's exploration team, 1938                                184
Richfield's refinery at Watson upon completion                    187
The Richfield Eagles                                              188
Rollin P. Eckis                                                   191
Company executives turn out in force to watch drillers bring in
      Tupman-Western No. 1, at North Coles Levee, 1938            192
Members of Richfield's management at Tupman-Western No. 1         193
The operator of the A. M. Kelley Pump Station signaling to
      a pipeline patrol plane, 1938                               195
Richfield executives conferring at a Christmas-tree valve
      system at North Coles Levee                                 197
Six of Richfield's tankers requisitioned
      by the government in 1942                                   212
The Japanese submarine attack on Elwood Field                     215
Japanese shell damage at an Elwood rig                            216
Japanese shell damage on the Elwood pier                          217
The tanker *Charles S. Jones*                                     220
Russell No. 1, the discovery well at Cuyama Valley                245
Happy men after the discovery of oil on H. S. Russell's ranch
      in Cuyama Valley                                            246

Drilling in Cuyama Valley 247
Two views of Homan No. 81-35, the discovery well of South
    Cuyama Field 248
The first well on the Perkins lease in the South Cuyama Field 249
On hand to witness the discovery of oil on the Perkins lease 250
The main trunk line from San Joaquin Valley to the Watson
    refinery 260
Alaska's first commercial oil well, Richfield's Swanson River
    No. 1, on the Kenai Peninsula 286
Swanson River No. 23-3 289
Two Richfield tankships: *Cuyama Valley* and *Kenai Peninsula* 293
The Athabasca bituminous-sands region in Alberta, Canada 296
Miniature replica of Krupp's mining wheel 297
Pipeline from the Cuyama fields to Edison's Mandalay plant 301
Robert O. Anderson 311
Drilling equipment being loaded aboard a Lockheed
    Hercules C-130 320
The Hercules C-130 airfreighter supplying equipment for the
    Prudhoe Bay well 321
Anderson, Jones, and Eckis at the Prudhoe Bay Field 329
AIME Engineering Achievement Award presented to Rollin
    Eckis in 1969 330

## MAPS

Rio Grande Oil Company operations *Page* 56
Richfield's beacon lights on the Pacific Coast 114
Eastern Richfield distribution points 140
Cuyama Valley 242
Cuyama Valley development by Richfield Oil Corporation 258
Operations of Richfield Oil Corporation in Cuyama
    Valley, 1950 262

PART ONE
*The Legacy of Rio Grande*

# 1. PANCHO VILLA BRINGS A CUSTOMER

FROM its beginnings Richfield Oil Corporation had a way of getting involved in history. It was thus with one of its main predecessors, Rio Grande Oil Company, which was founded at El Paso, Texas, in October, 1915. In the same month the rebel Francisco ("Pancho") Villa was defeated by Mexican government forces under the command of General Plutarco Elías Calles at Agua Prieta, Sonora—an event that was to give Rio Grande its first big customer.

The incident began when President Woodrow Wilson permitted Mexican army reinforcements dispatched by General Álvaro Obregón to cross United States territory by rail from Eagle Pass and Laredo, Texas, to Douglas, Arizona, to join Calles. After

3

Villa's defeat at Agua Prieta, he swore that he would even the score with the gringos. Shooting became so common across the border that hotelkeepers advertised their establishments as bullet-proof. As a young accountant in El Paso, I saw bodies of American miners, who had been taken from their train in Mexico and massacred by Villa's men, brought into the railroad station stretched out on flatcars. Americans, reacting emotionally, invaded the Mexican quarter of El Paso and brought on martial law.

This was the setting in which Rio Grande was launched on the United States–Mexico border. It was a moment in time when the whole world was slipping near chaos. Since August, 1914, World War I had been tearing Europe apart. In czarist Russia a revolution was brewing that would shift the world's political balance. Nor did Europe confine its troubles: German submarines swarmed the Atlantic to attack British and French shipping. The *Lusitania* had been torpedoed with the loss of American and British lives. Despite public outcries President Wilson was keeping the nation out of war, but the trend was ominous.

From the Mexican border to the Atlantic it was also a time when petroleum was coming into its own as a motive fuel. In civilian life, if not in military, the truck was replacing the wagon, the auto was succeeding the horse. Employed for heat, light, and factory power since the discovery of "rock oil" in Pennsylvania in 1859, petroleum products were now entering an undreamed-of era when they would power a world on wheels.

On hand to supply this need were new turn-of-the-century oil discoveries in Texas and Oklahoma. New companies were springing up to discover, refine, or market petroleum products. Whole sections of the country—particularly the West—were still without gas stations or even wholesale bulk plants. The opportunity was limitless.

Among those to seize it was Lloyd Earnest Lockhart, a native of the black-earth country of Central Texas. He was born at Rockdale, in Bell County, on February 5, 1881—the first of six sons. His father, Charles H. Lockhart, had been born in Pennsylvania and had had some experience in the oil industry before moving to Texas.

4

*Lloyd E. Lockhart, about 1922*

*The Van Horn Trading Company, Lloyd Lockhart's general store at Van Horn, Texas, 1915*

After starting business in Rockdale with a general store, Lloyd was attracted to the oil boom in Oklahoma and opened a store in the Kiefer Field, in the Glenn Pool area. Moving again, he settled in Van Horn, in West Texas, where he opened another general store, the Van Horn Trading Company.

In the meantime he had become a salesman for the Waters-Pierce Oil Company and had learned petroleum marketing. He had long wanted to enter the oil business, and he saw the oil potential in the world of 1915. In that year the Texas Company built a new bulk plant in El Paso, abandoning its original plant in the same town. Upon hearing this news, Lockhart caught a train to El Paso with borrowed capital—about $2,500—intending to buy the old plant and operate it. In his mind he planned the beginnings of a new oil company in the Southwest.

*An early Rio Grande tank truck, El Paso, 1916*

When the train pulled into the station at El Paso, Lockhart was slow to get off. He was looking out the car window at the Rio Grande—a bigger, if muddier, river than its headwaters in Colorado, where he had hunted and fished. Lockhart decided that its name was suitable for his own enterprise—the Rio Grande Oil Company.

With that decision made, he left the train, looked up the Texas Company offices, and bought the old bulk plant for $6,500, using most of his grubstake—$2,000—as the down payment. Lloyd Lockhart, impressionable, decisive to the point of impulsiveness, had an eye to the main chance.

Quickly Lockhart got in touch with one of his younger brothers, Arthur Mills Lockhart. "Come to El Paso," Lloyd urged, "and help start this new company!" Arthur came, and the two established their business in a small office at the corner of Kansas and Seventh

7

streets. To make deliveries from their bulk plant, they bought a chain-drive Ford delivery truck and equipped it with a three-compartment, 202-gallon tank. The first motor-drawn oil tank truck in El Paso, it was laughed at by competitors, who were still using horse-drawn wagons. The Lockharts housed it in a small converted warehouse, and with three employees they were ready for business.

On October 25 the Rio Grande Oil Company began advertising "kerosene, gasoline, lubricating oils, cup greases," and other products and invited the accounts of "dealers throughout West Texas, New Mexico, and Arizona." Opening his plant on November 1, Lloyd Lockhart moved quickly to expand the business. Among his first agents were two of the Ravel brothers, Sam and Louis. For six years the Ravel family had owned a general store at Columbus, New Mexico, about fifty miles west of El Paso. They also owned the main hotel and had an interest in the bank. They were among the leading citizens of Columbus.

In this sleepy town of several hundred Americans, the Ravel store looked pretty much like all the rest: a false front, a wooden awning over the sidewalk, and big front windows through which one could see dry goods, hardware, ladies' garments—everything from pot-bellied stoves to lightning rods. The Ravels even traded in animal hides—deer, cow, and goat—brought in by local hunters and stockmen. After Lockhart visited them, they also began handling Rio Grande's products.

Early in March, 1916, less than three miles south of Columbus, across the border in Mexico, Pancho Villa gathered about five hundred men. Now he would even the score with the Americans for helping Mexican government forces defeat him at Agua Prieta. Probably he chose Columbus for his target because it was the home of the Thirteenth Cavalry Regiment, garrisoned south of the El Paso & Southwestern Railway tracks that split the town. Pancho intended to sack Columbus and make off with arms and ammunition, including the few early-type French machine guns that equipped the Thirteenth Cavalry.

Well before dawn on March 9, 1916, Villa and his men, leaving their horses in Mexico, moved silently through the mesquite and

*The Ravel general store, Columbus, New Mexico, 1916. Courtesy Columbus Development Board, Inc.*

cacti. At 4:20 A.M. they opened fire on the army sentries and charged the town, shouting, "Viva Villa!"

Caught off guard, the garrison scrambled to the defense. But the Villistas had the advantage of surprise and overran the town. They broke into stores, homes, and Ravel's Commercial Hotel, routing their victims. They ripped rings from the women's fingers and took the men outside and shot them in the street. They knew of Sam Ravel and burst into his room at the hotel. But Sam was in El Paso, and in his place the bandits seized his brother Arthur, who was about seventeen. Despite the pleadings of the women in the hotel, they took him and W. T. Ritchie, the hotel manager, downstairs to a Villista mob milling in the street. There they shot and killed Ritchie and then turned to Arthur.

9

"Wait, don't kill him yet!" one of the bandits shouted in Spanish, which the boy understood.

"What shall we do with him?"

"Take him down to the store and let him open the bank, and then do with him whatever you please."

Two Mexicans—one on each side—took Arthur up the main street toward the Ravel store. Fighting was at its height, and shots were crisscrossing the street. One of the two bandits fell at Arthur's side.

"Don't get scared," the other told the boy. "We will get to the bank yet."

Arthur, not convinced, managed to croak, "All right." They had gone but a few more steps when the other bandit was shot. Left alone, Arthur lost no time darting off the street. Later he recalled that he ran for three miles.

By this time the Villistas had broken into the Ravel store. They searched feverishly for Sam Ravel, possibly to force him to open the bank and its vault. Sam's brother Louis, awakened in his bed at the back of the store, slid under a pile of animal hides. There he watched as they scattered through the store, probing every pile. They did not find him, but they left with a huge load of Rio Grande kerosene. They poured it on the buildings of Columbus and put them to the torch. That proved a mistake, for it broke the darkness, lighting up the main street and silhouetting the Mexicans. The American soldiers concentrated their fire on the clear targets and turned the attack.

Though Villa sacked Columbus, he failed to capture it. At 6:30, just at dawn, his bugler called the retreat. The cavalrymen, with the advantage of horses, pursued them out of town and across the border, killing at least seventy-five in Mexico before returning to Columbus.

They found the town a shambles, the main street littered with bodies, the survivors moaning their losses. Dead were 8 American soldiers and 10 civilians; 6 soldiers and 2 civilians were wounded.[1] Villa had left behind 215 of his 500 men. Their bodies were hauled

1 Haldeen Braddy, "Pancho Villa at Columbus," *Monograph* 9, Spring, 1965, El Paso, Texas Western Press.

10

*General Pershing's troops loading supplies at Columbus for the expedition into Mexico in pursuit of Pancho Villa. Courtesy Columbus Development Board, Inc.*

out of town and piled together on the desert. Rio Grande oil proved an effective fuel for cremation.

Rio Grande products played a more constructive role in the sequel to Villa's raid on Columbus. Within hours President Wilson decided to send a punitive expedition into Mexico against Villa. The Mexican government agreed but forbade the Americans to enter Mexican towns or use Mexican railroads. Thus, while the expedition would be a cavalry operation, it would be supplied and reinforced with some six hundred trucks—1½-ton Whites and 3-ton, 4-wheel-drive Jeffery Quads—purchased especially for the expedition. To carry supply officers and perform other tasks, 75 automobiles—mostly Hupmobiles and Dodge touring cars—were added. Supplying this contingent on the route south from Columbus were 57 motor tank trucks hauling water, gasoline, and oil. Altogether, Uncle Sam spent more than $2 million to put the motorized column on the road.

Quick to seize this new opportunity, Lockhart secured the largest contract to supply the army's petroleum needs. He built new and bigger facilities at Columbus, the staging point for the expedition, and began shipping in oil and gas by the carload from El Paso and from North Texas and Oklahoma refineries. He was joined by hundreds of others, who rushed in to participate in the Columbus boom. Almost overnight the town rose from ashes, frame walls replaced with brick ones. On the site of their burned Commercial Hotel the Ravels built the new and larger International.

So it was that Pancho Villa gave Rio Grande its first big customer. Establishing a pattern that would be followed again and again, Richfield's predecessor was already in the thick of history.

## 2. FUEL FOR PERSHING'S WHEELS

CHOSEN to command the punitive expedition into Mexico was Brigadier General John J. ("Blackjack") Pershing, a hero of the Spanish-American War and the Philippine insurrection. Since 1914 he had been commander of two infantry regiments at Fort Bliss, near El Paso, part of the border army strengthened to meet the threat of Mexican insurrectionists. Pershing had once been host to Pancho Villa himself during a dress parade at Fort Bliss— staged specifically to overawe the Mexican leader.

To take advantage of the hot-pursuit rule of international law and of the agreement with the Mexican government, Pershing mounted his campaign to pursue Villa into Mexico with astounding speed. Taking command two days after Villa's raid on Colum-

13

*Pershing's cavalry assembling at the Rio Grande, 1916. U.S. War Department, General Staff Photo, National Archives.*

bus, he led his column across the border five days later, on March 16, 1916. As his men rode south, they found mementos of the raid along the way. Stolen Rio Grande oil drums were scattered alongside the trail. Some had served as water barrels; others, with ends knocked out, as culverts in irrigation ditches; still others, halved lengthwise, as bathtubs.

When Pershing crossed the border, he rode horseback. An old cavalryman, he would have ridden down the whole state of Chihuahua, but he quickly realized that he needed more mobility to maintain contact with all the elements of his command. He commandeered four Dodge touring cars for himself and his staff and began moving southward as fast as Rio Grande gasoline and tank trucks could supply him. With Pershing went correspondents Robert Dunn from the *New York Tribune* and Floyd Gibbons of the *Chicago Tribune*, who pooled their funds to obtain a Model T Ford. "You can sign for gasoline," Pershing told them. The Asso-

*A United States Army border-patrol biplane being serviced with Rio Grande's "Speedene" gasoline, El Paso, 1916*

ciated Press started out with a Hudson, which broke an axle in an irrigation flume after the first eight miles, leaving the news gathering to passengers in the *"Tribune*'s armored car."

Roads were dirt or nonexistent. What roads there were became so rutted from the heavy traffic that in level spots the cars and trucks fanned out as much as half a mile to avoid the ruts. When it rained, every wheel stopped until the sun came out and dried the earth. Despite all obstacles, however, the trucks averaged more than 60 miles a day at a cost of about 70 cents a ton-mile—a figure considered favorable in 1916.

Dumps were established along the route to supply the trucks. Other gas bases were created to feed the "First Aero Squadron" of eight rickety biplanes that served as Signal Corps messengers. Aviation gasoline was still unknown, and the Rio Grande "Speedene" gasoline that went into the trucks powered the flying machines.

From an original contingent of 10,000 men Pershing's expedition had grown to a force of 15,000. The motorized force required about 60 tons of fuel a day—a large part of it supplied by the Rio Grande Oil Company.

Though Pershing failed to capture Villa, he encountered some of the outlaw's forces in several skirmishes and weakened Villa's strength in northern Mexico before the expedition was recalled in 1917. Probing 300 miles into Mexico—almost the entire length

15

of Chihuahua, Mexico's largest state—Pershing hammered out a fighting force on the anvil of hardship, exposed many of the army's shortcomings, proved the value of motor transport even under the worst conditions, and brought forth swift improvements that helped prepare the armed forces for participation in World War I. Incidentally, but importantly, he provided unexpected business for a struggling new oil company.

## 3. THE KAISER PROVIDES A MARKET

WHEN Blackjack Pershing returned to El Paso in February, 1917, he was greeted with a parade, a formal banquet, and the gift of a silver service. I was present when the Toltec Club, the leading men's social organization in El Paso, honored Pershing with a special fried-chicken breakfast. No effort was spared to please the general, whom most of the members regarded with awe. Sensing their formality, Blackjack broke the ice when he rose to speak.

"For nearly a year in Mexico," he began, "I ate nothing but beans, hardtack, and alkali. Everywhere I've been invited since, I've had nothing but fried chicken. What I want to know is, where in hell can a man get some ham and eggs for breakfast?" Needless to say, he brought down the house and won the gratitude of the

17

men of El Paso. Before the applause died down, he got what he wanted for breakfast, and Tom Lea, the mayor of El Paso (and the father of the artist Tom Lea), served it to him.

In the same month that Pershing returned from Mexico, the Kaiser began unrestricted submarine warfare—and incidentally handed Rio Grande Oil Company a wartime market. Within two months the United States was at war, and within three months Pershing was on his way to France as commander of the American Expeditionary Force. Lloyd Lockhart soon had his hands full supplying the growing number of army trucks and automobiles at Fort Bliss and elsewhere along the border in Texas and New Mexico.

When President Wilson sent Pershing into Mexico, he also deployed 150,000 regular troops and national guardsmen near the border to forestall further Mexican raids. When the United States entered World War I, Fort Bliss and other southwestern army bases became training and staging camps for the fighting forces, and a large cantonment was established at Deming, New Mexico. By 1919 army airplanes were patrolling the border, using Rio Grande fuel, improved in quality and colored red to identify it as "aviation" fuel.

Lloyd Lockhart found himself with more business than he could handle with his existing organization. Earlier, on January 11, 1916, he had incorporated Rio Grande in Texas with a capital of $20,000. His original directors were, besides himself, C. Ligon, a brother-in-law; J. Y. Canon, a friend and cattleman; Dan M. Jackson, his lawyer; and J. M. Daugherty, his father-in-law, who had endorsed Lloyd's note for his initial credit in starting the company.

Soon afterward Lloyd began bringing his other brothers into the business. In 1917, Herman L. Lockhart, two years younger than Lloyd, joined the company to operate a new service station at Deming. Herman soon became first vice-president of Rio Grande. Arthur Lockhart, second-youngest of the six brothers, who had been with Lloyd from the beginning, left the company to serve in the American Expeditionary Force but returned in 1919 to become second vice-president. In 1918, Leslie Marion Lock-

18

*The Lockhart family. Top row, left to right: Herman L. Lockhart, Mrs. Frank H. Pierce (a sister), Arthur M. Lockhart. Center row, left to right: Lloyd E. Lockhart, the founder of Rio Grande Oil Company, and Charles H. Lockhart (the father). Bottom row, left to right: Cecil H. Lockhart, Leslie Marion Lockhart, and Lynn L. Lockhart. From* National Petroleum News, *1922.*

19

*The Lockhart brothers. Left to right: Lynn, Leslie, Cecil, Arthur, Lloyd, and Herman.*

hart, the third-youngest brother, sold his dry-goods business in Chicago and transferred his capital and his talents to Rio Grande as the company's secretary. Lynn L. Lockhart, the youngest brother, returned from the war and joined the company in 1919. Finally, Cecil H. Lockhart, the third-oldest brother, became Rio Grande's agent at Las Cruces, New Mexico, in 1920. Such family cooperation and loyalty were a hallmark of the Lockharts. They worked hard and well together, and when one had a problem they all joined forces to solve it.

By 1917, Rio Grande was beset by the auditing, tax, and financial problems typical of a growing young company. At the time

20

I was a public accountant in El Paso, and I was called in to recommend new business and financial methods. I became a director of Rio Grande in 1918 and in 1923 gave up public practice and joined Rio Grande on a full-time basis as vice-president and treasurer.

As early as 1916, Lockhart had negotiated contracts with refineries in the so-called Group Three Area—southern Oklahoma and North Texas. Since these refineries had few outlets west of Fort Worth, Lloyd had little competition and an adequate supply of products. But with the military buildup of 1916 and 1917 the market soon exceeded his supplies. Potential relief came in 1918 with the discovery of the Ranger and Desdemona fields. This was the beginning of a continual discovery pattern of oil fields west of Fort Worth.

Oil from these fields had to be shipped east to be refined and then shipped back west to Rio Grande's market. The freight rate on refined products from North Texas to El Paso was about $1.62 a barrel, while the crude-oil rate from West Texas to El Paso was $.90 a barrel, a favorable difference of $.72 a barrel. Lockhart knew that, with a refinery at El Paso, he could meet his growing market demands at a competitive price. He also knew that he could build gathering lines from the new oil fields to the railroad and gain substantial revenue for this service.

To build and finance the new refinery, the Lockharts began increasing their capital. In 1918 the company charter was amended, and the capital stock was increased from $20,000 to $100,000. The capitalization was raised again to $200,000 in February, 1919, and to $750,000 in October of the same year. For the first time outside capital was included: $200,000 from El Paso bankers who had become interested in the company's future.

During World War I, Rio Grande needed considerable bank credit to finance its deliveries to the army. The government had a habit of waiting an inordinate time to pay its bills. At one point when Rio Grande had reached its bank-credit limit but needed more money immediately, I discussed the matter with Winchester Cooley and T. M. Wingo, the chief officers of the Rio Grande Valley Bank & Trust Company, our principal bankers, explaining

21

*The executives of Rio Grande Oil Company gathered in front of the*
*El Paso office, 1923. Left to right: Lloyd Lockhart, Arthur Lockhart,*
*R. W. Millar, Leslie Lockhart, Charles S. Jones, Lynn Lockhart,*
*Fletcher Etheridge, and Frank Morgan.*

23

*Desdemona, Texas, in 1919, a rough-and-tumble West Texas oil camp nicknamed "Hog Town"*

to them how slow the government was in its payments and how much it owed us. The bankers, somewhat annoyed, questioned the amount. I suggested that one of them call the depot quartermaster at Fort Bliss. Wingo did so, and the quartermaster gave him a figure half again as much as the amount I had claimed the army owed Rio Grande. From then on our relationship with the bank was a very warm one.

The new 1,000-barrel refinery, designed to fit the local market, was situated near the Rio Grande, adjoining Chamizal (a long-disputed piece of real estate later returned to Mexico). It was the first refinery between Cisco, Texas, and Los Angeles, California.

With the $750,000 capitalization of 1919, we were soon able

24

*Rio Grande Oil Company's first refinery, built in 1918 along the Rio Grande at El Paso*

to double the refinery capacity to 2,000 barrels a day. The refinery was profitable from the beginning and continued to prosper for many years until major companies producing in the ever-advancing West Texas oil fields extended their pipelines and built large refineries at El Paso.

Unlike many companies, which began as oil producers and moved into refining and then marketing, Rio Grande started at the other end. The Lockharts began selling other refiners' oil products just in time to win Pershing's expedition as a major, if temporary, customer. Then, to meet the demands of Uncle Sam's mobilizing army in World War I, they took the next step into refining. The Kaiser had handed Lloyd Lockhart a military market large enough to enable Rio Grande to become a real force in southwestern oil.

25

By 1919 the fighting in Europe was over, but in that year Rio Grande's young refinery received its own baptism of fire. On the evening of June 14 a Mexican rebel army—composed mostly of Pancho Villa's men—attacked the border town of Juárez, across the Rio Grande from El Paso. The rebels captured most of the city that night but fell to such reveling that they were easy prey to a government counterattack the next morning. Falling back to the Juárez racetrack, the rebels fired all day at the city.

The action was visible from rooftops in El Paso. Stray bullets sped across the river, striking buildings and wounding six Americans. At the Rio Grande refinery, situated alongside the river, several bullets struck oil tanks. Rio Grande's employees climbed atop a nearby school building to get a better look. A bullet chipped a brick on a chimney not six inches from one of the spectators. The next moment all of them were scrambling down again. The refinery closed down on June 15, and the employees took cover.

Late on the same day American troops—a battalion of infantry, two regiments of cavalry, and a battalion of artillery—jogged across the border to stop the Villistas from firing into El Paso. Laying down a barrage on the rebels at the racetrack, they sent them retreating southward. Within twenty-four hours the Americans were back on United States soil.

It was Pancho Villa's last battle. Assassinated four years later, he probably never knew that he was indirectly a benefactor to Rio Grande Oil Company.

26

# 4. THE LOCKHARTS MOVE WEST

BY 1920, Rio Grande's El Paso refinery was supplying products to all but one of the major competitors in the El Paso market area. While the competitors' advertisements made claims of superior quality, all of the gasoline came out of the same Rio Grande tanks.

With an unchallenged position on their home ground, the Lockharts decided that it was time for expansion. This time they moved westward to the Pacific Coast. The first step was Arizona, which at that time was being supplied principally from Texas and Oklahoma by tank car on the Texas & Pacific, Southern Pacific, and Santa Fe railroads. Much oil was being produced in California, but that state was growing so fast that it needed all its own products

27

*Rio Grande's refinery at Phoenix, Arizona, 1922*

29

and more, and the industry was reluctant to ship products to Arizona. Only two major companies, Standard Oil Company of California and Union Oil Company of California, were operating in Arizona. They were not truly competitive in their prices because of the shortage of oil products at their source in California. In 1920, Rio Grande opened a wholesale distributing plant in Phoenix, managed by Lynn Lockhart, and quickly gained a strong number-two position in the important Arizona market.

When Rio Grande began marketing in Arizona, the difference between the tank-wagon and the tank-car prices of gasoline was 12 cents a gallon (today there is no differential—the prices are the same). Again Lloyd Lockhart realized that a refinery was the answer. In 1922, Rio Grande built a small 500-barrel plant in Phoenix, the first refinery in Arizona. The first raw material for the refinery was petroleum tops—a combination of gasoline, kerosene, naphtha, and so on, distilled from crude oil—and was purchased from Richfield Oil Company and shipped from California. This was Rio Grande's initial contact with Richfield, which was then managed by Fred R. Kellogg and Gilbert J. Symington. Soon we were also buying crude oil from Continental Oil Company and from Ohio Oil Company, now the Marathon Oil Company, which had discovered a new field in Lea County, New Mexico. Some of the oil was shipped to the El Paso refinery, and some to the Phoenix plant. We were also buying Continental's very-high-gravity oil from the small Rattlesnake Dome Field in Farmington, New Mexico. Rio Grande's Phoenix plant continued to be profitable until 1929, when again the movement of West Texas oil westward pushed the price structure so low that the refinery operation became uneconomical.

Even while it was planting the flag in Arizona, Rio Grande was marching on to California. The world's oil products were in short supply in 1920, and in California, which had been an important oil producer since the 1880's, gasoline was rationed. Automobile owners were issued cards entitling them to three gallons a week—an open invitation to Texas oil. Quickly Lloyd Lockhart sent fifteen railway tank cars of gasoline over the Southern Pacific from El Paso to Vernon, California, at a price of 32.5 cents a gallon (in

*The Rio Grande refinery at Vinvale, California, opened in 1923*

those days there was no tax on gasoline)—a more than competitive price in oil-short California.

Rio Grande's advantage could hardly last, for at this same time the geography of world oil changed rather suddenly and dramatically in favor of California. Between 1919 and 1921 great new discoveries were made at Santa Fe Springs, Huntington Beach, and Signal Hill, all in southern California. Standard of California had been building a fleet of tankers to import oil into California, but instead the maiden voyage of the first tanker carried a cargo of oil from California to the Atlantic seaboard. By 1923, California was producing one-fourth of the world's oil. Local prices tumbled below Lockhart's shipped-in product, and even Arizona became the trade territory of California instead of Texas.

31

In this situation Rio Grande began looking at California as a possible new base of operations. In June, 1922, I went to Los Angeles to scout the situation for the Lockharts. On the basis of these firsthand observations the decision was made: move to California.

Purchasing one hundred acres near Downey, California, in 1923, Rio Grande began building its new Vinvale refinery. For its crude supply it built a pipeline five miles to the booming field at Santa Fe Springs and contracted to purchase J. Paul Getty's oil; later it built an extension to tap Signal Hill. I undertook to raise money for these developments, but I quickly found that Los Angeles bankers were cool to independent oilmen, who were regarded as fly-by-night gamblers. It was not even possible to borrow money on proven production.

Rebuffed in this quarter, we turned to more equity financing. The capital was increased to $1.5 million in March, 1923, and again to $3 million in April, 1924. The corporation commissioner of California gave approval for 18,000 shares, which raised approximately $1.8 million. Owing to the glut of speculative oil stocks on the market, new issues were difficult to sell in those days, but we made a favorable contract with William H. Daum & Company, which successfully sold the shares. Rio Grande was listed on the Los Angeles Stock Exchange in June, 1923.

After the Vinvale refinery began making its first test runs in November, 1923, the Lockharts could compete with local manufacturers' prices. Throughout the 1920's the Vinvale plant was expanded with the widening market the Lockharts developed in the nation's fastest-growing state. And they had an almost unlimited supply of local crude oil from two of California's largest oil fields.

In June, 1923, Rio Grande solidified its position in California by moving its headquarters from El Paso to Los Angeles. In eight years the company had grown from a one-truck, five-man operation (including Lloyd and Arthur Lockhart) in the desert Southwest to a three-refinery, four-state enterprise and from a capitalization of $2,500 to $3 million.

But it was a long way from the banks of the Rio Grande to what

*Rio Grande tank cars at the loading rack at the Vinvale refinery*

was, in the 1920's, the oil capital of the West. The days of Pancho Villa were long gone, but doing business in the rough-and-tumble oil industry of Los Angeles proved just as hectic and a lot more complicated.

## 5. FORAY INTO MEXICO

AFTER moving to California, Rio Grande launched its first and only venture into Mexico. In 1926 the company completed a small topping plant below the border in Nogales, Sonora, mainly to produce kerosene for the lamps and stoves of Mexico.

According to the license from the Mexican government, the products would be classified *productos nativos* ("native products"), subject only to the 5 per cent consular fees. At that time Mexico maintained an import duty on kerosene of 20 cents a gallon in gold. This duty afforded adequate protection for Rio Grande's comparatively high costs in operating a small plant.

The company established agencies at Guaymas, Navojoa, Los Mochis, Culiacán, and Mazatlán. It was impractical to expand

34

farther south, for, while the Southern Pacific Company was building a railroad line from Mazatlán to Guadalajara for a connection with National Railways of Mexico, construction was unfinished beyond Tepic.

From the beginning the business prospered. Within six months almost all of the plant's capacity was being marketed. Rio Grande began thinking of expanding and decided that it would be wise to find a leading Mexican citizen who would associate himself with the project. It was decided to ask Álvaro Obregón to become general agent for the west coast of Mexico. A retired army general and former president of Mexico, Obregón was a veteran of the revolutions and counterrevolutions that had rocked his country since 1910.

Enthusiastic about the prospects of this interesting venture, I visited the general at his beautiful west-coast ranch at Ciudad Obregón, Sonora. The general treated me with generous Latin hospitality, and no business was discussed on the evening I arrived. The next morning we rose with the sun for a drive around his ranch. The place was a beehive—workmen were digging ditches, drilling holes for fences, planting castor-bean plants, and otherwise improving his huge property.

It was during this tour that we discussed the business at hand. General Obregón was receptive to the offer, and we concluded an agreement in principle. He would act as Rio Grande's general agent in return for a commission of one cent a gallon on kerosene and gasoline and 10 per cent of the market value of lubricating oils.

The proposed contract was referred to our respective lawyers. When it was completed, it was signed by Rio Grande and sent to General Obregón for his signature. Considerable time passed without word from him. I decided to visit him again at Ciudad Obregón and remain until I had obtained his signature.

One morning not long before my scheduled departure, I opened a Los Angeles newspaper and read that General Obregón had just signed an agreement with Standard Oil Company of California to be its general agent for the entire Republic of Mexico. Jim Douglas, Standard's manager in El Paso, had learned of our activities and had also visited Obregón. In making his arrangement with the general, he had used almost the exact wording of our proposed contract, except that Standard Oil of California was substituted for Rio Grande and the agency territory was enlarged from the west coast of Mexico to include the entire country.

At that moment Rio Grande knew that all its Mexican investments were worthless. The only question was whether Standard would build one or more refineries in Mexico to manufacture the products there or whether the Mexican government would rescind the import duty, thus enabling Standard to make the shipments directly to Mexico from its California refineries.

The answer was not long in coming. About ten days later the import duties were rescinded. Of course, there was nothing left for Rio Grande to do but salvage what it could out of the Mexican venture, and as quickly as possible. That was accomplished by selling the plant and the plant site in Nogales to Standard Oil Company for construction of its bulk plant.

Rio Grande had learned something about investing where political protection may be withdrawn without notice. The vagaries of Mexican politics were further emphasized some months later, on July 17, 1928, when Obregón was assassinated soon after having been re-elected president of Mexico.

# 6. RIO GRANDE LOOKS FOR OIL

THE Mexican venture was, of course, a relatively small incident in Rio Grande's headlong expansion during the mid-1920's. Successfully established in marketing and refining from Texas to California, the Lockharts next turned to oil production. They meant to build a fully integrated company with its own source of products.

Accordingly, in 1924, Rio Grande employed Eric A. Starke, a practicing geologist, to advise the company about possible production acquisitions and leasing and drilling opportunities in California. Later, on March 23, 1925, a wholly owned subsidiary named Lockhart & Company was organized to explore for oil, primarily in Texas. Several discoveries were made in Texas in 1925: none were of magnitude, but collectively they were profit-

37

able. They included strikes in Loving, Howard, and Glasscock counties. Some of these fields were sold in 1928 to raise needed additional capital.

In 1925, following Starke's advice, Rio Grande began acquiring production and leases in California. It purchased from W. R. Ramsey the Reservoir Hill Gasoline Company and a group of leases in Signal Hill, known as the Reservoir Hill area, which were owned by Ramsey. The purchase price was $2.5 million. To finance this purchase, Rio Grande reorganized under the laws of Delaware, increased authorized capital to $10 million, and sold a $3 million convertible-bond issue, underwritten by Alvin H. Frank & Company, a Los Angeles investment house.

To continue to finance new exploration, as well as to raise capital for other activities, we decided to try New York. Los Angeles bankers were continuing to take a dim view of wildcatters. I was in New York concluding a satisfactory arrangement when I received a telegram from W. H. Ferguson, vice-president of Continental Oil Company at Denver, asking me to come to Denver before making any final credit arrangement. I promptly did so and found to my pleasant surprise that Continental had already discussed the matter of a loan with United States National Bank in Denver. A meeting was arranged for me with E. T. Wilson, the chairman of Continental; Ferguson; and A. C. Foster, the vice-president of the bank.

The bank provided the credit we needed, and Continental purchased a portion of the notes. It was the beginning of a warm relationship with the bank, and we continued to buy Continental's crude until major pipelines began serving the company's New Mexico fields several years later.[1]

Besides funds for exploration the new financing provided $455,-000 for the purchase of a small refinery in Sour Lake, Texas, in 1925. To supply this refinery, Rio Grande arranged contracts with

---

[1] Because of his extreme persuasiveness, I had a chance to show my appreciation to Foster, who was also president of the Cherry Hills Country Club, then under construction. My contribution to the club building fund was a substantial one, but I was more than repaid in 1953, when, during a round of golf at the club, Barry Leithead made a hole in one and President Eisenhower, whose handicap entitled him to a stroke on the hole, shot a birdie and tied him. I was a member of the winning foursome.

John R. Suman to buy crude oil from his Rio Bravo Oil Company. Specializing in lubricating oil, this plant supplied Rio Grande's needs at El Paso and its contiguous market.

Expansion was, in fact, the order of the day throughout Rio Grande's refining and marketing divisions in 1926 and 1927. The El Paso refinery was expanded to a 5,000-barrel daily capacity and the Los Angeles refinery to a 10,000-barrel capacity. Bulk plants were constantly being built in new areas, stations were leased in areas served by the plants, and where necessary new stations were built.

During the same years Rio Grande was pursuing its exploratory program in California in partnership with the Ramsey brothers. We drilled several very expensive holes that turned out to be very dry. The most expensive wildcat the partners drilled—the Canet Ranch wildcat near Ventura—was abandoned early in 1928. But while this wildcat took an inordinate bite, it did not discourage Rio Grande. On the contrary, it encouraged the company to seek a new partner in drilling the Elwood Terrace wildcat, west of Santa Barbara, on property which had been leased in 1927. And that, in turn, brought on a new upward spiral in Rio Grande's fortunes.

## 7. THE ELWOOD FIELD

BY 1927 the Santa Barbara coast had been fairly well explored, and a number of important fields had been discovered. Among them was the Santa Maria District's Orcutt Field, discovered in 1904, which had brought a lusty oil boom to the quiet-loving citizens of Santa Barbara County. The Orcutt discovery well was a 12,000-barrel-a-day gusher, California's most spectacular to that time and not to be exceeded until 1910 at Midway-Sunset. Other fields had been opened along the coast in the early years of the century, and much exploration had been done along the shore west of Santa Barbara around Goleta—mostly to no avail.

In 1909, Associated Oil Company of California drilled a well in the Elwood area near the beach east of Campbell Point. It

40

reached 3,600 feet without any oil showings. The sharp angle of a major fold in the strata, together with extensive faulting in the area, made most geologists skeptical of the Elwood Terrace. They wrote it off as nonproductive.

Even before 1927, Frank A. Morgan had explored the Santa Barbara and Ventura coast for oil. Born in the mining town of Sonora, in California's gold country, Morgan had received a degree in geology from the University of California in 1920. Four years later he had joined his father-in-law, Eric A. Starke, whom Rio Grande had hired as a consulting geologist the same year.

Late in 1927, Rio Grande sent Morgan farther up the coast to Elwood Terrace, twelve miles west of Santa Barbara. The site was named for Elwood Siding on the Southern Pacific Railroad, which in turn had been named for one Ellwood Cooper, the original owner of one of the local ranches.

Morgan's investigation centered on the possibility of oil in the Vaqueros sand, a blanket sand fairly well known to California oil geologists and the object of previous unsuccessful tests elsewhere. On September 17, 1927, Frank Morgan reported his findings. "The chances seem to be extraordinarily good for commercial production of some kind or another," he wrote, "and for this reason, the area is recommended for acquisition and complete testing." On the strength of his recommendations, Rio Grande leased acreage belonging to several ranchers in the area. Working with Morgan on the project was Fletcher H. Etheridge, the land manager for Rio Grande. Then, in accordance with the accepted practice of sharing the risk of wildcatting, Rio Grande gave Frank Morgan the task of finding a drilling partner. He was rebuffed by one major company after another, who dredged up all the old prejudices against Elwood and the Vaqueros sand:

"There is no oil in the Vaqueros."

"The nearest fields at Goleta and Summerland are small."

But the Lockharts and their people were wildcatters at heart. They kept looking and turned finally to Barnsdall Oil Company of California, whose main attraction was an idle drilling rig about five miles west on the coast. Barnsdall had drilled a dry hole there and was preparing to move the rig south to Los Angeles. Rio

41

Grande offered an undivided one-half of the leases it had taken, plus half of the drilling costs. Barnsdall had been finding oil from Pennsylvania to California for thirty years. The company's chief geologist, Richard W. Sherman, turned out to be the only other professional who had enough faith in Morgan's conclusions to recommend going ahead with the venture. Even so, Barnsdall agreed somewhat dubiously. R. A. Broomfield, the president and general manager, told the officers of Rio Grande: "We'll drill to three thousand feet and pay half the costs. If the corings aren't favorable by then, we're through."

On May 31, 1928, Barnsdall's crew spudded in the Luton-Bell No. 1. I remember Mrs. Caroline Bell Luton (one of the four lessors—see Chapter 8), a lovely woman, asking rather plaintively whether we could not "put off the drilling for a time" so that she could continue collecting the $400 a month we were paying her for the lease.

Notwithstanding Mrs. Luton's disarming naïveté, there was work to be done. For days the drill went through highly fractured shale. At about 2,600 feet the hole caved in repeatedly, and the drill pipe was nearly lost several times. But the drillers passed through this section, and in three weeks the bit was down to 3,160 feet—well past the agreed-upon 3,000 feet—with no significant oil sign. On Friday, June 29, Broomfield telephoned me at Los Angeles.

"We've shut the well down," he announced. "It's getting too deep and needs a string of casing." It was obvious what was coming next.

"There is no use going any farther, and we are through. We recommend abandonment." At that moment Rio Grande faced one of its major decisions.

"What do you want to do?" pressed Broomfield. "If you want to go ahead, we will rent you the rig for one hundred dollars a day, but we won't go."

"We'll send Frank Morgan up to have a look," I replied. "If he advises us to pull out, we will."

That night Frank drove from Los Angeles to the Elwood site. He arrived at the well about 9:00 P.M., to find the crew sitting around awaiting orders to abandon the hole and fold up the rig. Frank went into the doghouse and picked up the last core, taken at a depth of 3,150 to 3,160 feet. It was composed of temblor shale, which was known to be the layer just above the Vaqueros sand. As Morgan later recalled:

"I broke it open along a faulting plane. It had a good odor of sweet light oil."

Morgan did not say much about his discovery to the Barnsdall crew. Taking some of the core pieces, he left the same night for Los Angeles. On the way he telephoned me and described the core samples: "I think we are very close to the top of the sand." We agreed to hold a meeting with the Lockharts at the Rio Grande offices in Los Angeles the next morning, a Saturday.

There we examined the cored shale samples. Noting that the oil odor and strongest indications were in the faulting planes, we reasoned that the oil showing must come up from the Vaqueros sand below and must be very close.

The next move was to telephone Broomfield and take over Barnsdall's interest. If he wanted out, we would be happy to oblige. But by that time it was Saturday afternoon, and the Barnsdall offices were closed. Morgan and Etheridge tried unsuccessfully to reach Broomfield. After conferring again with us, they decided to let it go until Monday. That was a monumental error. Saturday evening Sherman telephoned Morgan from the Elwood site. He was breathless with excitement.

"Our crew decided to work out the rest of the daylight shift before we abandoned the well," he said. "They went into the hole to circulate and took a short core."

Morgan could hear the news coming.

"The bit dropped into oil sand at 3,168 feet. We've got a gusher trying to blow out on us!"

Obviously Barnsdall was now in the game to stay. Rio Grande had come within an ace of having the whole Elwood strike to itself.

For nearly a month the Barnsdall crew worked to bring in the well without letting it get out of control. Continually fighting the pressure, they finally got pipe set, water shutoff completed, and the Christmas-tree control valve installed.

43

On the morning of July 26, with the casing forty feet into the Vaqueros sand, the crew began swabbing the well. On hand to see the well brought in were officials and wives of both Rio Grande and Barnsdall, as well as a number of Elwood property owners, Goleta residents, and Santa Barbara newsmen. Among the last was Thomas M. Storke, publisher of the *Santa Barbara Daily News* (later the *News-Press*) and for half a century one of California's most respected and active citizens. He had an interest in one of the Elwood properties leased by us, and he and I were later to become warm friends.

During the day's operations the security guards at the gate of the Luton-Bell property were busy keeping out sightseers. All at once a man and woman on horseback brushed past the guards and approached us. They were William C. McAdoo and his wife, Eleanor, the daughter of Woodrow Wilson. Residents of Santa Barbara and close friends of Storke, they were out for a ride and were handsomely dressed for the occasion. We welcomed them to the group, and McAdoo showed a keen interest in the operations.

At that time McAdoo, Edwin Pauley, and other leading Democratic politicians were dabbling in the oil business.[1] Among the interests of McAdoo and his group was a block of stocks in Rio Grande, which they had bought on the strength of the Elwood strike. Thus McAdoo's visit that day to Luton-Bell No. 1 turned out to be more than a casual horseback ride.

Early in the afternoon, with the last run of the swab, the pressure broke through with a roar. Oil and mud blew to the top of the derrick. Then, through the Christmas-tree valve, the flow was sent into the sump hole. With a cheer the onlookers rushed for the sump to see the first oil splash at their feet.

Tests immediately showed the pressure to be very high, yielding an initial flow rate of 4,300 barrels a day. Though tanks had been installed at the well, the flow was so fast that six tank trucks and

---

1 They later raised a large sum of money among oilmen to support John Nance ("Cactus Jack") Garner for president. However, in the Democratic convention of 1932 the McAdoo forces threw their support to Franklin D. Roosevelt (McAdoo seconded his nomination), and Garner was left with the vice-presidential position. In 1933, McAdoo, who himself had twice tried for the presidential nomination, became United States senator from California.

*Luton-Bell No. 1, the Elwood Field discovery well, July, 1928*

Rio Grande oil field at Elwood (Calif.) famous for its exceptionally high gravity crude oil.

*By the early 1930's, when it was discovered that the Elwood Field extended well out to sea, the shore was lined with wharves to accommodate wells of competing owners and operators. This photograph was taken before the height of the drilling craze that robbed Elwood of perhaps half its recoverable oil.*

trailers were kept busy throughout the first two days hauling the excess oil to the nearby Summerland Field. After that a pipeline to Elwood Siding on the railroad enabled tank cars to carry the production to Rio Grande's Vinvale refinery.

It was also very-high-gravity oil—as the *Santa Barbara Daily News* put it, "a quality never before found in California." Four months later Frank Morgan estimated an ultimate recovery of 110 million barrels from Elwood—a major field by any standard.

Already a phenomenal success in its first thirteen years, Rio Grande was now in the big time. Neither the company nor its

*The location of the Elwood Field on the California coast favored the transportation of its products. This photograph shows tankers in the Santa Barbara Channel being loaded from Elwood's marine crude-oil pipeline (foreground).*

people would ever be quite the same again. As for Mrs. Luton, she was happy to forgo the $400 monthly lease money when she saw her first royalty check.

## 8. ELWOOD'S BOOM AND BUST—
## A CASE HISTORY

ON the same afternoon that Luton-Bell No. 1 came in, Tom
Storke's Santa Barbara newspaper announced the story in banner
headlines: "4300 Barrel Oil Gusher Brought in at Goleta." For
several days previously oil indications from the well had sent
rumors along the Goleta coast and brought lease agents swarming
into the area. Now the activity increased to fever pitch as new
leasers descended on adjacent land and made offers on property
far off the oil structure.

At the same time the two discovery companies began further
drilling and production, according to the best conservation methods then known. We were rapidly approaching the time when
markets in both the East and the West would be glutted. The great

48

Kettleman North Dome Field was discovered in July, 1928, and a tide of crude oil was soon flooding California. In Oklahoma, the rapidly developing Oklahoma City Field (a town-lot field) was soon to be shut down by martial law while the state hammered out amendments to its conservation law. Conservation-minded elements throughout the industry were struggling to keep production within bounds.

At the Elwood Field, Rio Grande and Barnsdall commenced production in an orderly way. A ten-acre spacing plan was adopted, and the wells were drilled in accordance with engineering practices designed to produce the ultimate barrel of oil. If the policy could have been continued, Elwood would have been a monument to oil conservation. But that was not to be. Legal technicalities coupled with human greed soon appeared to make offshore drilling the villain at Elwood. The structure of the Elwood oil field lies at right angles to the shoreline, and about one-third of the field was offshore in the Santa Barbara Channel.

The Luton-Bell lease was part of a large parcel of land inherited and owned by four persons: Mrs. Caroline Bell Luton, Charles D. Bell, Mrs. Katherine Bell Cheney, and Mrs. Mary Bell Cheney. They were grandchildren and heirs of Nicholas A. Den, an Irishman who settled in Santa Barbara in 1836. In 1842, Den secured a land grant from the governor of California for thousands of acres west of Santa Barbara, including the Elwood Field.

Under state laws existing in 1927, the tidelands could be leased in parcels measured at right angles to the shoreline, with riparian or preferential rights to the upland owners. On behalf of the four owners Rio Grande filed on four tideland parcels on July 26, 1927, using the names of Frank Morgan, his children, and other dummy owners for each tideland lease. When Etheridge, Morgan, and the company lawyers posted the notices on the property, they filled out the year, month, and day of filing but neglected to include the time of day, as required by law. The company's personnel failed to recheck or verify the accuracy of the notices. According to law the filers had twelve months to rectify such an error. During this period a Los Angeles attorney, David Faries, learned about the discrepancies and made ready to post filings on the same parcels.

*Rigging up an all-steel derrick, preparatory to tidelands drilling at Elwood Field, 1929*

Exactly one minute after the twelve-month period expired, Faries and others posted their own notices on the tideland parcels. The validity of these adverse filings was upheld by the courts.

To combat this intrusion, the four heirs of Nicholas Den filed on the tidelands parcels in their own names. To support their filings, they also divided their upland property into four parts. But the courts ruled that, because the property was not divided at the time of the discovery, the four landowners were entitled to riparian rights for only one of the permits. Thus they were denied the full riparian rights for all the permits offshore from their jointly held lands. This ruling left the Faries interests in possession of the other three tidelands parcels. Quickly they leased the properties to the Bankline Oil Company, the Honolulu Oil Company, and later to the Signal Oil and Gas Company.

About this time still another interest entered the scene. Tecolote Ranch, which adjoined Elwood on the west, was owned by Mr. and Mrs. Silsby Spalding. Spalding was an associate of Edward L. Doheny, and Mrs. Spalding was a daughter of Charles A. Canfield, of California oil fame. Ironically, the Spaldings had bought their ranch after being assured by geologists that there was no oil on the property and no reason to believe that their privacy would be invaded. They now secured their preferential rights on the offshore permit adjoining their property and leased it to Pacific Western Oil Company. The property turned out to be highly productive and later played an important part in Richfield's history.

Coupled with these developments was the fact that Elwood was an unusually rich, high-pressure field. Part of its oil could be produced quickly and in high volume. The stage was set for the rape of Elwood.

The first offshore well at Elwood was brought in on October 11, 1929, and within seven months thirty-six wells had been located on the beach or in the ocean. Wells were produced wide-open, through both tubing and casing. More wells were drilled to increase production on one property, and to offset them others were drilled elsewhere. Some wells produced steadily at 12,000 to 14,000 barrels daily. Pressures soon dropped, and water flooded the rich sands.

Since its discovery the field has produced over 100 million barrels of oil. At least another 100 million barrels have been destroyed for all time. Such is the end product of the law of capture. California, alone among the major oil states, still has no law to prevent this form of waste and destruction to a natural resource on private property.

## 9. THE THROES OF SUDDEN WEALTH

UNEXPECTED riches bring many problems, and certainly the Elwood discovery brought its share of them. Suits were launched against Rio Grande by many people claiming to be heirs of Nicholas Den, but the claims did not prevail. Others laid claim to the tidelands through the use of "Valentine scrip," which had been issued in 1872 by the United States government to a man named Valentine as compensation for the condemnation of his rights to an old Mexican land grant. The scrip could be used to claim government land elsewhere, and much of it was sold on the open market. The whole spectacle was like the opening of a fresh steer carcass on the desert. Blowflies and vultures come from all directions.

The discovery well also made the tax collectors happy. In the spring of 1929, as vice-president and treasurer of Rio Grande, I appeared before the Board of Supervisors of Santa Barbara County with a tax expert and a lawyer to protest a tax bill of some $650,-000. We pointed out to the chairman of the board that the method of computing the tax was clearly wrong. He ended the hearing with a friendly, frank, and completely disarming answer to me:

"Charlie, we are building a new courthouse, and you are going to pay for it. Now please redo the tax bill in any way that pleases you, as long as you don't change the amount of tax on the bottom line. We may even name the courthouse for you." It was the beginning of a long, pleasant, but expensive relationship with that august body. In retrospect, few worse things could have happened to Rio Grande than the Elwood discovery. The company and its executives were totally unprepared, either economically or psychologically, for the trauma of such a large oil strike.

Up to this time the executives were a close-knit, hard-working group—cut one and all of them would bleed. They were all young, and no task seemed too great. They owned 40 per cent of the stock. They were alert, keen, and ready to recognize opportunity and take advantage of it. For several years they had made a reasonable profit and had plowed practically all of it back into the business. The publicly owned shares were well distributed, and there were no large holdings.

In July, 1928, when the Elwood discovery well came in, a group of people arrived at Los Angeles in a private railroad car on their way to the Bohemian Grove, an exclusive club in northern California. They included Robert Law, director of the Barnsdall Corporation and a son-in-law of its founder, T. N. Barnsdall; Amon G. Carter, publisher of the *Fort Worth Star-Telegram*; Sam Blythe, a popular magazine writer; and several big-time stock-market operators from Boston and New York. Heading the last-named group was Matthew C. Brush, one of the builders of the Boston Elevated Railroad, chairman of the Barnsdall Corporation, president of American International Corporation, and an officer or director of many railroad, banking, and other firms. He was an astute stock-market manipulator on a large scale.

53

While in California, Brush and his associates visited the Elwood Field. There, seeing an opportunity to apply their talents, they promptly acquired a large position in Rio Grande stock. Before we could bring in the second well, New Yorkers were on the board, the stock was split five for one, and the company was selling for about $80 million on the New York Stock Exchange, which until a few months before had been as remote as Peking. Rio Grande was suddenly one of the hottest items in the market, and its executives were abruptly cast in the roles of big operators.

Up to this time the official social lives of the executives had been limited to company activities. "Society" for its own sake had not even been considered. Now everyone at Rio Grande was besieged with invitations to affairs which soon became a way of life. Local bankers, with whom company officials had earlier had difficulty getting appointments, now invited us to their homes. Appointments with smart tailors and chic dressmakers became the order of the day. Executive $X$ hired a chauffeur; executive $Y$ hired two chauffeurs. Bigger and better homes—or, rather, bigger and more expensive homes—were purchased. More bootleg whiskey was acquired for ever-larger parties. Thus, little by little, the hard-hitting group was softened and transformed into VIP's.

On October 24, 1929, the stock-market crash came upon us, arriving as suddenly and unexpectedly as the Elwood strike fifteen months before. While none of the executives understood the significance of the events of October 24, we very quickly understood the significance of a great misfortune that befell one of our number.

Like many others, Leslie Lockhart had been trading in the stock market. His account was with H. J. Barneson and Company, with whom he had put up securities and other collateral to cover his trading activities. Lockhart had also employed an investment counselor to advise him and had given the counselor power of attorney to buy and sell. As part of the arrangement, the investment counselor was to carry accounts in his own name but on behalf of Lockhart and based on Lockhart's credit. On October 29, according to Lockhart's books, he was out of debt and had over $3 million market value of collateral in his Barneson account.

*Matthew C. Brush, New York financier (second from right), visiting the Elwood Field in July, 1928. Charles S. Jones is at the left; next to him, in the plaid jacket, is Frank A. Morgan.*

55

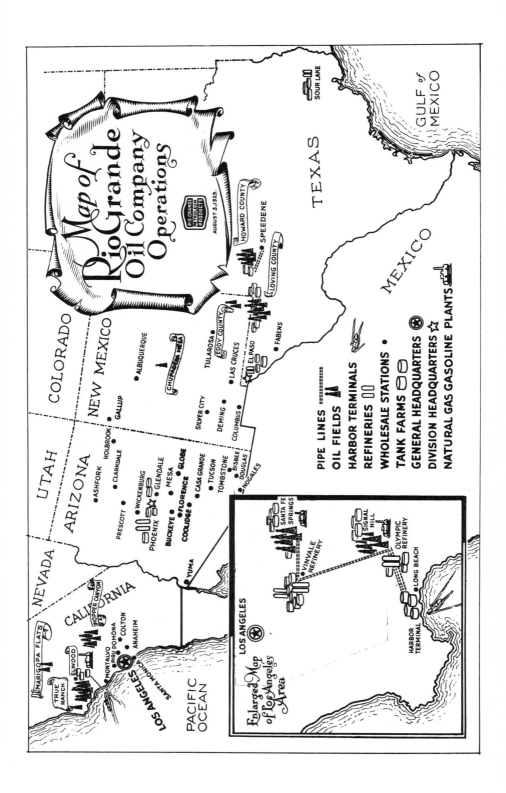

About midnight I was awakened at home and asked to go to Lockhart's home at once. Assembled there were Lockhart, Lionel Barneson (incidentally, one of God's noblemen), an accountant from Barneson and Company, a lawyer, and Lockhart's investment counselor. As the story unfolded, the investment counselor had used Lockhart's power of attorney and his credit to speculate for himself in Rio Grande stock. The series of accounts that he had created in his own name had been used for his own benefit. Then with the stock-market crash, the value of the stock had plummeted. The accounts were now undermargined because of the loss in value of Lockhart's collateral, and Barneson was calling for more margin. The total indebtedness to Barneson was over $3 million, and Lockhart's fortune was in jeopardy. There was no money to pay the margin.

How could Barneson recover his advances? He realized that he could not sell the stock in the open market—and the shares represented about 15 per cent of the company.

By sunrise we had made an arrangement with Barneson. I put up a substantial amount of personal securities to help margin the stock, and we arranged to give Barneson a note for the total amount, signed by Lockhart, Lloyd Lockhart, and me. We also agreed to set about trying to borrow the money at once. The following week I went to New York and called on Elisha Walker, of the Bancamerica-Blair Corporation, who later arranged an introduction to Ned Tinker, head of Interstate Equities, a new investment trust with $25 million in capital. Tinker was willing to make a loan on the shares, provided we would be willing to discuss merger with some larger company. We were conditioned for this, because the Elwood production was larger than we could market. Rio Grande agreed to Tinker's proposal, and we set out to find a merger partner—a step that was to open an entirely new era in the history of Richfield's predecessors.

# 10. ENTER HARRY F. SINCLAIR

WHEN we first began contemplating a merger, we hoped to join some California company that could provide a market for our huge oil production—or at least had empty storage tanks. I returned to California to pursue the quest for such a company. By coincidence, James A. Talbot, chairman of the board of Richfield Oil Company of California, was also thinking along merger lines. Richfield was deficient in crude-oil production, and Rio Grande had more than it could handle. At the instance of Gordon Crary, a partner in E. F. Hutton & Company, Talbot invited me to his office one evening early in December, 1929. After three hours spent in exploring possibilities, it became apparent to both of us that a merger of our respective companies was not feasible. Rich-

58

*Harry F. Sinclair, one of the titans of the American oil industry. He acquired Rio Grande Oil Company in 1932 and was chairman of Richfield Oil Corporation from 1937 until his death in 1956.*

59

field wanted our production but not our refineries and marketing facilities.

Rio Grande concluded that California offered no opportunities for merger, and I returned to New York in mid-December. Elisha Walker took me to the office of Harry F. Sinclair, president of Sinclair Consolidated Oil Corporation. Born in West Virginia in 1876, Sinclair had been in the petroleum business since the turn of the century and was one of the oil magnates of the world. I had first met him several years earlier, while he was on a visit to El Paso. At that time—unknown to those of us associated with Rio Grande—he was engaged in the activities that led to the Teapot Dome scandal and to his brief imprisonment for contempt of court. He had been released from prison only two months when I met him again in New York in 1929.

It soon became apparent to me that Sinclair was a nocturnal worker. He commenced his day when most offices were closing. His imprisonment had left its scars: he was hard, relentless, driving, and unforgiving. In a conference that lasted most of the night, we agreed in principle on a merger between Sinclair and Rio Grande. Sinclair was also working on merger possibilities with Prairie Oil and Gas Company, Parco Oil Company, and Pierce Petroleum Corporation. He wanted to postpone the merger with Rio Grande until some of these larger negotiations could be concluded. This was logical, and we agreed to it. But as a result of our understanding with Sinclair, Interstate Equities made a personal loan of $3.5 million to clear Leslie M. Lockhart's account with Barneson and Company. By that time the markets had somewhat improved, and the collateral had a quoted market value of better than $5 million.

In January, 1930, Sinclair organized a group to inspect the Rio Grande properties. The group included Sinclair himself and some of his executives, lawyers, and bankers, as well as Sam Fitzpatrick, chairman of Prairie Oil and Gas, and John Markham, president of the Petroleum Corporation of America.

We left New York in Sinclair's private railroad car, and Rio Grande's Fokker plane was put at our disposal. We inspected the properties in West Texas, New Mexico, and Arizona. Stopping

*One of the first company planes, this trimotor Fokker, purchased by Rio Grande in 1929, was used principally to fly executives to the company's plants and operations in Texas and California.*

over at both El Paso and Phoenix, we arrived in Los Angeles about January 30 and made side trips to the California properties, the producing fields, and the refineries.

While we were in Phoenix, Sam Fitzpatrick inspected our small refinery there. On returning to the hotel that evening, Sinclair asked Fitzpatrick what he thought about the refinery. Fitzpatrick replied, "You know, Harry, this is the finest refinery I have ever seen." He added, "There is absolutely no room for expansion."

At the time Rio Grande was building steel tanks to store unsalable Elwood crude oil, and the need for money had become acute. A loan of $5 million, underwritten by Sinclair, was arranged through Bancamerica-Blair Corporation, and Sinclair was later elected to Rio Grande's Board of Directors. From that time on, all important policy matters were discussed with Sinclair, and close contact was maintained. In fact, I was asked to assist in the discussions between Sinclair Consolidated and Prairie Oil and Gas.

These negotiations progressed well on both sides until midsummer, 1930, when the Great Depression hit in force, trying the souls and fiber of men and institutions throughout the world. The situation in the oil industry changed almost daily. When the negotiations with Sinclair commenced in 1929, crude-oil prices had averaged more than $2 a barrel throughout the country. By August, 1931, crude-oil prices were as low as 5 to 10 cents a barrel—about 15 cents in California. To curtail overproduction, the militia had shut down wells in Oklahoma and in the great East Texas Field. The latter field had only been discovered in late 1930 but by August, 1931, was producing more than 1 million barrels a day.

Those were trying times. The Depression continued on its downward plunge, and the nation's oil production rose still further above market demand.

Since 1930, Prairie had been in financial trouble as production declined in Oklahoma and West and North Central Texas—the company's principal sources of crude oil. Moreover, the various Standard Oil companies, which Prairie had served exclusively, were still busy reintegrating after their divorcement following the dissolution decree of 1911 against the old Standard Trust. They were consequently finding their own sources of crude oil. Standard Oil Company (New Jersey) had participated in building the great Ajax pipeline from Oklahoma and Texas fields to the eastern market. The pipeline was a body blow to Prairie. Then, in September, 1930, Standard Oil Company of Indiana bought Sinclair's half-interest in their jointly owned pipeline. Prairie had been handling all this business for Standard of Indiana, and that move alone cost Prairie some $13.5 million in traffic.

By the end of 1931, Prairie was operating at 28 per cent of capacity and losing money. It became more and more receptive to the proposed merger with Sinclair, which was completed in 1932. Shortly thereafter, in September, 1932, Rio Grande was also merged with Sinclair Consolidated. By that time Harry Sinclair had changed considerably. The bitterness which had seemed to consume him two years earlier was gone, although his drive was undiminished.

After Rio Grande merged with Sinclair, most of the Lockharts retired from the company; they found it difficult to adjust to the discipline of a large corporate complex. Lloyd and Leslie re-entered the oil business in East Texas and were highly successful there (Leslie was reported to have sold some of his oil-production holdings in 1946 for $25 million). Arthur remained in California and built a profitable refining and asphalt plant in Long Beach. Lynn continued with Rio Grande for several years, after which he entered politics and became a highly respected businessman in Arizona. Herman and Cecil withdrew from the company in 1930 to enter private business. I stayed on to become president of Rio Grande, which continued to operate as a distinct unit within the Sinclair empire.

Thus ended the saga of Rio Grande as an independent company. Like many others, it had started as a shoestring enterprise, founded mainly on the nerve and drive of a few highly motivated men. But unlike most of the others, it had survived the vagaries of oil economics to become—through the added impetus of a major strike—a potent name in petroleum.

In the meantime, two other young companies, United Oil Company and Richfield Oil Company, had also been making their way through the thickets of the oil industry toward a juncture that would create the modern Richfield.

PART TWO
*The Heritage of Richfield*

# 11. THE UNITED OIL COMPANY

IN 1916, the same year that Lloyd Lockhart filed incorporation papers for Rio Grande, Colon F. Whittier was ending his sixth year as president of United Oil Company, which had just resumed dividends after four long, hard, unprofitable years.

Destined to play an important part in Richfield history, United was organized as a crude-oil–producing company on November 19, 1909. Three days later the seven directors, of whom J. M. Danziger was chairman, held their first meeting in Bakersfield, California. Up to that moment United had no property, no oil, and no capital stock, but it seemed that almost anything could happen in the California oil realm of that day, particularly in the boom fields around Bakersfield.

*An early photograph of the Midway-Sunset Field, discovered in 1894
and still producing*

McKittrick, Coalinga, Kern River, Midway-Sunset—such fields
in southwestern San Joaquin Valley were pouring forth a stream
of oil. When United's founders met in 1909, Union Oil Company
was drilling what would soon be the greatest oil well in the world—
Lake View No. 1, a gusher which sprayed black gold for miles
over the Midway-Sunset Field. Such excitement naturally brought
a horde of enterprisers to Bakersfield, among them the founders
of United. Their object was to raise capital through a stock issue
and then acquire some producing property that would support
still another round of capitalization and expansion.

Among United's developers—though not among its original
incorporators and directors—was Colon F. Whittier, a native of
Maine who had been active in the lumber business before coming
to California in 1898 at the age of twenty-nine. Restless and ambitious, Whittier joined the gold rush to the Klondike, in Canada's
Northwest Territory. But a year later he returned to join the black-
gold fever gripping California. His older brother, M. H. Whittier,
had been a drilling contractor in the Los Angeles oil boom of the

*Colon F. Whittier,*
*founder and first president*
*of United Oil Company*

1890's, had gained interests in the San Joaquin Valley fields, and was one of the founders of Associated Oil Company.

Approaching the industry from a different direction, young Colon Whittier joined with C. P. Campbell in forming the Whittier-Campbell Company, a stock-brokerage firm in Los Angeles dealing mostly in penny oil stocks. They also bought a controlling interest in at least one firm, Midway Six Oil Company, which had some producing land in the Midway-Sunset Field. But at a time when oil was a magic word to the investing public, Colon also realized the gains to be made from founding one's own company. The standard procedure was pretty much followed by Whittier and his colleagues in November, 1909.

Step 1: At the November 22 meeting Whittier conveyed to the new company all his equities under an oil lease made by him to one W. E. Jeske. In return he received the sum of $2 million, which was paid by issuing 2 million shares of $1 par-value capital stock.

Step 2: A branch office of United was immediately established at Whittier's brokerage office in Los Angeles, and on the day after Whittier had received the 2 million shares for his interest in a worthless oil lease, he donated the stock back to the company, less 700 shares, which were retained as directors' qualifying shares.

Step 3: Five of the original directors, including Danziger, resigned, and Whittier was elected director and president. His partner, Campbell, became a director and vice-president. J. B. Hedrick, secretary of Whittier-Campbell, was named a director and secretary-treasurer, and two others were elected directors. Thus United Oil Company was organized with $2 million of fully paid capital and all except $700 returned to the company as treasury stock to be disposed of at the directors' discretion. The next move was to acquire some producing property and raise some working capital.

Step 4: Traction Oil Company, owned by several of the directors and former organizers, was acquired by exchanging 2½ shares of United for 1 share of Traction.

Step 5: Midway Six Oil Company, largely owned by Whittier-Campbell, was acquired by an exchange of 1¼ shares of United stock for each share of Midway Six stock. The oil properties thus acquired included twenty acres of patented land in the Midway-Sunset Field near Fellows, California. Producing wells were drilled on this property, which became the backbone of the company and sustained it through years of tribulation. By December 31, 1966, the field had produced over 6.3 million barrels of crude oil—the oldest property (acquired in January, 1910) operated almost continuously each year by United and its successor, Richfield.

Also acquired along with the Midway Six Oil Company were several hundred acres of unpatented government mineral claims. These lands, together with some similar acquisitions a few months later, would prove a heavy burden on the company and a severe trial of its stamina. But as time passed, it developed that stamina; patience and perseverance were qualities with which Whittier was heavily endowed.

70

*From 1910 until the 1920's this twenty-acre parcel in the Midway-Sunset Field near Fellows, in California's San Joaquin Valley, was the mainstay of the United Oil Company.*

Step 6: Working capital was raised by employing Whittier-Campbell to sell 100,000 shares of treasury stock at 25 cents a share, at a commission of 20 per cent. In August, 1910, United stock was listed on the Los Angeles Stock Exchange and on the California Stock and Oil Exchange in San Francisco. By November, 1910, approximately 997,000 shares had been sold for a total of $554,000, at an average of 56 cents a share. The last sales in November averaged 71½ cents a share.

Step 7: Sale of the stock was aided when the board declared a dividend of 1 cent a share, payable each month starting in May, 1910. This dividend was maintained through the stock-selling period.

Thus, with little more than a few strokes of the pen, Whittier had acquired oil land and was running an oil company in addition to his brokerage business. On January 31, 1912, he addressed a report to his stockholders, outlining the good and meeting the bad head on. In 1911, he reported, the nine wells on the twenty

71

acres in the Midway-Sunset Field had produced nearly 500,000 barrels, bringing in sales of $215,000. On the other property, which was surrounded by gushers yielding from 2,000 to 30,000 barrels a day, four wells were being drilled when one of them encountered "very heavy gas pressure." As Whittier graphically described it: "The gas blew the mud over the derrick and embedded the rotary drill pipe in the hole in such a manner that it was impossible to loosen it. It is now being redrilled." Drilling on two of the other wells was "temporarily suspended when curtailment was found necessary."

The high cost of the blowout and redrilling could not sustain the company's monthly dividend. At the annual meeting held in the company's office in the Midway-Sunset Field on November 25, 1911, three new directors were elected. "Acting upon the advice and counsel of these new members," wrote Whittier, "the Board of Directors discontinued the payment of dividends." Whittier forgot to mention in his report that the new directors owned over 400,000 shares of stock and that he had reduced his holdings to 3,200 shares. Extremely astute in his personal financial matters, Whittier was merely rolling with the punch. When the dividend was resumed in 1914, he had reacquired 175,000 shares of stock. His lament to the stockholders had simply meant that he would keep on working and reacquire his stock position at a prudent time dictated by the financial signs.

It should be noted that the year 1911, when Whittier found himself in such distress, was a bad year for the entire industry. In 1910 the Midway-Sunset Field had produced over 20 million barrels and in 1911 more than 27 million barrels. Contributing some 9 million barrels of this (over 4 million barrels of which was wasted) was Union Oil's great Lake View gusher, which blew out of control. It was asking too much of the industry to absorb that much additional oil in so few months. Thus, in addition to Whittier's problems with gas blowouts, dry holes, high drilling costs, and such annoyances as the cancellation by the federal government of a large number of his placer-mining oil claims because of illegal filing, he had the problem of getting a price for his product.

At this juncture the company's fortunes appear to have been

saved by one of the three new board members, Austin O. Martin, who also served as second vice-president of United. Martin, a Los Angeles realtor, was highly regarded in business circles and brought stability to the floundering company. He owned more than 275,000 shares of stock in the company and pledged his personal credit to obtain large sums of money to tide United over the crisis. Three years later the board gave extraordinary recognition to this and other services by a grant of $7,500 to Martin, "to be paid at such times and in such manner as to best serve the interests of the company." The association proved a good example of free enterprise working in its own interests. Martin devoted his best efforts to the welfare of the company and succeeded in saving it from financial disaster, thus making the stockholders happy, furthering Whittier's career and the destiny of the company—and making quite a bit of money for himself.

During this period of crisis, however, the stockholders decided to sell the company. For several years the board tried to find a purchaser. In July, 1913, the directors voted to assess the stockholders 5 cents a share and thus raised $100,000 to pay off pressing debts. But by the end of 1914 the fortunes of the company had turned upward somewhat. United was free from its heavy drilling expenses, and the onset of World War I had brought an increase in the price of oil. The board resumed dividends of one-half cent a share on the outstanding stock. By early 1915 most of the debts had been liquidated, and at the end of that year the company had earned $100,000 and had $27,000 in the bank. In a meeting held on May 8, 1916, the directors concluded that the company could even afford to pay a salary of $100 a month to President Whittier.

Owing to expenses in connection with various oil properties, United's fortunes dipped in 1917 and 1918, but by the end of 1919 the company had $200,000 in cash and Liberty bonds. Reflecting United's improvement, the stock rose from 25 to 90 cents a share. Whittier, taking advantage of these fluctuations, sold 103,000 of his shares, retaining 72,000 shares.

At this point United was further strengthened by the arrival of Jerre M. Kent, who appeared as a 50,000-share stockholder at the annual meeting on November 30, 1918, and was elected a director

74

*Signal Hill Field, near Long Beach, California*

at that time. Kent had the confidence of the Los Angeles oil community in general and of fellow board member Martin in particular. At the directors' meeting held on May 5, 1919, Martin called for the appointment of Kent as general manager, to concentrate on securing oil leases to strengthen United's production. Kent agreed to assume the position, on the condition that he would not be saddled with any office duties. At a salary of $350 a month he immediately set out on a lease quest that took him as far as Texas and Louisiana. It was soon apparent that Kent was Whittier's strong right arm in managing United.

By the end of 1920, United had cash and bonds on hand of $172,000 and was out of debt except for small current accounts. The company was in excellent shape to participate in the exciting new era of oil that was to begin on a small hill north of Long Beach, California. In May, 1921, rumors raced through the Los Angeles oil community that Shell Oil Company had found oil showings on Signal Hill and was about to bring in a well. The site had recently been subdivided, and leasers began taking up town lots even before Shell brought in its gusher on the southeast slope on June 23. In January, 1922, General Petroleum Corporation brought in an even bigger gusher on the northwest side— spraying oil all over the hill and defining it as one of the world's great oil fields.

The frenzy mounted as royalty offers reached an unprecedented one-half and the hill took on the appearance of a mammoth porcupine. Every alert oil company was scrambling for a share of what was to prove the richest field per acre in the world. Among the first leasers to invade the hill were Colon Whittier and Jerre Kent of United. Apparently the first leases Kent secured were signed in July, 1921, for land owned by Louis Denni. The property proved to be a giant producer and sent United's $1.00 par-value stock to $1.75.

In 1922, Whittier and Kent acquired the Jones, Malcom-Davis, and Hass leases—names which became famous on Signal Hill. Proving up the fabulous Hass lease laid the foundation for major changes in financial structure and transformed Whittier from a penny-oil stockbroker to a big-time developer. For the first nine

*The Hass lease (Hass Well No. 6 in foreground), acquired in 1922 on Signal Hill. Revenues from this and other leases on the hill helped provide the funds for the United Oil Company to purchase Richfield Oil Company in 1923.*

77

months of 1922, United's profit was $303,000, and it had a surplus of $272,000.

At the stockholders' meeting held in October, 1921, Irving H. Hellman had been elected a director, and his arrival had signaled the beginning of a new era for United. Hellman was surrounded by able and vigorous stock promoters, most of them associated with the brokerage firm of Aronson & Company. The group had acquired a sizable stock interest in United, and in October, 1922, James A. Talbot and R. I. Rogers, two members of the powerful Hellman group and partners in Aronson & Company, were also elected directors.

A shipbuilder in World War I, Talbot was a rising star in the Los Angeles business world. Like many others, he had been attracted to the excitement of Santa Fe Springs and Signal Hill. The Denni and Hass leases had apparently convinced him that United had caught the tide of fortune. He and the other new director, Rogers, lost no time. Their first move was to have the board vote salaries of $700 monthly to President Whittier and General Manager Kent—something of a softening-up procedure. The second step was to forgo the issuance of a report to stockholders for 1922 and to order a new appraisal of the company's properties that would greatly increase its stated capitalization.

The resulting financial statement, dated April 30, 1923, was sent to stockholders a month later. As Whittier proudly wrote, "This shows the present state of the company's affairs and speaks for itself." The statement indicated a profit for the first four months of 1923 of $298,000—more than the profit of most previous full years. Net property accounts were listed at $8,385,000; current assets (including cash of $97,000), $350,000; current liabilities, $124,000; capital stock, $2 million; and a surplus of $6,611,000. Thus, by having the company's holdings reappraised, the board had been able to pump $6 million additional water into the situation as of April 30, 1923. Added to the original $2 million put in at the time the company was organized in 1909, this made a total watering in the balance sheet of $8 million.

The stage was now set for some adventures in high finance. In March, 1923, the stock had been listed on the San Francisco Stock

*James A. Talbot, 1928*

Exchange, and on April 13, 1923—even before the publication of the new financial statement—the authorized capital stock had been increased from 2 million shares of $1 par value to 10 million shares of $25 par value. On June 20, $1 million of the new stock was offered to stockholders. Again on October 1, 1923, the board declared a 50 per cent stock dividend, on the ground that the surplus was now more than $1.5 million. The new $25 stock was selling at $75 a share. Earnings for the year 1923 were $719,000, and cash dividends, which had been resumed in October, 1922, were $330,000. Signal Hill had catapulted United to a new level of success.

At a meeting of the stockholders on January 5, 1924, held on the company's property near Fellows, a $3 million convertible-bond issue was authorized. The ease of the sale and the rapid conversion of these bonds had a profound influence on the promoters. They had hit upon the open-sesame, and they adopted this means of financing as a way of life—sell convertible bonds, . . . jiggle stock, . . . convert bonds, . . . sell more convertible bonds.

Within two and a half years after becoming a United director in October, 1922, James Talbot was president of the company and was helping steer it through the reefs and shoals of high finance. Ambitious to achieve oil eminence, he began pressing to make United more than a producer of oil. Refining and marketing were needed for a fully integrated company. At this point the history of United began to converge with that of Richfield Oil Company, which in the same years had been rising in an even more dramatic fashion.

# 12. RICHFIELD'S BEGINNING

THE Richfield saga began one day in 1902 when an Iowa farmer
named Frederick Ranney Kellogg got off the train in Los Angeles.
He was one of thousands flocking to California from the Middle
West and particularly from Iowa. Like so many others, he was
ready to start a fresh business in his new home. In his late thirties,
Kellogg was still flexible enough to take a new direction—petroleum. In 1905, Kellogg joined G. J. Symington and S. R. Roseberg to form the Kellogg Oil Company.

The Los Angeles Field, discovered by E. L. Doheny and Charles
A. Canfield a decade earlier, was in flush production in those days.
The principal business of the new company was to operate a
small refinery in Vernon, then on the outskirts of Los Angeles. The

*Frederick Ranney Kellogg, about 1920*

entire plant was about the size of an experimental unit in a modern refinery. Aside from the plant, the partners' principal working asset was a contract with the Atchison, Topeka and Santa Fe Railway Company for all the lighter products (tops) from the railroad's topping plant at the Maricopa Field in southern San

*At the Maricopa Field, in southern San Joaquin Valley, wooden derricks stand as silent monuments to a hell-roaring oil boom at the turn of the century.*

Joaquin Valley. The railroad needed heavy fuel for its steam engines, and at Maricopa it distilled crude oil into two parts, heavy fuel and tops. It was then necessary to distill the tops and separate them into their various components—gasoline, naphthas, kerosene, stove distillate, and so on—in order to market them directly to the consumer.

Kellogg and his little company contracted to ship the tops from Maricopa. Some of the products were delivered to buyers along the line, and the remainder went to Kellogg's refinery at Vernon. As an illustration of the lenient rules under which railroads then operated, the contract called for delivery of the products at any point on the company's system at a constant price. Most of the time Kellogg's little still ran twenty-four hours a day. One Kellogg employee did all the selling, delivering, and collecting, and the quickening pulse of the business enabled him to keep orders three or four days ahead of the company's manufacturing capacity.

83

*The original Los Angeles Oil & Refining Company (the large white building at the left in front of the tanks). The first floor housed the offices of the company. On the second floor was the lubricating-oil and -grease blending plant. Gravity fed the products from the top to the bottom floor into barrels, cans, and packages.*

At that time distillate was an important item of sales. Electricity had not extensively replaced stationary engines, and almost every kind of business that required power was a fuel customer. Gasoline was actually a troublesome by-product for which there was a limited market. As gasoline surpluses accumulated, they were unloaded to Standard Oil Company of California. The partners attributed much of their early success to Standard's paternal and accommodating attitude, since periodic sale of the gasoline inventories enabled Kellogg to keep its products moving and its capital liquid. Gasoline was not taxed in those days, and the retail price was 9 cents a gallon, below which no one wanted to bother handling it. (Exactly the same price prevailed in the Los Angeles area in June, 1932, with one-third being extracted for taxes.)

In 1909 the Los Angeles Oil & Refining Company was formed by T. A. Winter, J. R. Jacobs, and George Gillons, who had entered the oil business as brokers of eastern lubricants. They operated an 80-barrel-a-day still and performed a general sales and brokerage business similar to that of Kellogg Oil Company. Their small refinery was situated on Twenty-fourth Street in Los Angeles, where one of Atlantic Richfield's downtown warehouses and distributing centers now stands.

Soon the six owners of the two companies decided to cooperate in assuring themselves a larger supply of tops, a logical expansion of their business. In 1911 they jointly financed a plant to top more Santa Fe Railroad crude from the Olinda Field in Orange County. The plant was built at Richfield Station, a railroad siding about three miles south of Olinda. The station, consisting of a grocery store and a railroad watering tank, provided the name for the new corporation—Richfield Oil Company.

Without realizing it at the time, Kellogg and his associates had become the owners of the most easily merchantable trademark in the oil business—"Richfield"—a great name, good to look at, pleasant to say and to hear.

By 1913 the three companies were prospering in a small way. Then General Petroleum Corporation's pipeline was completed from the great new Midway-Sunset Field in San Joaquin Valley to Los Angeles. After securing a contract from General Petroleum to market this oil under a 5 per cent commission arrangement, the owners launched a fourth organization. They named it National Petroleum Company, a somewhat grandiose name for a concern with just $30 capital.

85

*The railroad station on the Santa Fe line, three miles south of Olinda Field, California, originally called Richfield Station. The name was later changed to Atwood Station.*

About this time Clarence Mark Fuller joined Richfield to manage the road-oil and asphalt business. Fuller, twenty-five years old, had been born in Lawrence, Kansas, the son of a minister. He had gone to California as a youth and was working for Adeline Consolidated Road Oil Company at Bakersfield when he was hired by Richfield at an initial salary of $150 a month. Ambitious and energetic, Fuller was advanced within a few months to assistant general manager and took charge of all sales.

By 1915, with World War I under way in Europe and oil demand mounting in the United States, General Petroleum found that it could sell its products directly. It canceled the sales contract with Kellogg and his associates, who then decided to market their own products. Actually, General Petroleum did them a favor. As it turned out, the Richfield people did far better as entrepreneurs than as commission agents.

Up to this time the two groups that owned Richfield had sep-

*Clarence Mark Fuller,*
*1925*

arately refined and sold the output of the Richfield topping plant. They now undertook to merge Kellogg Oil Company and Los Angeles Oil & Refining Company. Neither group could resign itself to the loss of identity and finally compromised on the jointly owned name, Richfield. It was a wise and fortunate decision, though neither group thought so at the time. The assets of the other two companies were turned in to Richfield, and T. A. Winter was named president. The National Petroleum Company, which was actually little more than a sales staff, was also taken over. Clarence Fuller became general manager.

From its incorporation in 1911 to the merger in 1915, Richfield's capital had remained at $18,000, owned equally by the six partners. Now the stockholders authorized a capital increase to 150,000 shares at a par value of $1 each. On November 23, 1915, in return for their properties, 23,603 shares were issued to the Kellogg Oil Company and 23,603 shares to the Los Angeles Oil & Refining Company. In addition, a sale of 5,000 shares was

87

*The first Richfield tank wagon, about 1915. The Model T Ford (shown in the background) and its sister automobiles were beginning to replace kerosene lamps and oil-burning machines as the principal customers of petroleum products.*

authorized to Fuller on credit. Richfield was now capitalized at $70,206.

The new company's assets consisted of the topping plant at Richfield Station, the two small refineries in Los Angeles, one tank wagon, a team of horses—and aggressive salesmanship. Deliveries were restricted to the area within easy reach of the refineries. If dealers from such distant points as Santa Monica or Redondo Beach wanted products, they had to travel twenty-five miles on dirt roads to get them.

For ten years the venture launched by Fred Kellogg had remained small. But a new era was dawning in the oil business, one which would profoundly affect such men as Kellogg and Fuller, as it would Colon Whittier and Lloyd Lockhart.

# 13. THE EAGLE TAKES FLIGHT

THE year 1915 was a good one for a fresh start in the oil business. A seller's market had begun that was to last for six years. Fuller was a young and energetic marketer. His problem in those first years was supply: he could sell faster than the refineries could produce. Soon after the merger, Richfield purchased the Yosemite refinery in Los Angeles for $8,500. A year later the 2,800-barrel Phoenix refinery at Bakersfield became a Richfield property for $23,000. For a long time it operated almost entirely on crude oil from Fellows, running enough gasoline for the local market and shipping the remaining tops to Los Angeles or to the Utah Oil & Refining Company at Salt Lake City.

Obviously Richfield had taken off well and was fast gaining

*Richfield's Phoenix refinery at Bakersfield, where in 1919 Richfield produced a fuel with the unheard-of octane rating of 75.*

altitude. Each of the six owners began receiving $1,000 to $1,500 a month in salary and dividends, and Fuller was advanced to a corresponding salary. Two of the owners, Roseberg and Gillons, dropped out in 1916, selling their stock to the remaining stockholders. Upon Winter's death in 1917, Kellogg became president.

At that time the company's principal source of crude oil was royalty oil withheld by the government receiver of certain properties from operators holding oil-and-gas interests under disputed title in government-owned land in Kern County. The oil was occasionally sold in large quantities, and other bidders saw to it that Richfield paid heavily for it. This defenseless position tempted Richfield's owners into their one and only effort to develop their own production: they lost $80,000 on a wildcat at Newhall, north of Los Angeles.

The seller's market continued strong. Although Richfield com-

*Richfield's fifth delivery truck, purchased about 1919, a 4-cylinder Moreland tank truck with three compartments and 849 gallons' capacity.*

*A Richfield railroad tank car at the Western Tank Car Company plant, September, 1928.*

plained about paying premium prices for crude oil, the refined prices more than compensated for the higher costs. In 1917 the company paid a stock dividend of 115 per cent and in December, 1920, a stock dividend of 233 per cent, meanwhile continuing generous cash dividends. Thus in five years the merged company had earned and saved over ten times as much as in the ten years preceding the merger.

In 1920, during the gasoline shortage and resultant rationing in California, Richfield made one venture into the San Francisco market. To salvage an uncollectible account, it took over and for some months operated the Pacific States refinery. A few service stations were built, and an attempt was made to capture business in the Bay area. The attempt proved premature. Local politics and a shortage of refinable oils forced Richfield to withdraw from the area for the moment. Meanwhile, Richfield was cultivating the marketing territory around the Bakersfield and Los Angeles refineries and the area between the two cities. Eight bulk distributing plants were built to provide more effective service in southern California.

In 1921, with the flush production of the new fields at Signal Hill and Santa Fe Springs, prices for both crude and refined products suddenly started downward. The seller's market disappeared. New refineries were built, and price competition became severe. But by this time Richfield had established good customer and dealer relationships. Despite the tight market, it managed to add $80,000 to its surplus during 1921 and 1922. Capital and surplus on November 1, 1922, were $500,000 and $328,000, respectively, and the company paid a 50 per cent stock dividend. In seven years the company had earned and plowed back ten and one-half times its capital at the time of the 1915 merger and had paid liberal cash dividends. Thus even while prices were dropping, Richfield was climbing higher.

Fuller's salesmanship was not the only reason for this financial success. It was also the result of closely controlled management by the owners. The five-man board of directors met each Monday, and the executive committee of three at first met once a week and later twice a week and even oftener when called by the president.

93

Through such continuous attention the group kept a tight rein on the business, down to the smallest details. The directors approved all contracts for the purchase of crude oil and the sale of refined products. They authorized all check disbursements and other transactions, even to such items as the purchase of Christmas cards to be sent to customers of the company and the rental of a signboard in Pomona for one year at a cost of $15.50 a month. On one occasion it tabled the expense account of President Kellogg and placed a limit of $20.00 a day on the officials' expense accounts other than travel costs (which included railroad fare and sleeper accommodations). On February 19, 1923—in the midst of the postwar recession of that year—the board decided to suspend all capital expenditures temporarily.

Richfield's leaders were following two elementary rules for profit: increase sales and cut costs. On this basis Richfield flew successfully through the clouds of the early 1920's and soared into the blue sky beyond.

# 14. THE "GASOLINE OF POWER"

TO Clarence Fuller, an increase in sales necessitated a liberal dose
of showmanship. As early as 1919 he was seeking out the auto
racers to publicize Richfield gasoline. It was racing's golden age,
when the feats of the gasoline-powered vehicles captured the enthusiasm of America's male population and the names of Barney
Oldfield, Ralph DePalma, and Teddie Tetzlaff were as widely
known as those of movie stars. If racing drivers used Richfield to
win victories, Fuller reasoned, the average motorist would want
to use it, too.

In January, 1919, on a westbound train Fuller happened to
meet a young racing driver from Indiana named Roscoe Sarles.
With his black-painted Roamer loaded on the same train, Sarles

*Ascot Speedway, Los Angeles, where many famous auto racers began their careers. Upper left: view from the air. Upper right: the starting lineup for a race. Lower left: the start of a race. Lower right: Omar Toft goes into a short-lived skid as Roscoe Sarles takes over the lead in the first race of Richfield's great racing history, January 26, 1919. Clarence Fuller told the story on billboards (center left, bottom right).*

was heading for the 100-mile midwinter race at Ascot Speedway, held near the corner of Slauson and Central avenues in Los Angeles. The race was one of the dozen leading auto events in the country. Lacking the customary sponsorship of an automobile manufacturer, Sarles had retreaded tires and near-empty pockets as he headed west on a gamble. Impressed by the young racer's quiet confidence, Fuller talked him into using Richfield gas and oil in the Ascot race, though Sarles was unfamiliar with Richfield.

Fuller was promoting a new blend of gasoline developed at Richfield's refinery by its superintendent, Tony Panero, and by the young and imaginative head of Richfield manufacturing, Albert Kelley. Joining Richfield in 1914, Kelley had plunged into the task of developing a powerful gasoline. With Panero he had designed a still with one of the first bubble-cap fractionating columns in the industry. To their blend of California products they had added a special casinghead gasoline from Texas and Oklahoma that provided an extra dose of power. Through trial and error they had blended a fuel with the unheard-of octane rating of about 75. They were ready to road-test it when Fuller met Sarles, and on the morning of January 26, 1919, Sarles fueled up with the new gasoline before a crowd of 25,000 at Ascot.

At the starting line a field of six drivers switched on their engines. Among them were two of the most experienced champions of the day, Eddie Hearne and Omar Toft. At the starting flag the cars roared down the speedway in a flurry of dust. In the first few laps of the mile-long oval track, Toft, Hearne, and Sarles were running close together in the lead. On the seventh lap another driver crashed through the inside rail; but before the ambulance could reach him, he had backed the car onto the track and was off again.

Until the twentieth lap Sarles fought for the lead with Toft, who was driving a Miller Special. Then Sarles began to pull ahead. On the thirty-first mile one of Toft's front tires blew out, forcing him to his pit for a change. Sarles lapped him and Hearne to take a strong lead. But Toft was never counted out that easily, and on the fifty-second lap he rushed past both Hearne and Sarles in the backstretch, bringing the spectators to their feet. He came thunder-

97

ing out of the lower turn ahead of the field, only to lose speed when one of his cylinders began missing. Sarles passed him, was in turn overtaken on the sixty-fourth mile, and again drew past the sputtering Miller Special to regain the lead. He crossed the finish line with an average speed for the race of 71 miles an hour—impressive enough in 1919. Racing fans had a young new hero.

For Clarence Fuller the victory was especially sweet. An upstart driver using Richfield gasoline had beaten the veterans. Unlike Toft, Sarles had maintained a steady pace throughout the race, never straining his engine and never faltering. It was as good a testimonial as a gasoline salesman could ask for. Fuller was ready with some newspaper advertisements hailing the victory, and Richfield had found a formula to prove publicly the superiority of its gasoline.

Richfield-sponsored drivers went on to win other races in 1919 and again in 1920. In the latter year the company hired an auto-racing expert, Edward F. ("Big Ed") Wintergust, to represent the company with drivers and track officials. For the following twelve years Big Ed was a familiar figure at the nation's speedways and the friend and colleague of the top racing names in the country.

On Memorial Day in 1921, Richfield made its first strong bid at the Indianapolis Speedway. Richfield gasoline and Richlube oil were used not only by Roscoe Sarles but also by Tommy Milton, a racer from Minneapolis who for several years had been piling up victories at dirt tracks throughout the country. A year earlier Milton had set a new world's speed record of 156 miles an hour in a Duesenberg at Daytona Beach, Florida. Later in 1920 he had come in third on the brick track at Indianapolis.

The night before the 500-mile race Milton and his crew stayed up until 2:00 A.M. installing a new set of thirty-two connecting-rod bearings on his American-made Frontenac, the same car in which Gaston Chevrolet had died in a crash a few months earlier.

When the race started, Ralph DePalma roared to an early lead in his French Ballot and for the first 250 miles set a furious pace for the field. By that time he had lapped Milton and Sarles twice. But suddenly his engine began to falter. Sarles was boxed in behind him, and Tommy Milton sprang into the lead. DePalma

98

*Roscoe Sarles (above right, with his mechanic), the first Richfield winner, who led the field in the Ascot Speedway race at Los Angeles in 1919.*

stopped to change plugs and resumed the race for two more laps before a connecting rod broke—thus justifying Milton's late-night work—and put DePalma out of the race. From then on Milton was unchallenged as the leader. With Sarles finishing second, Richfield-sponsored drivers won both top places in the race. The order was the same in the ranking for national champion in the same year.

That was not the end of Richfield's honors in 1921. Jimmy Murphy, a protégé of Milton's, went to France and entered the Grand Prix at Le Mans—the world's most important auto race—using Richfield gasoline. A week before the event Murphy was injured in a practice run. With several cracked ribs and bandaged from waist to shoulders, Murphy left his hospital bed and was

*Jimmy Murphy, who won the Grand Prix at Le Mans, France, in 1921 and the Indianapolis 500 in 1922. In this photograph, taken in Indianapolis in 1923, Richfield's racing representative, Edward F. ("Big Ed") Wintergust, is second from the right.*

helped into the driver's seat on the day of the race, July 25. At the start of the thirty-lap race Ralph DePalma in his Ballot took the lead. But on the second lap Murphy passed him in his Duesenberg. In the first hour the rough traffic ruined the road surface, and in many places the cars were running on the rocky roadbed. Tires were being chewed up, and stones were flying through the air, puncturing gas tanks and radiators.

On the twenty-ninth lap a rock broke through Murphy's radiator core, and one of his tires blew out. He drove the car, spewing water, to his pit. After adding water and changing the tire, Murphy roared on. But the water kept gushing from the radiator, and another tire blew out eight miles from the finish. Still Murphy pressed on and came in fifteen minutes ahead of second-place winner, Ralph DePalma. It was the first Grand Prix won by an American driver and the first Grand Prix won in an American-made car.

100

Tommy Milton
1921 National Champion.

Jimmy Murphy
and his dog "Pal"
National
Champion 1922 + 1924

Eddie Hearne
1923 National Champion

Peter De Paolo
National Champion
1925+1927

1926
HARRY HARTZ
National Champion

Billy Arnold
1930 National Champion

1928 +
Louie Meyer, 1929 National Champion

Louis Schneider

National Champion 1931

1932
BOB CAREY
National Champion

*The national champions, 1921 to 1932.*

*Fred Frame, the 1932 winner of the Indianapolis 500. Standing next to Frame is Harry Hartz (holding the hat), the owner of the car, a front-drive Miller 8. The riding mechanic (on the opposite side, next to the car) is Jerry Houck. In the race the car averaged 104.144 miles per hour.*

With this victory there was no stopping Clarence Fuller and his promotion of Richfield—the "Gasoline of Power." The advertisement headlines "Richfield Wins Again" and "Winners Use Richfield" were repeated year after year as drivers using the company's gasoline won race upon race. From 1921 to 1932 (the year Fred Frame won the Indianapolis 500) Richfield was used by the winners of all but one of the Indianapolis races. In most races the drivers who came in second, third, fourth, and fifth also used Richfield. In those years Richfield was used by all the national champions—Tommy Milton, Jimmie Murphy, Eddie Hearne, Peter de Paolo, Harry Hartz, Louie Meyer, Billy Arnold, Louis Schneider, and Bob Carey. Most of the other important races in the United States were won on Richfield gas and oil. As the advertisements put it, "Richfield has won more speedway victories and world's

102

*A sculptured racing car, one of many erected to exploit Richfield's auto-racing victories.*

records than all other gasolines combined." Along highways and at major Richfield stations sculptured racing cars were erected to remind motorists of these facts. Harry Hartz stated in a 1926 testimonial advertisement: "Richfield is unquestionably the finest motor fuel that is made. I would never think of using any other."

Tens of thousands of motorists were won to Richfield's banner by such dramatic evidence. By 1926, Richfield's annual gasoline sales had climbed to 130 million gallons—a 50 per cent increase over the preceding year. Richfield had achieved third place in California marketing—only slightly behind the second-largest seller.

Not content with such achievements, Al Kelley and Tony Panero continued to improve their racing and stock-car fuels. For many

103

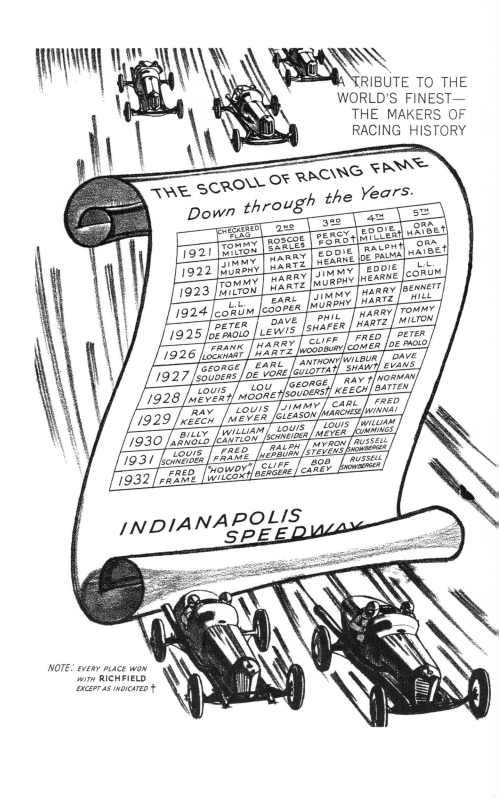

*In the 1928 season* Miss Rioco, *piloted by Ralph Snoddy, the famous hydroplane champion, using Richfield Gasoline and Richlube Oil, won an impressive string of victories. Snoddy won at Palm Beach, Sarasota, Winter Haven, and Miami, Florida, and at Havana, Cuba—five victories out of seven starts. Both world's records for 151-class hydroplanes—the limited and the unlimited—were established with Richfield products, and this combination won scores of victories in the major regattas of 1927–28, including the famous Duke of York Trophy in the International Regatta at Southampton, England. Shown above are a few of the trophies won by* Miss Rioco.

years they led the industry in matching gasoline to the ever more powerful engines coming out of Detroit. During this period Fuller was also promoting Richfield as a marine fuel. Supplying boat racers with gasoline, Richfield began setting new speed records and winning race trophies on the water.

Richfield, by the record, was a pioneer; it was always willing to lead in developing a new area. Now that it led on land and water, it took to the air. In 1926, Richfield helped establish Western Air Express, the world's first commercial airline. The planes flew the Los Angeles–Salt Lake City route on Richfield oil and gas. In 1926 and 1927, when George Hubert Wilkins of Australia made trial flights preparatory to his first two attempts (both aborted by

*Arthur C. Goebel standing beside his single-engine Waco biplane while a Richfield employee fuels the tank.*

*A study in contrasts: Refueling President Harry S Truman's plane,* The Independence, *in Los Angeles, about 1950.*

# From Coast to Coast in 14 Hours, 45 Minutes, 32 Seconds

## ... and COLONEL LINDBERGH establishes the newest Transcontinental Record with RICHFIELD

AT EXACTLY eleven minutes, fifty two seconds past 11 P.M. Easter Sunday, a speeding Lockheed Sirius plane powered with a Pratt & Whitney Wasp motor, piloted by Colonel Charles A. Lindbergh with Mrs. Lindbergh acting as co-pilot, appeared over Roosevelt Field, Long Island, circled the field three times, touched the ground in a perfect three-point landing and another Transcontinental record had been made with Richfield.

Colonel Lindbergh, Technical Advisor of the T.A.T.-Maddux Lines, made this flight to test the possibilities of using higher altitudes for air transport.

Lindbergh took off in the early dawn Sunday, his plane carrying 446 gallons of Richfield gasoline in the tanks. He followed the "great circle" route, flying at altitudes ranging from 10,000 to 15,000 feet . . . streaking through the sky at an average speed of more than 175 miles per hour.

Richfield joins with the nation in saluting the "Flying Colonel" and Mrs. Lindbergh. Once again Lindbergh demonstrates the superb courage and flying skill that made possible his history-making flight across the Atlantic.

# RICHFIELD
## THE GASOLINE OF POWER

*This 1930 Richfield advertisement was one of many in a highly successful campaign to promote Richfield gasoline through association with pioneer aviators and champion auto-racing drivers.*

107

*Dudley M. Steele (left), the first head of Richfield's pioneering aviation department, shown with Colonel Charles A. Lindbergh.*

bad weather) to fly over the North Pole, Richfield supplied the gasoline. In 1927, Arthur C. Goebel and W. V. Davis won the Dole Race from Oakland to Honolulu using Richfield.

In 1927, after Lindbergh's dramatic flight from New York to Paris made Americans air-conscious, Fuller was convinced that aviation was going somewhere. He looked for an aviation manager and found Dudley Steele, who contributed much to Richfield's success in developing, producing, and marketing aviation fuel. Richfield established a separate department for aviation sales and service on October 13, 1927, the first oil company to take this step.

Richfield continued to furnish gasoline to intrepid flyers seeking records. Among them was Wilkins, who in 1928 on his third try succeeded in flying over the polar ice cap from Point Barrow

*Hand pumps on drums succeeded the hand-can fueling of early airplanes. A Richfield pilot, Rufus Pilcher, holds the funnel in this photograph, taken about 1928.*

to Spitsbergen, a feat for which he was knighted. Another example was the record-setting endurance flight over Los Angeles in January, 1929, by an air corps crew that included such notables as Carl Spaatz, Ira Eaker, and Elwood Quesada. Their trimotor Fokker, *Question Mark*, set an endurance record of 150 hours, 40 minutes, using Richfield products. This record was soon beaten by others in Texas but in July, 1929, regained by the *Angeleno*, a Buhl Airesedan, in a sustained flight of 246 hours, 43 minutes, 32 seconds, again on Richfield gasoline and oil. Needless to say, Fuller's advertising and publicity department capitalized on these feats.

In 1929, Richfield took an expensive step in the promotion of aviation. It spent $750,000 building a string of thirty-four beacon towers along the Pacific Coast from the Mexican to the Canadian

109

*George Hubert Wilkins (right) and his copilot, Carl B. Eielson, in 1928, at the time of their successful flight across the polar ice cap from Alaska to Spitsbergen. The plane was an orange-and-blue single-engine Lockheed Vega. Courtesy of Lockheed Aircraft Corporation.*

borders, marking the route for the night-flying airmail pilots. Standing 125 feet high, the tripod towers bore the name Richfield in neon letters on two sides and a code sign for the location on the third side. Each of the towers situated near an airport had an 8-million-candlepower light on the top. Some years later, when the United States Department of Commerce established such beacons across the United States, Richfield turned over its Pacific Coast string to the government without charge. Meanwhile, Richfield had established special "beacon" service stations—its show-window outlets—beside many of the towers.

The tower of the Richfield Building in Los Angeles, completed in September, 1929, was originally designed as an aid to aviation

# RICHFIELD WINS AGAIN

**First in both Class "A" events of the world's greatest air derby! Three new aviation records!**

Leading a field of 37 starters in every lap except one during the entire flight, Earl Rowland in a Scarab-motored Cessna Monoplane covered the 2939 miles of the Class "A" transcontinental air race from New York to Los Angeles in 25 hours, 14 minutes and 6 seconds elapsed time—a new record for planes of this class!

Rowland used Richfield Aviation Gasoline exclusively, competing with practically every well known brand of gasoline that is sold.

Immediately following Rowland's sensational feat, H. S. Myhers in a Simplex Monoplane powered with Richfield Aviation Gasoline and Richlube Motor Oil

won the Class "A" San Francisco to Los Angeles race with an elapsed time of 3 hours, 10 minutes and 20 seconds; while the huge tri-motored Fokker Monoplane, *"Richfield"*sped down from San Francisco with a load of 10 passengers in 2 hours and 13 minutes establishing still another aviation record.

Rowland's and Myhers' great victories follow on the heels of Art Goebel's record breaking non-stop Coast to Coast flight and Captain Wilkins' hazardous 2300-mile dash over the Polar Ice Cap both made with Richfield.

*Richfield continues to demonstrate its great winning qualities in competition—the qualities which have won more speedway victories and records than all other gasolines combined.*

A 1928 advertisement in which Richfield capitalized on its impressive victories in air races.

*The* Angeleno *setting a new endurance record in July, 1929. Richfield's "aerial service station" refueled the* Angeleno *in midair thirty-one times, transferring 2,922 gallons of aviation gasoline and 60 gallons of oil.*

112

Two of the string of thirty-four beacon towers Richfield built along the Pacific Coast. The beacon stations built in California were of Spanish design like the one below, in Capistrano Beach. Those built in Oregon and Washington were of Normandy style, like the one on the left, in Grants Pass, Oregon.

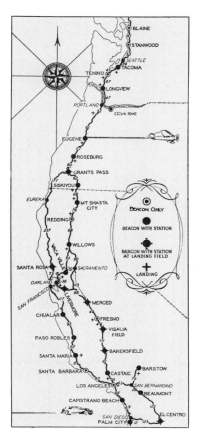

# FROM BORDER TO BORDER
## BEACON LOCATIONS
### WASHINGTON

BLAINE—1 mile south Canadian Border on U. Highway 99.
STANWOOD—1 mile north on U. S. Highway 99.
TACOMA—7 miles south on U.S. Highway 99.
TENINO—4 miles south on U.S. Highway 99.
LONGVIEW—4½ miles southeast on U.S. Highway 9

### OREGON

CROWN POINT—15 miles east of Portland on Colum bia River Highway.
EUGENE—7 miles north on U.S. Highway 99.
ROSEBURG—4 miles north on U.S. Highway 99.
GRANTS PASS—1½ miles north on U.S. Highway 9
SISKIYOU SUMMIT—At Summit on U.S. Highway 9

### CALIFORNIA

MT. SHASTA CITY—1 mile south on U.S. Highway 9
REDDING—7½ miles south on U.S. Highway 99.
WILLOWS—1 mile north on U.S. Highway 99.
SANTA ROSA—3 miles north on U.S. Highway 10
VACAVILLE—3 miles east on U.S. Highway 40.
LIVERMORE—1 mile west on U.S. Highway 48.
MERCED—2 miles north on U.S. Highway 99.
CHUALAR—11 miles south of Salinas on U.S. Hig way 101.
FRESNO—9 miles north on U.S. Highway 99.
VISALIA—6½ miles west on U.S. Highway 99— junction Visalia and Hanford Highways.
PASO ROBLES—3 miles south on U.S. Highway 9
BAKERSFIELD—4 miles north on U.S. Highway 9
SANTA MARIA—2 miles south on U.S. Highway 10
SANTA BARBARA—10 miles south on U.S. High way 101.
BARSTOW—At east city limits on U.S. Highway 6
CASTAIC—4 miles south at junction Ventura High way and U.S. Highway 99.
LOS ANGELES—On Richfield Building, 555 South Flower Street.
BEAUMONT—2½ miles south on U.S. Highway 9
CAPISTRANO BEACH—At Capistrano Beach on U.S. Highway 101.
PALM CITY—5 miles north Mexican Border on U. Highway 101.
EL CENTRO—4 miles north on U.S. Highway 99.

*Above: Map show ing the locations of Richfield's beacon towers. Left: A corner in a Santa Maria station rest room—charm, con venience, and clean liness typical of Richfield's beacon stations.*

114

*Two views of the black-and-gold Richfield Building in Los Angeles, completed in 1929. The building was one of the architectural marvels of its day—the second-tallest structure in the city (second only to the City Hall). The photograph on the right, showing the lighted tower at night, was made some years after the photograph on the left.*

115

*The launching of the Transcontinental Air Transport, July, 1929. On hand for the arrival in Glendale were public officials, company executives, and movie stars, including Douglas Fairbanks and Mary Pickford (seated, center). Lindbergh is the tousle-headed young man standing at the left.*

and as a mooring for dirigibles, though it was never used for the latter. The tower, the tallest structure in Los Angeles except for the City Hall, served for many years as a 40-million-candlepower beacon to night pilots.

While such activities as these were impressing Richfield's name on the flying fraternity, Dudley Steele was leaving nothing undone to serve the young airlines that began springing up in the late 1920's. Richfield was the first company to place underground pits at airports to service airplanes. It was the first in southern California to provide tank-truck fueling service to passenger airlines. It also arranged financing and supplied fuel for a new company, Standard Airlines, operating from Los Angeles to El Paso.

116

In another pioneering venture Richfield supplied the aviation gasoline for the remarkable train-plane trip across the country launched by Transcontinental Air Transport in July, 1929. Passengers traveled by train from New York to Columbus, Ohio, where they boarded a fourteen-passenger Ford Trimotor, which, with its limited fuel capacity, had to make four stops to reach Clovis, New Mexico. From there another train ride took the travelers to Albuquerque and a second flight into Los Angeles after two stops in Arizona. Lindbergh piloted the plane on its last lap, from Winslow, Arizona, to Grand Central Air Terminal in Glendale. The trip across the continent took forty-eight hours, in that day a real improvement over the four-to-five-day train trip.

By 1929, two years after Richfield established its aviation department, the company was supplying gasoline and oil for approximately 40 per cent of all the airline miles flown in the United States. Among its customers were Western Air Express, Inc.; Transcontinental Air Transport; Mid-Continent Airlines, Inc.; Transcontinental and Western Air, Inc.; West Coast Air Transport; Maddux Air Lines; and other early carriers. The Richfield eagle was a familiar sight at every airport on the Pacific Coast.

## 15. EXIT COLON WHITTIER

WHILE Fuller was engaging in the most aggressive publicity and marketing drive in the West Coast oil industry, his company continued to be handicapped by lack of crude production. Richfield paid bonuses as high as $1.10 a barrel for crude oil. In one year the company spent $480,000 in such bonuses. As early as 1922 the handicap sent Richfield looking for a partnership with a producing company.

A natural candidate was United Oil Company, whose rise as a producer in San Joaquin Valley and Signal Hill has been described. Short on refining and marketing capabilities, United was also seeking a partner. One of those pressing for a merger was James A. Talbot, who became a director of United in 1922.

118

As the story goes, one night Talbot was sitting with Fuller in the smoking car of a San Francisco train. As they talked shop, Fuller mentioned that Richfield was "looking for some producing properties with the intention of merging interests." Talbot replied that United was "equally desirous of obtaining an assured outlet." He suggested that Fuller delay any move toward such a merger until United could make an offer.

Soon United did make an overture to Richfield, but the response was cool. By early 1923, however, with lowered gasoline prices putting Richfield at a further disadvantage, its owners looked at United with new interest. One day J. R. Jacobs, secretary-treasurer of Richfield, met Talbot in the Merchants National Bank and told him of Richfield's change of heart.

"If United ever seriously intends to deal with Richfield," he confided, "now is probably a good time to act."

Soon afterward Talbot renewed negotiations through the mediation of a San Francisco firm represented by Fred Thompson, an old friend of Talbot's. Thompson secured a ninety-day option to buy Richfield for $1,250,000, and on July 2, 1923, Talbot presented a proposal to United's board to buy Richfield for $1,750,-000. According to the proposal, the Richfield stockholders would receive $1,250,000, and the intermediaries represented by Thompson would receive $500,000 as a commission. The United board approved the proposal.

The commission alone, representing 40 per cent of the amount paid Richfield, was approximately one-half the amount that the Richfield group had earned in eighteen years of hard work. Such a feat, accomplished overnight, must have greatly impressed Clarence Fuller. It was this kind of new world into which he found himself plunging headlong. It was an abrupt transition from the days of weekly board meetings and semiweekly executive committee meetings held by directors who deliberated over $15.50 items.

In July, 1923, United took over Richfield, and its president, Fred Kellogg, resigned. At the outset, Colon Whittier was clearly impressed. In his report to United stockholders for the year 1923 he declared:

119

*Five Richfield stations. Above left: The first station operated by Rich-field, at Slauson and Central avenues in Los Angeles, in the early 1920's. Its equipment included three hand-operated five-gallon pumps. Customers could see the gasoline gurgling in the glass bowls on top of the pumps.*

*Above right: Double canopies and an octagonal office marked this station in San Marino, California, which typified the stations of the middle 1930's.*

*Below: Larger, more sweeping lines were featured in this station in Portland, Oregon, representative of the post–World War II period of the late 1940's.*

120

*Above: Bathed in light, the expansive design and landscaping of a typical station in Sacramento, California, built in the late 1950's.*

*Below: A new program to blend Richfield's stations with their suburban surroundings is shown in this station in Los Altos, California, built in the early 1960's. The shingle roof, brick walls, and picture windows are a far cry from the stark design of the 1920's.*

121

The entire capital stock of the Richfield Oil Company was acquired on August 1st, 1923, and the interests of the two companies were merged. This company has a large number of distributing plants advantageously located, as well as approximately 60 of its own service stations in California, and not less than 600 dealers are handling Richfield products. With an extensive program of market expansion for the current year and the completion of the new refinery near Los Angeles Harbor, the earnings from this source will be materially increased. The fact should not be overlooked that "Richfield" gasoline and "Richlube" motor oil and greases are well and favorably known throughout the state of California and have gained among all branches of the trade an enviable reputation for high quality and efficiency.

Whittier was not prepared, however, for the events that followed. Fuller lost no time taking advantage of the opportunities afforded by access to United's capital. Within weeks he had arranged the purchase of land at Hynes, near Long Beach, for construction of a 10,000-barrel refinery. The company employed David E. Day, a consulting refinery engineer, to help design the refinery. His design was called impractical at the time, but it proved successful and was indeed far ahead of its day. (Years later Day was to become a vice-president and director of Richfield Oil Corporation.) By the end of the first year after the merger Fuller had increased the number of dealer outlets from 600 to 1,450 and annual gasoline sales from 12 million to 32 million gallons.

During the early and middle 1920's the phenomenal growth of the automobile industry attracted large numbers of independent service-station dealers, men who owned and operated their own stations. It was to the independents that Fuller directed his efforts and salesmanship, and Richfield developed the best independent-dealer relationship ever known in the industry. Rio Grande, also competing for the independent-dealer business, felt the impact of Fuller's techniques. Many times Rio Grande salesmen reported that they were only able to close a deal because Richfield was unable to make deliveries for ninety days or more.

In 1924, Richfield again entered the San Francisco Bay region, this time on a scale that would assure success. A storage depot, a

*Richfield's storage depot, warehouse, and operating base for a tank-truck fleet built on the waterfront at Oakland, California, 1924.*

warehouse, and an operating base for a tank-truck fleet were built on the waterfront in Oakland. At the same time an extensive marine base was constructed at Long Beach. Thoroughly modern, with pipeline connections direct from shipside to the refineries, this terminal was equipped to load out gasoline at a rate of 8,000 barrels an hour and twice that quantity of fuel oil. The 3,500-ton, 28,000-barrel tankship *Brilliant* was purchased, rechristened *Richfield*, and brought to the West Coast by way of the Panama Canal. It was put into service in 1925, completing the coastwise transportation chain which, by economical distribution, opened northern California to Richfield's products.

These improvements pushed the marketing frontiers north to the Oregon line and eastward into Arizona and Nevada. By the end of 1926, Richfield had a chain of twenty-seven strategically placed bulk distributing plants—twenty of them company owned.

123

*Richfield's tankship* Brilliant, *built in 1913 and purchased and re-christened* Richfield *in 1925. Its capacity was 28,000 barrels.*

Through substations and contracts with independent wholesalers, the system served five hundred cities and towns.

The intensity of this sales and refining expansion had a sobering effect on Colon Whittier. He found himself in some rather fast company, and it seems evident that, although he was president of the company, he was somewhat out of his element—too far removed from the decision makers. One day while the Hynes refinery was under construction, Whittier and Kent paid a visit to a company lease on Signal Hill, overlooking the refinery site. Turning to Kent, Whittier said: "There is the damnedest piece of foolishness ever perpetrated—a ten-thousand-barrel refinery for a company with no more outlets than Richfield has is ridiculous. I'll bet you all the money in California that no more than five thousand barrels a day will ever go through it."

Whittier found a way out. Over the years his practice of selling his stock in United, buying it back at a lower price, and again re-

124

The Richfield, *bound for Oakland, California, formally inaugurates the newly dredged direct-to-sea channel at Long Beach Harbor, April, 1926.*

The self-propelled barge Richlube, *built in 1926 and used for bunkering ships in the San Francisco area.*

*Richfield's refinery at Hynes, California, completed in 1925, with a daily capacity of 10,000 barrels. By 1926, when Richfield had captured 10 per cent of the market in its area, the capacity had been increased to 50,000 barrels a day.*

selling had brought him a personal fortune. On February 18, 1925, he notified the United board that he had sold his interest in the company and was resigning as president and director. A month later he was followed by his long-term associate, Kent, who resigned as vice-president and general manager.

On the same day Talbot was named president. Now Talbot's control over the destiny of Richfield was formalized. He commanded the production, refining, and marketing facilities of a fully integrated company, freed of the limitations under which he and Fuller had previously had to function. For an ambitious man like Talbot, it was time to tilt at the windmills of the gods.

# 16. THE EAGLE FLIES HIGH

BY 1926, Fuller's remarkable success in marketing and the constant publicity attending his sales efforts had largely obscured the name of the parent company, United, whose securities were owned by the public. The stock-market possibilities demanded a change in name to Richfield. Only by this measure could Talbot and the financiers take full advantage of the good will and publicity Richfield had won. Accordingly, the board decided upon reorganization.

Instead of simply changing the name from United to Richfield, the board created a new company, Richfield Oil Company of California, which was incorporated in Delaware in August, 1926. Its authorized capital of $60 million was divided into 400,000 shares of 7 per cent cumulative preferred stock with a par value of $25 a share and 2 million shares of common stock of $25 par value, together with an authorized bond issue of $20 million. The company issued $12 million in 15-year, 6 per cent convertible bonds.

To help market the new company's securities, Talbot ordered a reappraisal of the properties of United Oil Company and Richfield Oil Company, following the same pattern he had established for United in 1923. The appraisers reported a value of more than $16 million above the book value, to which Talbot added another $1 million, preferring his judgment to that of the appraisers. On the strength of the appraisal the new common stock of Richfield of California issued for the old stock of United Oil Company was capitalized at $24,415,000. By then, less than $5 million had actually been paid in, and more than $19.5 million had been pumped in. Talbot neglected to mention these important data in his report to the stockholders of October 23, 1926.

With the new company organized and the consolidation completed, the impressive new balance sheet and the fabulously popular name Richfield on the certificates made the securities easy to sell. Talbot was now also in the stock-promotion business.

Sales continued to rise. In 1926, with only 20 bulk plants as compared to Standard's 703, Richfield captured more than 10 per cent of the market in its area and was in fourth place in sales (in third place in California). This remarkable achievement is illustrated in the following table of sales as of June 30, 1926, in the territory covering California, Washington, Oregon, Nevada, and Arizona:

| Company | Bulk plants | Service stations owned and operated by marketer | Percentage of sales |
|---------|-------------|--------------------------------------------------|---------------------|
| Standard Oil Company of California | 703 | 720 | 28.7 |
| Shell Oil Company | 179 | 505 | 15.0 |
| Union Oil Company of California | 283 | 392 | 12.3 |
| Richfield Oil Company of California | 20 | 80 | 10.3 |

These figures speak volumes for the creative energy of Richfield's marketing staff, who were serving their customers from meager California facilities, mostly through independent dealers and jobbers.

Shored up by the new financing, Fuller drove on with his expansion program. The capacity of the Hynes refinery was increased to 50,000 barrels daily, while four Cross cracking units could handle 14,000 barrels of charging stock a day. In 1927, Richfield built service stations in Oregon and Washington, constantly pushing northward to the Canadian border. Richfield was also extending its market to foreign countries, taking advantage of the ocean terminal built in Long Beach Harbor to serve the tanker traffic to San Francisco. By the end of 1927 the tankers were also serving Portland and Seattle. Southern California remained the major market for Richfield, however.

In the meantime Richfield was acquiring still more production, including expensive town-lot leases on Signal Hill. In 1927 the company purchased a group of leases from Delaney Petroleum Corporation for $3,290,000 and made many smaller purchases for cash or stock or a combination of both.

Richfield also bought several producing companies in which some of its present and former directors and close associates were controlling stockholders. In 1926 it purchased Southwestern Petroleum Company, half of whose shares were owned by Talbot, Whittier, Kent, and George W. Newberger (a Richfield director). Largely as a result of these acquisitions, new stock of $11 million was issued for cash or property, bonded debt was increased to $12,650,000, and net property accounts were increased $18.5 million. The expansion was headlong.

While such growth was bold and imaginative, it was becoming unrealistic from a financial standpoint. By the end of 1927 it was clearly apparent that such a thing as a budget was completely unknown to Richfield's management. Fuller was busy expanding his markets, the production department was busy buying oil properties, and Talbot was busy selling stocks and bonds. The idea of setting up a budget and financing to meet it simply never occurred to those in control. The eagle was beginning to fly too high for comfort.

131

## 17. THE MILLS OF THE GODS GRIND
## A LITTLE FASTER

IN his report to the stockholders for 1927, Talbot said: "There are stages in a company's history when expense within reason must be disregarded, to build a market. When the market objective has been gained, the management naturally turns its efforts toward increased profits. Richfield reached this point during 1926." Whether or not he actually believed that Richfield had reached that point in 1926, he certainly forgot it. After that, sheer valor seems to have taken precedence over shrewdness and enterprise.

Early in 1928, Richfield was selling preferred stock, issuing new common stock for properties, and retiring all outstanding funded debt by payment and conversion. Inventories were under $5 million and manageable. Richfield was producing and had

132

contracted for crude oil to the full extent of its market requirements. Like other small independents, however, it had to pay a bonus for most of its purchases.

Riding the crest of the business boom of the 1920's, Richfield seemed sounder and stronger than ever. Talbot commented in his report to the stockholders of April 25, 1928: "We believe that the oil industry on the Pacific Coast faces a period of greater stability and prospective earnings and all factors point toward the most successful year in the history of your Company." With this confident statement Talbot decided to relax a bit. To help relieve the boredom of success, he ordered a 175-foot yacht, the *Carissima*—almost as large as the *Casiana* owned by the West Coast oil king, Edward L. Doheny.

A calm also descended upon Richfield's fiscal waters. Practically all of the authorized capital stock was disposed of. There was no reason to sell bonds. The month of April, 1928, passed without a single board resolution authorizing stock sales or purchase of companies. Talbot's investment bankers, probably pinched by having nothing new to sell, amused themselves by manipulating pools in Richfield stock.

But for a man of Talbot's ambitions this calm was only a lull before new and more imaginative assaults. A classic definition of an expert is one who avoids all the small errors on the way to the grand blunder. Talbot graduated as an expert cum laude on May 24, 1928, when he presided over a special meeting of the board and pushed through a resolution which was to bankrupt the company. The resolution authorized Talbot to purchase control of Pan American Western Petroleum Company and "other properties" from Doheny for $7.5 million in cash. That was the "cover charge." To finance the purchase, the board authorized the sale of 100,000 shares of Richfield common stock at $35 a share and $5 million of convertible three-year, 5½ per cent notes.

A shrewd businessman, Doheny had entered the oil business in 1892 with a shovel and a strong back and had become one of the giants of the industry. Talbot, seemingly bent on becoming a new Doheny, viewed the Pan American purchase as a big step in that direction.

133

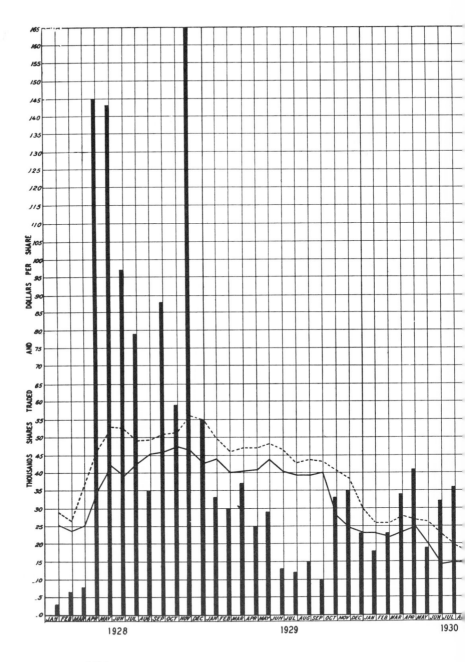

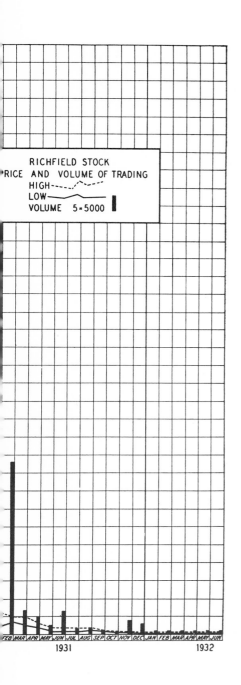

RICHFIELD STOCK
PRICE AND VOLUME OF TRADING
HIGH-----.../^-----
LOW
VOLUME 5-5000

1931          1932

Common stock of the Richfield Oil Company of California was one of many issues manipulated by speculators in the stock-market boom and crash. The chart at the left shows the wide fluctuations in volume of trading, largely the result of large pool operations which took advantage of and in turn affected the price of Richfield stock.

135

*Edward L. Doheny, one of the oil giants of the early 1900's*

Pan American had outstanding stock of 500,000 shares, 100,-000 of which were voting shares. Doheny owned all the voting shares and 50,000 of the nonvoting shares, which together equaled 30 per cent. After acquiring Doheny's shares, Richfield's board authorized 116,667 shares of Richfield common stock to be offered to Pan American class B nonvoting stockholders at a ratio of 1 share of Richfield for 3 shares of Pan American.

The class B stockholders of Pan American raised quite a fuss about the provision that they would receive $7.5 million in cash for 30 per cent of the company while they were offered only $2,-917,000 par value of Richfield stock for the remaining 70 per cent. But they finally gave in and exchanged the stock.

What did Richfield get for what was then a huge capital outlay? Pan American represented properties that Doheny had withheld and mobilized as a separate unit when he sold Pan American Petroleum and Transport Company (no relation to our Pan American) to Standard Oil Company of Indiana. It consisted of a large refinery, ocean terminals, and a myriad of facilities—all duplications of everything Richfield owned. Those facilities included a pipeline built to carry government oil from Elk Hills to Los Angeles (but no oil to go through it), a ten-year operating deficit, a $10 million inventory, $24 million of bonded debt, and a judgment for over $5 million plus the interest against it issued by the United States government in an Elk Hills lease squabble (see Chapter 23). There were a few representative service stations, but they were owned by Doheny and leased for one year to Pan American. The other property included in the deal was a contract with Doheny's Petroleum Securities Company to purchase all of its oil production from whatever source at Standard of California's posted price. No producing properties of value were included. Doheny had seen to it that the worthwhile producing properties were owned by Petroleum Securities Company, the family corporation. It was a truly bleak picture. Thorough research down through the years has failed to disclose any benefit to Richfield from the deal. The negative side was overpowering.

The reasons motivating the Richfield board will probably never be known. It is difficult, however, to believe that even a group of promoters would walk blindly into such a trap. Yet the minutes of the meetings show no dissent among the qualified oil men on the board. One is tempted to conclude that Talbot's earlier successes had charmed the board into this grand blunder.

137

Whatever the reason, when the Richfield board members and management personnel settled down to count their blessings, they found themselves operating five refineries with a total capacity of 159,000 barrels a day. That was more than 4.8 per cent of the national total and 22 per cent of the California total—nearly as much capacity as that of Standard Oil Company of California. They found themselves more than $50 million in debt, with unmanageable inventories approaching and soon to exceed $20 million and firm contracts to purchase oil they could not sell.

When Richfield formally took over Pan American, J. C. Anderson, Doheny's righthand man, was still president of the company. Incidental acquisitions in the purchase were large amounts of obsolete and worthless oil-field supplies that had been crammed into Pan American warehouses by a purchasing agent who also had an interest in a supply house. The story is told that Anderson personally took inventories for Doheny, counting the bolts and nuts with Richfield's warehousemen. To be sure that Richfield got only the junk that it bought, Anderson brought his lunch and would not leave the scene when the Richfield warehousemen went to lunch.

Despite the acquisition of this huge white elephant, Richfield's board of directors seemed to share Talbot's own belief that he could do no wrong. In fact, in December, 1928, the board voted to create the office of chairman of the board, a move approved by the stockholders at their annual meeting on March 21, 1929. Speaking to them on that occasion, Talbot publicly assumed that "your directors may see fit to elect me to the office of Chairman of the Board," adding that the position, "carrying with it the Chairmanship of the Finance Committee and the Executive Committee, will place me in the position of much more efficiently administering the business and financial affairs of your company."

## 18. THE MOVE EASTWARD

WHILE Chairman of the Board Talbot was devoting his time "more efficiently" to the financial affairs of the company, Fuller, the new president, was desperately trying to dispose of the incoming oil. At the time of the Pan American merger Richfield's sales had achieved a balance in its production and purchase contracts. But the huge Pan American inventory, its small crude production, and its daily refinery operation proved immediate embarrassments.

The situation was greatly aggravated by a contract with Pacific Western Oil Company, managed by William C. McDuffie. Shortly after the Richfield–Pan American deal, Doheny sold a portion of the producing properties of his Petroleum Securities Company to

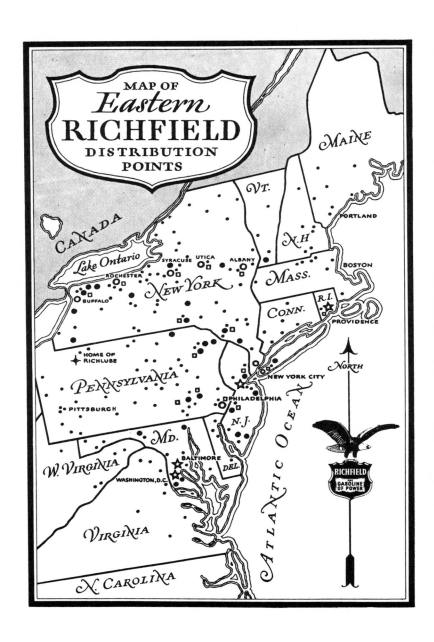

MAP OF
*Eastern*
RICHFIELD
DISTRIBUTION
POINTS

CANADA

MAINE

PORTLAND

VT.

N.H

Lake Ontario

SYRACUSE  UTICA  ALBANY

ROCHESTER

NEW YORK

MASS.

BOSTON

BUFFALO

CONN.

R.I.

PROVIDENCE

HOME OF
RICHLUBE

PENNSYLVANIA

NORTH

NEW YORK CITY

PITTSBURGH

PHILADELPHIA

N.J.

MD.

ATLANTIC OCEAN

RICHFIELD
THE
GASOLINE
OF POWER

W. VIRGINIA

BALTIMORE

DEL.

WASHINGTON, D.C.

VIRGINIA

N. CAROLINA

140

## LEGEND

★ STAR . . . WATER TERMINALS
    (Regular Tankers
    Accommodated)
Curtis Bay, Md. (Baltimore)
Port Everglades, Fla. (Miami)
Bayonne, N. J.
Providence, R. I.

O CIRCLE . . . BARGE DELIVERIES
Long Island City, N. Y.
Mt. Vernon, N. Y. (L. I. City Br.)
Schenectady, N. Y.
Ilion, N. Y. (Utica Br.)
Syracuse, N. Y.
Rochester, N. Y.
Buffalo, N. Y.
Philadelphia, Pa.

● DOT . . . OTHER BULK PLANTS
                (Company Operated)

| | |
|---|---|
| Camden, N. J. | Middletown, N. Y. |
| Newark, N. J. | Lockport, N. Y. |
| Vineland, N. J. | Barker, N. Y. |
| Absecon, N. J. | Canandaigua, N. Y. |
| Avon, N. J. | Hamburg, N. Y. |
| Harrisburg, Pa. | Jamestown, N. Y. |
| Reading, Pa. | Port Jervis, N. Y. |
| Scranton, Pa. | Albion, N. Y. |
| Carbondale, Pa. | Central Sq., N. Y. |
| Honesdale, Pa. | Fort Plains, N. Y. |
| Athens, Pa. | Norwich, N. Y. |
| Binghamton, N. Y. | New Hyde Park, L. I. |

SHERWOOD BROS., INC.

★ STAR . . . WATER TERMINAL
Baltimore, Md.

● DOT . . . OTHER BULK PLANTS
Highlandtown, Md.
Washington, D. C.
Hagerstown, Md.
Perryville, Md.

WHOLESALE OUTLETS

☐ SQUARE . . . 15 Branches

More than 6800 retail station outlets are
supplied from the points shown on this
map.

*Clarence Fuller built an instant empire for Richfield on the Atlantic
Coast, which by 1930 had achieved an over-all gallonage as large as
Richfield had on the West Coast.*

141

Pacific Western Oil Company, a new firm promoted by Blyth, Witter & Company. Blair & Company, Inc., representing Doheny, persuaded Talbot to cancel the crude-oil purchase contract with Petroleum Securities Company and substitute a contract with Pacific Western under which Richfield would buy all of Pacific Western's oil, present and future. Later Pacific Western acquired from Mr. and Mrs. Spalding a lease on their Tecolote Ranch, along with tideland permits. The latter turned out to be a goodly portion of the Elwood Field discovered by Rio Grande Oil Company in July, 1928.

By mid-1929, McDuffie, like the rest of the operators, was busy exploiting the field. Fuller's problems were magnified by having to buy the flush production from Pacific Western's unexpected bonanza. Such an excess of production could not be sold on the Pacific Coast without a disastrous effect on the market. The company had reached and passed the point of diminishing returns in local marketing; new outlets were taken on only under great pressure and at ruinous prices. Nor could the company accept export business at current offshore-product prices, since the prices for California crude made a substantial loss inevitable.

Standard Oil Company of California had absolute power to hold a minimum price on crude oil, meanwhile watching product prices decline under competitive selling pressures to a fraction of the cost of raw material. As mentioned earlier, independents generally had to purchase crude oil at a bonus over Standard Oil's posting, and it was the usual practice for landowners to require settlement for royalty at the highest market price with Standard's postings as a floor. In a prolonged price war with an imbalance of supply and demand, any inordinate delay by Standard in reducing crude prices as rapidly as product prices were dropping was certain to injure the small refiner. Only the integrated refiners with large production and adequate financial liquidity could survive.

Under the extreme pressures of the moment Richfield decided to develop a market for its products on the Atlantic seaboard. Richfield Oil Corporation of New York was organized as a subsidiary. Fuller set about building a market from Cape Hatteras north, with the principal terminals at Baltimore and New York—

142

almost five thousand nautical miles from Los Angeles. The move eastward naturally required large outlays of cash for the acquisition of going concerns and the introduction of a new product in a sharply competitive market.

In April, 1930, I visited Fuller at his New York headquarters in the Ambassador Hotel. His suite was pulsing with activity. Bellhops were rushing in and out with telegrams. Too busy to tip each one personally, Fuller had placed near the door a large cut-glass bowl which he kept filled with quarters. As each bellhop left, Fuller would wave in the direction of the bowl and say, "Help yourself." He didn't know—and probably didn't care—whether the bellhop took one quarter or a handful.

Working at this feverish pace, Fuller had bought up various large distributors; had acquired ocean terminals in Baltimore, New York, Providence, and Boston; and had achieved an over-all gallonage as large as Richfield had on the West Coast. When I talked to him, he was elated by his success. It was plain that he had reverted to the company policy expressed by Talbot in his 1927 report: "There are stages in a company's history when expense within reason must be disregarded, to build a market."

In the early days of the Royal Dutch–Shell group of companies, Sir Henri Deterding said, "The advantages of having production not concentrated in only one country but scattered over the whole world so it may be *distributed* under favorable geographic conditions have been clearly proven." The Richfield board forgot to consider the geographical hazards of developing a market five thousand miles from home without nearby sources of production or supply. The geography of oil production can, and in this case did, change very rapidly. In 1930, Columbus M. ("Dad") Joiner brought in an oil well at Kilgore, Texas, discovering the great East Texas Field, which for more than thirty years was the largest oil field discovered in the United States. Before Fuller could even think of serving the extensive market he had put together in the East, the prices of crude oil and oil products were less than the freight costs from California to the Atlantic seaboard.

143

## 19. THE EAGLE FALTERS

WHILE Fuller was building an instant empire on the Atlantic, Talbot was dancing on the peaks of high finance. He was merrily pursuing his practice of issuing convertible bonds, juggling the market, and bringing about quick conversion of the bonds to stock or paying them off before maturity from proceeds of subsequent issues. There seemed to be no doubt in his mind that this cycle of bond issues, conversion, and still more bonds could continue indefinitely. On May 22, 1929, the Richfield board authorized a bonded indebtedness of $75 million and the sale of 25 million 6 per cent bonds at $93 each to Bond & Goodwin & Tucker, Inc.; Blair & Company, Inc.; Hemphill, Noyes & Company; and Hunter, Dulin & Company.

144

Amazingly, while crude inventories were burgeoning and large sums were being spent and committed for Richfield of New York, only a fraction of the bond-sale monies was being used for these and other corporate purposes. Rather, it was used mostly to pull Doheny's chestnuts out of the fire. When Talbot made the Pan American deal with Doheny, Pan American had two outstanding bond issues totaling $23,927,000. These included $13,393,000 in first-mortgage, fifteen-year convertible 6 per cent sinking-fund gold bonds, due in 1940, and $10,534,000 in fifteen-year, 6 per cent sinking-fund notes, also due in 1940. Doheny owned $2,500,000 of the first-mortgage bonds and all the unsecured gold notes. In addition, Pan American owed Doheny $3,050,000 on current notes.

For some unexplained reason, $13,600,000 of the $25 million in bonds sold by Richfield went to buy from Doheny the unsecured gold notes he held in Pan American and to pay off his current notes of $3,050,000. Additional proceeds from the sale of Richfield bonds were used to pay off Doheny's $2.5 million in first-mortgage bonds. Finally, Richfield paid Doheny $2 million for two tankships, the *Pat Doheny* and the *Larry Doheny*.

The canny Doheny was home free with cash. A year earlier he had rid himself of an extremely unprofitable and vulnerable refining and marketing complex with some production of doubtful value and had sold his voting stock in Pan American to Richfield for $7.5 million, over twice his cost. He had forced the dismayed, protesting, but impotent class B stockholders, who had put up over 70 per cent of the total capital, to accept on a one-for-three basis Richfield's stock, which a short time later had no value. In all, he had received $25.6 million in cash and in addition had made Richfield contract to buy all the crude-oil production of his Petroleum Securities Company—truly a remarkable transaction.

There is no suggestion in the records why Talbot bought Doheny's unsecured notes and first-mortgage bonds. Perhaps Doheny charmed him. In any case the fabled Doheny luck—probably better described as innate shrewdness—was as potent as ever. Doheny had his money in the bank with the Great Depression only months away.

More than any words could do, these acts seem to prove that Talbot had unbounded confidence in his ability to operate as usual. He may have fancied that by these acts he had become a great man in Doheny's eyes—or perhaps even that he was stepping into Doheny's shoes. In a sense, of course, he did just that, but he chose some old ones full of holes and troubles. If the amount Talbot sank in the purchase of Pan American had been spent for sound oil reserves, the results might not have been as exciting, but they would have had a very different effect on Richfield.

No further attempts were made to sell bonds or stocks before the market crash in October, 1929, although some stock was used to buy the eastern-seaboard companies for Richfield Oil Corporation of New York. After the crash all efforts to sell stock and bonds failed. Gone was the pattern of financing that had worked so well for Talbot. He turned to the banks, found fertile ground to plow, and by December 31, 1930, owed them over $10 million.

In the midst of this high-flying finance Richfield's other mistakes were helping produce the inevitable financial crisis. In their six-month report to the stockholders of September, 1930, Talbot and Fuller said: "Richfield of New York sustained a net loss of $909,000 after charging to expense more than $800,000 of non-recurring introductory expense." Talbot's third-quarter report, released on December 1, 1930, was still more revealing:

> The company's sales have progressed very satisfactorily, especially on the Atlantic coast, where gasoline gallonage equal to that on the Pacific coast has been built up. The company now has a domestic distribution in excess of 400,000 gallons per year. During the first nine months of 1930, however, unsatisfactory prices for products have prevailed on the Atlantic coast, in spite of which your company is netting back more per gallon for its gasoline sold through the eastern company than it could secure by selling offshore in cargo lots. It is expected that the price situation on the Atlantic coast will be adjusted early in 1931.

Beset by low retail prices, Richfield was flooded with crude it did not need. Talbot's report continued:

> As a result of voluntary production curtailment program that has existed during the nine months in California, Richfield has

146

been obliged to close in 45% of its own production and to purchase at the posted market price approximately 70% of its crude requirements, producing only the remaining 30%. Richfield is the second largest buyer of crude oil in the state of California.

At the same time the company was frantically opening other outlets around the world. Earlier in 1930 Talbot had reported: "Richfield products are now being sold in most of the principal countries of the world, including South America, Australia, Africa, New Zealand, India, China and Japan." It was an ambitious undertaking. At Richfield's California refineries 70 per cent of the crude supply was purchased from other producers, and over two-thirds of that amount was purchased at an average bonus of 10 cents a barrel over prices set by Standard Oil Company of California. At the same time Richfield was attempting to market in competition with Standard and the Royal Dutch–Shell group throughout the Pacific and on the Atlantic seaboard.

Even without the pressures of the time Richfield could not have won such a competition, and the effort can only be ascribed to unbelievable boldness (probably enhanced by the effect generated by the rich Cuban cigars of the time). The problems were intensified by Richfield's need to rid itself of the crushing burden of operating 4.8 per cent of the nation's refining capacity on a shoestring without ownership of the raw material or the ability to buy it at par. Richfield had not yet realized the soundness of Sir Henri Deterding's philosophy of matching markets with geographical ownership of production.

147

## 20. THE DESPERATE MONTHS

ON December 18, 1930, just seventeen days after Talbot sent out his report on the achievements of Richfield of New York, his board decided to try to sell the organization which Fuller had just put together so successfully. This decision was not taken lightly, and was born of the pressures of the Depression.

The outlook had grown darker and blood pressures had risen on May 7, 1930, when Richfield's board authorized the officers to borrow up to $10 million and pledge inventories and receivables. There was no suggestion where the money would come from, and in fact none could be found. The company continued to pay the dividend, however, in the desperate hope that, by so doing, more stock could be sold.

By June it was certain that there would be no more stock or bond financing. The banks would lend no more and were extending the outstanding loans from day to day, pressing for payment. The investment bankers and investment bank directors who had participated in securities sales in the past were either helpless or unwilling to continue doing so; they had many problems of their own. Talbot grabbed at a straw when James C. Willson & Company, a New York banking firm, began issuing bullish statements about Richfield, and at the same time the board reduced the price of the stock offering to $17 a share. But before the proposed sale could clear the office of the California corporation commissioner, the price sagged further, Willson & Company lost interest, and that hope faded.

For some time decisions had been based on expediency or desperation, and the tempo of desperation was increasing. Other efforts having failed, the management now decided to shore up Richfield by taking advantage of the resources of its employees. In August, 1930, a subsidiary company was formed and capitalized at $2 million, with the immediate objective of devoting its purchasing strength to all three classes of Richfield securities and thus of assisting materially in stabilizing the market price. Stock in the new company was sold to employees for cash down payments and monthly installments; Richfield made no contribution. In a bullish sales letter to employees on August 30, 1930, Fuller stated that, though he was unable to present the "employees' benefit plan" personally, having been called to the East, he believed it to be a real opportunity and added that no "coercive measures" were to be employed in obtaining subscriptions. About $1,310,000 was subscribed and $357,000 paid in, but, like other efforts, it was too late. The courts later took a dim view of the "opportunity" and allowed the employees general unsecured claims against the receivership estate for their payments.

At about the same time Richfield was indulging in still another financial caper. Sometime in the latter part of 1929, Richfield had paid $822,500 for 47,000 shares of Universal Consolidated Oil Company stock controlled by Joe Toplitzky, a director of Richfield. In his third-quarter report, dated November 3, 1929, Talbot

149

had said: "Control of Universal Consolidated Oil Company was recently acquired by Richfield. The company's [Universal's] financial position is very strong with ratio of current assets to current liabilities of approximately 8 to 1." Universal Consolidated's own report for the full year 1929, issued by Richfield on April 8, 1930, showed a current assets ratio of approximately 3.6 to 1 and advances made to Richfield of $769,540, which in 1930 increased to $1,305,960.

On January 28, 1930, the board authorized a contract for the purchase of 106,000 shares of Universal Consolidated capital stock from Toplitzky for some $221,000 in cash and 70,666 shares of Richfield stock, to be issued to Toplitzky or his nominees. The Universal Consolidated stock was controlled by H. Fleishhacker and R. W. Hanna, of San Francisco. With this deal and a subsequent exchange of stock, Richfield acquired 186,778 shares, or 52 per cent of Universal Consolidated stock. In a suit brought by the Richfield receiver against Toplitzky in 1931, Toplitzky's attorney stated that Richfield was in control of Universal Consolidated by prior arrangement with a three-man syndicate, of which Toplitzky was a member. He further stated that Richfield had borrowed about $1.3 million from the treasury of Universal Consolidated without the knowledge of the syndicate.

Although such a practice appears common now, at the time it was an adventure in high finance to buy control of a company and use its own cash to pay for the purchase. The courts later turned a jaundiced eye on the "borrowing," and Richfield lost its investment in Universal, which ultimately became a very prosperous company.

Meanwhile, the board was preparing to sell Richfield stock at whatever price it could get. On September 5, 1930, it authorized a change in the value of the common stock from $25 par to no par. But security prices were dropping more each day. Prices for petroleum products were going down even faster, and, still more ominous, the consumption of oil was also plummeting.

At a meeting of the Richfield board on October 2, 1930, the members for the first time discussed a "proposed change of management" but made no decision on the matter. In six meetings held from the third to the tenth, they decided on merger as the only hope. Director Sam Haskins was authorized to invite an offer from William F. Humphrey, president of Associated Oil Company of California, who had previously indicated an interest in acquiring Richfield.

Fuller's success in building a large distribution for Richfield of New York had awakened several larger companies to the possibility of acquiring Richfield so as to gain access to the New York company. Late in 1929, Harry Sinclair and Fuller had discussed the possibility, and Fuller had made Sinclair an offer to sell the Richfield company of California at $60 a share. Sinclair had made no counteroffer, however.

Sam Haskins now secured an offer from Humphrey of Associated to buy Richfield's assets (the price was never disclosed). Richfield's board accepted the offer, subject to certain amendments. It was a logical move for Associated, which was well entrenched in northern California, with a modern refinery and a strong market position, while Richfield was centered in southern California. The move apparently had the additional goal of strengthening Tide Water Associated Oil Company, which then held most of the stock of Associated and Tide Water Oil Company of New York. The latter could use Richfield's eastern marketing spread to advantage. With the acquisition of Richfield, Tide Water Associated Oil Company would be more attractive to Sinclair Consolidated Oil Corporation, with which it was conducting its own merger discussions. But, on November 21, Associated withdrew its offer. Conditions in the industry were deteriorating so rapidly that any estimate was valueless within a week's time.

Back in 1925, United Oil Company had bought several thousand acres of fee land in Belridge and Lost Hills (near Bakersfield, California), and now Talbot hoped that a successful well in Belridge would solve Richfield's problems. Mericos ("Max") Whittier, Colon Whittier's brother, had bought some land for his Belridge Oil Company in 1910 and in 1930 drilled a deep well and discovered a major oil field. Richfield was now drilling a well on its own lands in the region, about one and a half miles north-

151

east of the Belridge discovery well. In his report for the third quarter of 1930, dated December 1, Talbot said:

> It is expected that Richfield's Belridge well will be completed within the next 15 days at from 5,000 barrels to 10,000 barrels per day of 45 gravity oil. The completion of this well will be followed by the commencement of additional wells on the Belridge properties immediately, development work in other fields being temrarily suspended. For gasoline producing purposes, 5,000 barrels per day of this light oil is equal to from 10,000 to 15,000 barrels per day of the heavier oil.

Before the well was finished, the board voted that if a deal with Associated was not consummated the finance committee would have the power to sell one-half interest in the Belridge–Lost Hills property to Amerada Petroleum Corporation for $5 million. But the well turned out to be dry, and that dream too faded.

## 21. THE EAGLE FALLS

EVEN without the Pan American deal, 1930 would have been a year to try the souls of Talbot and Fuller. Gasoline was selling below cost in all categories; California oil wells were producing a flood of oil—887,000 barrels daily with a market for only 675,-000 barrels. Oil was being stored in anything that would hold it, and at least one company was pumping oil back into the ground on its fee lands. On October 13 the Richfield board authorized the sale of 3 million barrels of fuel oil at the specified price of 50 cents a barrel and an option for 2 million more barrels. On October 15 it took a step too long delayed. Fuller was authorized to address a letter to Pacific Western canceling the crude-oil purchase contract. On December 8 the dividends on the preferred shares were discontinued.

These final actions, though constructive, were too late. As the end of the year approached, the securities markets continued to collapse, Richfield's bank credit was exhausted, and hopes for merger on any terms vanished. The full import of Richfield's predicament became evident. Its management had overplayed its hand—a common enough error of the time. It was extremely difficult for men who had been riding on the crest to accept the cold fact that the financial world as they knew it had crumbled.

In mid-December the banks notified Richfield that they would extend the overdue notes to February 1, 1932, provided that the loans were secured by bonds of the corporation of $10.5 million and that contemplated changes in the management structure were satisfactory.

On December 24, 1930, the board authorized additional bonded debt to meet the banks' requirements. It also accepted the resignations of Clarence M. Fuller, president and director; R. W. McKee, vice-president and assistant to Talbot; and directors W. E. Dunlap, George W. Newberger, Thomas W. Streeter, and Joe Toplitzky. Talbot's own departure was delayed for a short time. At the same time the board elected William C. McDuffie as president and director and named five new directors acceptable to the banks: H. H. Cotten, Joseph F. Loeb, Harry J. Bauer, P. H. O'Neil, and John Treanor.

Three weeks later, on January 14, 1931, the board resolved that "this Corporation is unable to meet its current obligations as they mature, and it is the opinion of the Board of Directors that a Receiver is necessary to preserve and administer its assets for the benefit of all concerned." On January 15, 1931, McDuffie was formally appointed receiver. Shortly thereafter I had a talk with McDuffie and among other things suggested that the receivership might be a mistake—that with the new management (the new directors were tops in their fields) and with the confidence of the bankers the creditors would be better off not to resort to receivership. McDuffie replied that the accounts and the accounting procedures were completely unreliable and that he felt that receivership was the only way left. It was he who had recommended this course of action.

When Talbot, Fuller, and McKee left Richfield, each was considerably indebted to the company. In May, 1932, after a sensational trial, they were jointly convicted of grand theft and sent to prison. Fuller and McKee were later pardoned. Talbot died while on parole before his pardon application was acted upon.

Whatever opinion may be held of Richfield's wheeling and dealing, Fuller had created for the Richfield brands a public acceptance unmatched to that time in petroleum marketing. His skillful use of media, Richfield's near monopoly in racing competition, and his constant promotion of aviation had kept Richfield's name in the headlines both east and west. When the receiver took over, the Richfield of the future was endowed with invaluable assets in its loyal, satisfied customers.

## 22. ENTER HENRY DOHERTY

RICHFIELD'S receiver, William Chester McDuffie, had spent much of his business life with Royal Dutch–Shell. He was credited with having discovered the Signal Hill Field in 1921, while he was in charge of production for Shell. In 1928 he left Shell to assume the presidency of Pacific Western Oil Company, which had been organized by Blyth, Witter & Company to take over oil properties from Doheny (see Chapter 18). Because of Richfield's contract to buy all of the oil produced by Pacific Western, the latter company became one of Richfield's larger creditors. When McDuffie became Richfield's president on December 24, 1930, and its receiver on January 15, 1931, he brought to the company both experience in the oil industry and executive talent.

156

The final deflation of Richfield stock was a financial blow to a great number of employees, among them practically all the key men in the organization. In April, 1929, the Richfield board had authorized the sale to officers and employees of 10,000 shares of common stock at $40 a share, payable in cash or 5 per cent in cash and a note for the balance secured by the stock. When Vice-President John McKeon resigned in February, 1929, he had one-fourth interest in the executive-bonus arrangement shared by Talbot, Fuller, and assistant executives. Talbot ordered McKeon's share divided among the key employees. When the bonus was distributed, each employee received, instead of money, a note to be signed for the purchase of more stock, the bonus to be used as the down payment. These notes, together with the original notes of April 3 on which the employees had been paying, were still owing at the time of receivership, and the stock which they were given was worthless. This development, together with the wave of adverse publicity, the possibility of unjust implication in court proceedings, and the usual uncertainty that attends an abrupt change of management combined to lower employee morale.

When McDuffie took over, Richfield was purchasing 45,000 barrels of oil daily—over two-thirds of it at a bonus over Standard of California's posted prices—and refined-product sales were declining rapidly. Now that he was acting as a buyer of crude rather than as a seller, McDuffie gave the bonus contracts his first attention. In a matter of days he had prepared a new purchase contract by which Richfield agreed to refine and sell the producer's oil on a commission basis. Using the legal power granted him by the court order, he repudiated the existing purchase contracts, both bonus and non-bonus, and offered the new ones in their stead. The producers, among them Pacific Western, finding themselves unable to sell oil elsewhere, accepted the new arrangement. In a short time an adequate amount of oil was back in hand on a basis that gave Richfield a small profit instead of the previous devastating losses.

Next in line for modification were the hundreds of service-station and dealer agreements. In the recent drives for sales volume, many of these agreements had run the cost of doing business as high as 20 cents a gallon. Step by step the receiver used his

*Henry L. Doherty, a pioneer in electric and gas utilities. Doherty took an interest in Richfield early in its receivership through his Cities Service Company. When Richfield was reorganized in 1937, Doherty's firm shared control with Harry F. Sinclair's Consolidated Oil Corporation.*

powers to modify, or if need be cancel, contracts until the costs had dropped as far as he could possibly lower them and still remain a competitive purchaser. In 1931 a price war broke out that nearly wrecked the industry, and without these various cost-saving steps the receiver would probably have been forced into final bankruptcy.

During the early period of the receivership a number of companies expressed interest in acquiring Richfield. Among them was Cities Service Company, controlled by Henry L. Doherty. Cities Service had a large interest in the town-lot field in Oklahoma City and had been forced by competitive drilling to produce a flood of oil for which it had no market. The savage competition in Oklahoma City was damaging a great oil reserve and bringing anguish to Cities Service and indeed to the entire industry. (As mentioned earlier, the same forces were at work at Elwood, California, destroying that fine field and causing great financial distress to both Rio Grande as a producer and Richfield as a buyer of Pacific Western's oil.) The development of the Oklahoma City Field has been described as follows:

> There were few restrictions. . . . Derricks, slush pits, and steel and ground tanks invaded industrial and residential areas. Rigs reared their crown blocks in schoolyards, slush pits were dug on playgrounds, and storage tanks were built in alleys.
> Well into late summer and early fall of 1929, the field gave every promise of being one of the industry's most prolific flush discoveries. It was only after bitter conflict between oil producers, both integrated and non-integrated, that the field was voluntarily shut down for 30 days, a measure only temporarily effective. . . .
> In 1931, the Governor of Oklahoma was forced to declare martial law in the state's major oil field.[1]

At that time Cities Service had a refinery at Petty's Island, near Philadelphia, and the market that Richfield of New York had opened could provide the outlet for the flush Oklahoma City crude oil for which Cities Service had no market. In the fall of 1930, when prices were steadily dropping, Cities Service quietly began buying Richfield stock on the open market, rather than opening negotiations with Richfield's management.

On January 26, 1931, eleven days after Richfield was placed in receivership, Cities Service published an advertisement in the Los Angeles newspapers offering to exchange its common stock for Richfield common stock. On February 13, Cities Service joined a group of creditor banks to buy sufficient receivers' certificates to enable the Richfield receiver to pay gasoline taxes and fend off bankruptcy. That action was followed with an offer on March 2, 1931, to exchange Cities Service preferred and common stock for Richfield's preferred stock. An estimated 320,000 shares of preferred stock—about 80 per cent of the outstanding preferred—were tendered and accepted. By its exchange offer Cities Service also acquired about 60 per cent of Richfield's common stock.

[1] Harold F. Williamson, Ralph L. Andreano, Arnold R. Daum, and Gilbert C. Klose, *The American Petroleum Industry: The Age of Energy, 1899–1959*, Evanston, Ill., Northwestern University Press, 1963, 542.

Later in March, Doherty's company announced that the preferred offer had been withdrawn and that no more Richfield preferred stock could be accepted for exchange. Doherty's interest in the junior securities also quickly cooled when the receiver's first report was filed. In 1930, negotiating from a distance, Doherty had not sufficiently depreciated Richfield's mid-year and third-quarter statements of earnings. But his ardor for the junior securities cooled quickly as the true financial situation began to appear.

At this point a new figure—one destined to play a key role in Richfield's fortunes—entered the scene. He was W. Alton ("Pete") Jones, first vice-president of Cities Service. Born in Missouri in 1891, Jones had risen from a career as a financial officer in local utility companies to an important position in Doherty's business empire at a time when Cities Service was still principally a utility. Jones's sound judgment and high business principles had made him a leader in the oil industry as well. In March, 1931, as Henry Doherty's chief assistant, he took his staff to California for a close look at Richfield.

For the first time Jones and Doherty learned how greatly exaggerated were the published earnings and financial prospects on which Cities Service had based its offers for Richfield shares. Richfield's third-quarter report for 1930, dated December 1, had announced a net loss of $302,500 for the quarter and a net profit of $58,000 for the nine months. But, as the *Los Angeles Examiner*'s financial editor observed, "Where the old management announced the last year's operations would probably result in a small profit, it is understood that the latest audited figures show that Richfield suffered an operating loss of close to $14 million in the year 1930." This revelation, the editor correctly surmised, "is presumed to have come as a shocking surprise to the Doherty firm."

In a public statement issued on April 6, Jones said: "Certain information obtained in the more exhaustive analysis of the situation made in the last few weeks reveals less favorable data than had been anticipated from earlier reports." It was a cautious understatement of the situation.

At this point the financial world assumed that the receivership

*W. Alton Jones, of Cities Service, one of the leading figures in the history of Richfield Oil Corporation.*

161

was the problem of Cities Service alone, but Jones disagreed. Fully realizing the enormity of the problem, he decided not to send good money after bad by bailing out all the other creditors at his company's expense. Doherty and Jones were content for the time being to let the receiver deal with these problems and wait for a more auspicious time to make their move.

In fact, as time passed and the Depression deepened, Cities Service found itself confronted with other problems. It was soon to discontinue the dividend on its own common and preferred shares and prepare for the dark days ahead.

As for McDuffie, he was doing all that he felt he could do to maintain the receivership and avoid bankruptcy. Much of his time was devoted to negotiating with committees of creditors, looking to an ultimate end to the receivership. These activities were to develop into a six-year endurance contest.

162

# 23. HARRY F. SINCLAIR TAKES A HAND

IN June, 1932, the maneuvering for control of Richfield was complicated by the arrival of Harry F. Sinclair on the scene. Shortly after acquiring Prairie Oil and Gas, Sinclair went to California with Herbert R. Gallagher, the new president of Sinclair's company; Henry Lockhart, of Bancamerica-Blair; Forsyth Wickes, a New York attorney; and others of Sinclair's staff. Lockhart and Wickes were well known to Californians as the men who eleven years before had attempted to secure control of Union Oil for British-controlled Royal Dutch–Shell interests. Some of the leading citizens of Los Angeles had risen to the challenge and formed Union Oil Associates to secure a large portion of Union Oil stock, thus frustrating the attempted foreign takeover.

163

At the time of his visit Sinclair was chairman of the board of directors, and I was president of Rio Grande. Although Rio Grande would not formally merge with Sinclair until September, 1932, its policies were concentrated on ultimate combination with Richfield. Setting up headquarters in the Biltmore Hotel, Sinclair made an offer to buy Richfield's assets. The Reorganization Committee, composed of Richfield's creditors, conditionally accepted the offer on July 27, 1932, but left the way open by stating that they would consider other offers for forty-five days. Then, of course, the pot began to boil.

Doherty of Cities Service sent Sinclair a formal telegram (which I later learned was drafted by W. Alton Jones), saying that Sinclair's interference in the Richfield matter was considered to be an unfriendly act and that Doherty would leave no stone unturned to retaliate if Sinclair continued in his endeavor to take over Richfield. Sinclair's advisers and bankers counseled him to ignore the wire; in their judgment Doherty was powerless to cause any particular trouble. After all, owing to the receivership, Cities Service's stock position in Richfield was worthless and had no legal position. I remember well Sinclair's reply:

"Gentlemen, I have known Mr. Doherty for a long time. I have seen him in some pretty desperate financial situations. I have yet to see him fail to come out of them with adequate financing and adequate strength. I personally am going to take his threat very seriously."

When Sinclair made his bid for Richfield in June, 1932, Cities Service was prepared to protect itself. Doherty promptly reacted by purchasing enough of both classes of first-mortgage bonds of Richfield and Pan American to prevent a reorganization without his approval. This defensive move made it clear to Sinclair and everyone else that there would be no reorganization without the consent of Cities Service. Sinclair had been entirely right in his appraisal of Doherty's resourcefulness. Of course, the receivership could be transferred to bankruptcy courts and sold piecemeal "on the courthouse steps," but this approach did not suit anyone. Richfield's values needed to be preserved by treating the company as a going concern and reorganizing it as such.

164

During the early period of receivership Richfield of New York continued to receive products shipped from Los Angeles by the parent company, almost 5,000 miles away—and continued to lose money at the rate of $250,000 a month. In July, 1931, Mc-Duffie succeeded in negotiating a contract with the Arkansas Natural Gas Corporation, a Cities Service subsidiary, under which Richfield's eastern marketing organization secured its gasoline supplies at more favorable prices.

As a result of this agreement the New York company's losses became inconsequential, and in time it began to earn a profit. Moreover, Cities Service had provided concrete evidence that it intended to maintain a firm position in Richfield's future. In fact, the business provided by this sales contract was Cities Service's primary goal in buying Richfield stock.

Within a short time Standard of California stepped in and made an offer that was given serious consideration by the Reorganization Committee. Standard's move was bold enough and probably would have resulted in the acquisition of Richfield, but Standard's management appeared unable to resolve a disagreement between Richfield and the United States government over the latter's claims against Doheny in the Naval Oil Reserve at Elk Hills, California. This problem finally dampened the enthusiasm of Standard to the point where it was not really playing to win.

The disagreement with the government, perplexing to everyone, had to be settled before anything could be done about sales or mergers, and all concerned were devoting much time to the problem. Among those trying to resolve the conflict were Frank J. Hogan, representing Doheny, and groups of lawyers representing Richfield's receiver, Sinclair, and Rio Grande.

The controversy arose from the government's cancellation of leases in the Naval Petroleum Reserve No. 1 at Elk Hills, California, granted to Doheny's Pan American Petroleum Company in 1921 by Albert B. Fall, secretary of the Interior in President Harding's cabinet, and subsequently declared illegal by the United States Supreme Court. The controversy was not of Richfield's doing but had been inherited at the time of Richfield's purchase of Pan American in 1928. The judgment of the United States District

165

Court had been rendered against Pan American three years before Richfield bought the company. Later the lower court reversed itself, but in February, 1932, the appellate court reversed that decision, and in October, 1932, the Supreme Court made the adverse decision final. The receiver then filed his audit and accounting of the government claim, which showed an amount due the government of $9,277,666 for oil and other products extracted from the Elk Hills leases, together with accrued interest.

How to pay this huge claim was a problem which had to be resolved before any reorganization could even be planned. On January 8, 1933, after months of negotiations, a compromise was reached whereby Richfield would pay $5,001,500 as a preferred claim in the event of a sale of assets. Owing to political aspects of the issue, it was agreed that the settlement should be approved by Congress. In February the United States Senate approved it, and in April the House concurred with minor amendments that were quickly approved by the Senate.

While this settlement was being ratified, Standard Oil Company of California used it to justify an increase of $500,000 in its original offer. But the Standard offer was an idle exercise, because any transaction now had to have the approval of Cities Service.

Meanwhile, Doherty and Sinclair continued to spar with each other over the Richfield prize. Although well realizing that he would somehow have to make peace with Doherty, Sinclair was not yet prepared to think in terms of a joint arrangement. Having acquired Rio Grande in September, 1932, he wanted very much to have Richfield exclusively under the Sinclair banner as well. He settled down to watch carefully all of the maneuvering, alert to an opportunity to improve his chances.

## 24. RICHFIELD REBORN

ALTHOUGH a man of great patience, Sinclair had very little regard for people who lived on hope, and late in 1934 he realistically decided not to fight Cities Service but instead to try joining that company in a plan to reorganize Richfield. The Depression had bottomed out, and Sinclair would be working against his own best interests to delay action.

At that time Doherty was hospitalized with illness, and W. Alton Jones was in command of Cities Service. Jones was also looking after Doherty's hotels and personal properties in Florida. He was staying at one of Doherty's hotels, the Roney Plaza in Miami. Sinclair and members of his staff went to Miami and took up residence in the same hotel. Thus Sinclair and Jones met. Each knew that the other wanted to discuss Richfield, but though they saw each other at the cocktail hour every day for ten days, neither mentioned the subject. Sinclair was a man who did not like to open a pot, and Jones also had a sense for poker percentages. The visits ended without either side opening the subject, and the standoff continued.

The next move took place when Jones visited California to bring himself up to date on the receivership. Sinclair "happened" to be visiting Rio Grande at the time. I met Jones for the first time and had no difficulty becoming a catalyst for these two powerful elements. Jones stayed in California about ten days. The three of us traveled around the country in Jones's plane, looking at various properties, both Rio Grande's and Richfield's, and engaging in small talk—Jones and Sinclair each had an unusually well-developed sense of humor. When the pleasant days ended, neither side had made an opening gambit. But both men were convinced that time was running out. Richfield's oil properties were being rapidly depleted, and depreciation and obsolescence of the refineries and facilities was everywhere in evidence. The receiver was greatly handicapped by the legal restraints which prevented him from negotiating long-term leases or contracts, drilling wells, or building new plants. If the receivership continued much longer, there would be very little left to contend for.

Early in 1935, Sinclair notified the receiver that his company wanted to buy Richfield Oil Corporation of New York for cash. The offer promptly sent Jones to California. Sinclair had already arrived for his periodic visit to Rio Grande. Very quickly Sinclair's offer was the topic of discussions, which also quickly broadened to other subjects.

Cities Service had been having a difficult time in the securities markets and had run out of credit. Its bonds were selling very low, even though all interest had been paid. At the moment financing was out of the question. A Richfield agreement would be a logical step and a relief to both Jones and Sinclair. The agreement took the form of selling Cities Service a one-half interest in Rio Grande for all of Cities Service's interest in Richfield and, in addition, a few scattered oil leases which Cities Service owned in California. Rio Grande had Cities Service's dominant position in Richfield, and Cities Service and Sinclair each owned 50 per cent of Rio Grande.

With these negotiations completed, everyone began concentrating on winding up the receivership. The first step was the purchase of Richfield of New York by Sinclair for $5.1 million. Cities Service took an option from Sinclair to buy one-half of the New York company later in case it was still interested in the eastern distribution. In the meantime the problem of the flush oil in the Oklahoma City Field had been resolved by rapid depletion, as well as enforcement of the new Oklahoma conservation law and the federal Connally "Hot Oil" Act. At the same time the receiver added $400,000 to the $5.1 million received from Sinclair and in a revised compromise agreement paid the government its claim against Richfield in May, 1935.

Next was the problem of dealing with the various creditors' committees for a division of the proceeds from a sale of the company. There was a creditors' committee for each class of bonds and unsecured debts, and the Reorganization Committee had the task of deciding on the acceptability of any offers that might be made. After reappraisals of the company's assets Federal Judge William P. James, who had overseen the receivership since its inception, issued an order fixing an upset (minimum) price for the property of approximately $30 million. The formal invitation to bid was published on January 31, 1936. Each bidder could offer a cash price or a plan of reorganization. The Reorganization Committee could agree or object, and the court would have the final say.

To meet the court rules, if Rio Grande made a bid, any competitive bid would have to top it by at least 10 per cent. We were thinking in terms of a package deal that could be soundly evaluated at $30 million, but of course we dared not discuss this figure with the creditors' committees. We hoped that the figure would be sufficiently higher than any previous or suggested offers that a subsequent bidder would not go 10 per cent higher. We had a great deal to offer to a reorganized company: adequate financing and experienced management and, above all, competitive drive.

Sinclair, Jones, and I considered all the possibilities. The great

169

imponderable was whether competition would develop when the bidding opened. Would there be a surprise offer? And if so, by whom? A careful survey of local banking circles convinced us that no large amount of funds was being accumulated for bidding purposes. We could learn of no unusual developments among the creditors' committees; the receiver had not had any recent overtures. We realized that, despite these precautions, a good strategist could be keeping his plans well concealed.

On August 20, 1936, we appeared before Judge James to file our bid and participate in the bidding. In the courtroom were a number of our employees who had been instructed to keep a sharp eye out for strangers, and especially strange attorneys. But there were no other bidders. Our plan was approved by the Reorganization Committee, by the Sabath Committee[1] and other appropriate government agencies, by the ten banks who held the largest portion of unsecured claims, and by Judge James.

Only one incident marred the smoothness of the proceedings— and it could have proved serious. The attorney whom we had carefully groomed to make the presentation to the court got buck fever and became almost inarticulate. When he got to the words "thirty million dollars," they were nearly too much for him. We thought for a few minutes that we would have to replace him.

The formal plan was approved on December 23, 1936, but litigation by dissenting creditors held up the final implementation. At last, shortly before midnight on March 12, 1937, all the parties involved, accompanied by counsel, assembled in the board room of the Richfield building. The formalities of signing and delivering documents closing the receivership and bringing the new Richfield into being were concluded at 12:01 A.M., March 13, 1937.

Several months earlier, Judge James had approved the formation of Rio Grande Oil Corporation (incorporated in Delaware) for the purpose of carrying out the approved plan of reorganization. The closing agreements transferred all assets and business of the Richfield and Pan American receivership, as well as certain

---

1 The committee's official name was the House Select Committee to Investigate Real Estate Bondholders' Reorganization. The chairman was Representative Adolph Joachim Sabath of Illinois.

assets and business of the old Rio Grande, to the new Rio Grande Oil Corporation. The name of the new company was changed to Richfield Oil Corporation, thus preserving a valuable asset, the highly marketable name of Richfield.

The reorganization plan for the new company provided for capitalization as follows: $10 million in fifteen-year, 4 per cent convertible debentures; 1,250,000 ten-year stock-purchase warrants (expired by the terms thereof on March 14, 1947); and 7.5 million shares of no-par common stock.

Securities were issued as follows: 2 million shares of common stock were issued to all classes of Richfield's creditors for their claims; 865,000 shares of common stock were issued to Rio Grande for its assets; 1 million shares of common stock were offered and sold to creditors and the public at $10 a share (of these shares, 550,000 were underwritten by Kuhn, Loeb & Company; Consolidated Oil Corporation; Cities Service Company; Petroleum Corporation of America; Atlas Corporation; and Blyth & Company, Inc.); 45,000 shares of common stock were issued to Kuhn, Loeb & Company for services rendered; and 100,-000 shares of common stock were issued with the sale of $10 million of convertible debentures, which were underwritten by Rio Grande. No values were assigned to the common and preferred shares of the old Richfield Company, of which Cities Service owned the majority.

Thus, after the financing, the capitalization of the new company consisted of 4,010,000 shares of common stock and $10 million in fifteen-year, 4 per cent convertible debentures.

The original board of directors was composed of Harry F. Sinclair, chairman of the board of Consolidated Oil Corporation; W. Alton Jones, first vice-president of Cities Service Company; Charles S. Jones, president of Rio Grande Oil Company; George MacDonald, director of Consolidated Oil Corporation and director of Cities Service Company; P. H. O'Neil, director of Petroleum Corporation of America; Frederick H. Bartlett, a retired businessman of Chicago and Pasadena; Herbert R. Gallagher, president of Consolidated Oil Corporation; Alexander Macdonald, a partner in the Los Angeles law firm of Bauer, Macdonald,

*The first meeting of the Board of Directors of Richfield Oil Corporation, March 13, 1937. Left to right: Frederick H. Bartlett, member of the Executive Committee; Charles S. Jones, president; Homer D. Crot-*

*ty; William C. McDuffie, chairman of the Executive Committee; Harry F. Sinclair, chairman of the Board of Directors; M. R. Gross, treasurer; R. W. Ragland; Patrick J. Hurley; Francis S. Baer; H. R. Gallagher; and Alexander Macdonald.*

173

Schultheis & Pettit; Francis S. Baer,[2] banker and chairman of the creditors' Reorganization Committee; F. R. Coates, vice-president of Cities Service Company; William C. McDuffie, former receiver for Richfield and Pan American; and Joseph M. Schenck, chairman of the Board of Directors of Twentieth Century–Fox Film Corporation. The board elected Harry F. Sinclair chairman, I was elected president, and W. Alton Jones was named chairman of the Finance Committee.

Thus, on March 13, 1937, the great legacies of Rio Grande and Richfield became one. Infused into them were the financial and management strength of two oil giants, Sinclair and Cities Service. The result was a fully integrated company that had passed through the fire of the nation's worst depression and had emerged annealed and hardened. The long receivership had left many problems, but the new Richfield had the men and the means to solve them.

2 Baer, a court-approved director, filled the vacancy created by the death of G. Parker Toms, the original chairman of the Reorganization Committee and a source of strength throughout the long receivership.

PART THREE

*A Team of Eagles*

# 25. THE EAGLE ON ITS FEET

THE transition from receivership to corporate status presented many problems—none of which were unforeseen. Crude-oil reserves were depleted. The receiver's inability to provide capital funds for six years had left the refineries and other properties inefficient and even obsolete. But the immediate problem was personnel.

The organization which assumed responsibility for the new Richfield company on March 13, 1937, was composed of dedicated, hard-working men from the ranks of Rio Grande and Richfield and a few from Sinclair. All had been through the Depression, and those from Richfield had weathered the receivership. Most of them were eager to prove themselves with a going concern, and most of them did just that with the new company. They soon came to be called the "Richfield family," and there has probably never been a more closely knit group. Throughout the exciting years from early 1937 to 1966 about 120 men were involved in the decision-making process—men of varying skills and experience, but all dedicated to a common cause.

Describing the Richfield management, a competitor once said, "They are just a bunch of average people who have grown up together and understand each other." I do not know how to define "average people," but if it means a group of persons who work hard, play hard, take care of their civic obligations, bury their dead, and, above all, replenish their ranks from within, then I agree with the description.

From that team initial assignments of operating responsibilities were as follows: Charles S. Jones, president; W. T. Dinkins, vice-president, marketing; Albert M. Kelley, vice-president, refining and transportation; Richard D. Montgomery, manager, exploitation; Frank A. Morgan, manager, exploration; W. T. Autrey, comptroller; Cleve B. Bonner, secretary; and M. Richard Gross, treasurer. No separate staff was created; the line officers and the managers doubled in brass. During the nearly twenty-nine years of the company's existence, this management system worked extremely well, the managers running their separate departments and working closely with their colleagues. There was no time for introspection or the development of petty jealousies and, above all, no chance to build separate ivory towers. In my judgment, the first and most important quality in a successful executive is selflessness. Without it he will not really succeed in doing the best job. With it there is no real limit to his potential.

As the new team turned to its tasks, it was obvious that at least a temporary layoff of hourly rated employees would be necessary. The Richfield refineries were run-down and obsolete; the Rio Grande refinery, while new and efficient, was small. The closing of some refineries and the rebuilding of others was imperative. The director of purchases, H. H. Kelly, gave invaluable service in negotiating contracts for the rebuilding of our facilities. Fortunately, our ships and pipelines were adequate for our needs.

178

At this time Rio Grande had approximately one thousand employees, and under the receivership Richfield and Pan American had approximately two thousand. How to meld the two organizations so as to be fair to all was another problem. I felt that there would be no difficulty with the regular salaried employees, since we had prospects of an increasing workload which, coupled with normal attrition, would soon correct any surplus payroll.

In 1934, after passage of the National Industrial Recovery Act (NIRA), Rio Grande had signed a labor contract with the Oil Workers Union, the first in the California oil industry. The contract had worked well; the grievance procedures that had been established were satisfactory. James C. Coulter was the local head of the Oil Workers Union. I had come to know and respect him. We had discussed the problem of the hourly rated employees several times before the reorganization.

The proposal we made to Coulter was that when the new company came into being we would modify the present Rio Grande contract, changing the name to Richfield and adding a clause providing that seniority for union members would be limited to a maximum of ten years. For purposes of determining layoffs, all employees of Rio Grande, the old Richfield, and Pan American would be considered one class, and the grievance procedures incorporated in the present contract would govern.

Coulter was delighted with the proposal, and the arrangement worked so well that only one grievance of consequence was filed—curiously enough, a disagreement between a father and his son over seniority. All the laid-off employees who wanted to return to work were rehired within a short time. There were no more layoffs and only one strike interruption (see Chapter 35) between the opening day of the new company and the merger with Atlantic Refining Company almost twenty-nine years later.

By 1937 I had come to know most of the Rio Grande employees by their first names. Learning the names of all the people from Richfield and Pan American was impossible, but I decided to try to become acquainted with the enlarged general and district office staff—about six hundred additional employees. For this purpose one day of company time was set aside periodically for a picnic at

179

Will Rogers Stadium in Santa Monica. It became an annual affair and was highly successful until the onset of World War II made it necessary to discontinue it. After the war the company grew so fast that it was not feasible to revive the custom.

To cope with Richfield's obsolete refineries, it was decided to utilize the research facilities and patent position of Sinclair's Consolidated Oil Corporation. Among the able men who came to Richfield under this arrangement was Clarence R. ("Mac") McKay, who was managing a refinery at Sand Springs, Oklahoma, for Pierce Petroleum Corporation when Sinclair acquired that company in 1930. He became manager of Richfield's projected new refinery at Watson, near Wilmington, California. Mac was born in California and attended Stanford University, and he was happy to return to his native state. (At this time Albert M. Kelley was in charge of manufacturing, David E. Day was refinery engineer, and L. F. Strader was refinery foreman. Day and Strader in turn succeeded Kelley as manager of manufacturing in the years that followed, Day also becoming a vice-president and director of the company.)

The next step was to build the completely new refinery at Watson, on the site of the old Pan American refinery. Constructed by C. F. Braun & Company, it was completed in September, 1938, at a cost of $5 million. The most important improvements were two combination crude distillation and cracking units that employed De Florez heaters, with a combined charging capacity of 50,000 barrels a day. With the completion of the Watson refinery all the other Richfield refineries were closed. The old refinery at Hynes was converted to a fuel-oil loading facility for Union Pacific Railroad Company. Later the Hynes and Vinvale refineries were dismantled, and the sites were turned into large tank farms.

Although the old Richfield company had developed, and the receiver had maintained, excellent customer acceptance, the new company owned very few of the facilities in which its products were marketed. Sales were largely through wholesalers, distributors, and independent dealers who owned their facilities. The wholesalers' interest was not always the company's interest; the distributors might threaten to handle other products, and the in-

180

*The personnel in charge of Richfield's new refinery at Watson, California, September, 1938. Left to right: Frank Fontana, resident engineer; H. V. Goza, foreman, maintenance department; R. A. ("Tony") Panero, superintendent; Clarence R. ("Mac") McKay, manager of refineries; L. F. Strader, foreman, combination units; W. C. Farquhar, refinery engineer; and W. R. Davis, assistant superintendent.*

dependent dealers often adopted the "long-hose" technique—delivering an inferior competitive product to a Richfield customer.

It was not prudent business judgment to budget and build larger refineries without permanent marketing facilities to back them up. The company began a campaign to buy out wholesalers and distributors, to integrate them and their personnel into Richfield whenever possible, and also to build or lease service stations. Within a few years Richfield had built a base of company-owned outlets broad enough to justify the continuing expansion of its refining and service facilities. In the process an outstanding sales force was added to the organization. W. T. Dinkins, vice-president and general manager of marketing, had two especially outstanding assistants: W. G. King, Jr., manager of the Southern Division, and H. T. Hutchinson in the Northwest, each of whom was to succeed Dinkins years later as vice-president and general manager of marketing—King first, until his retirement, and then Hutchinson.

Building refineries and marketing facilities was largely a question of engineering and money. Discovery of new oil fields which would give the new company a supply of low-cost oil was quite another matter. It was decided to divide production responsibility into two parts; exploitation and exploration. Montgomery and his engineers were given the responsibility of drilling wells and developing proven areas. Two members of his staff were W. J. Travers and Stender Sweeney, field superintendents who were later to become vice-presidents and managers of production. Morgan and his geologists were given the task of finding new oil fields for Monty to drill. This was no easy task for Morgan; the opinion widely held in the industry was that all of the oil in California had been discovered. The key members of his team were Harold W. Hoots, chief geologist; Roy W. Carver, manager of lands and leases; and two district geologists, Rollin Eckis and Mason L. Hill. Eckis later became president of the company, and Hill became manager of exploration. Hoots and Carver later left the company after contributing much to its successes in discovery.

Morgan's job was a hard one, but his small, well-knit, hard-working exploration department, together with the equally efficient exploitation department, performed a remarkable job in the following years. It was one of the great records of American oil discovery, as will be seen in subsequent pages.

A fresh start was also launched in finance. We decided to use

182

a calendar-year fiscal period; thus the first report to stockholders was for a fractional year, March 13 to December 31, 1937. For accounting purposes the board decided to place a value of $49,-250,000 on all the capital assets as of March 13, 1937. The first report showed a net profit of $1,406,000. A dividend of $.25 a share was paid on the almost 4 million shares outstanding, and $4.6 million was invested in capital items. The balance sheet as of December 31 appears below.

RICHFIELD OIL CORPORATION AND SUBSIDIARY COMPANIES
CONSOLIDATED BALANCE SHEET, DECEMBER 31, 1937

*Assets*

| | |
|---|---:|
| Current assets (cash $18,231,000) | $34,633,000 |
| Investments and advances | 440,000 |
| Capital assets (net of reserves) | 50,100,000 |
| Deferred charges | 1,962,000 |
| | $87,135,000 |

*Liabilities*

| | |
|---|---:|
| Current liabilities | $ 4,811,000 |
| Long-term debt | 7,192,000 |
| Reserve for contingencies | 285,000 |
| Capital stock: | |
| Authorized: 7,500,000 shares without par value | |
| Issued:      3,986,637 shares | $74,437,000 |
| Earned surplus | 410,000 |
| | $87,135,000 |

Although the first fractional year of operation under the new Richfield company had generated a substantial profit and a dividend on the common stock, not all of this was due to Richfield's new management. In 1936 the California oil industry had made a determined effort to restore prices to something approaching a reasonable return on production costs. In 1935, following the United States Supreme Court decision in the case of *Schecter Poultry Corp.* v. *U.S.* (the "Sick Chicken" case), which ruled the NIRA unconstitutional, wholesale gasoline prices had quickly dropped to 1.5 cents a gallon in Los Angeles and had continued at that level for several months. In 1936 a number of responsible companies, including Rio Grande, bought up a large amount of surplus gasoline on the market, and the price of gasoline was re-

183

*Richfield's crack exploration team, assembled on Sisquoc Ranch, Santa Barbara County, California, 1938. Front row, kneeling, left to right: John L. Porter, R. K. Cross, Donald Birch, Drexel Dana, T. J. Fitzgerald, Manley L. Natland, and H. Allen Kelly. Back row, standing,*

*left to right: Rollin P. Eckis, Paul H. Dudley, Clifton W. Johnson, F. E. McPhillips, Lesh Forrest, Mason L. Hill, Sam Stasast, J. B. O'Flynn, K. M. Cook, R. Stanley Beck, Cordell Durell, Joseph Le Conte, R. T. White, A. J. West, Harold W. Hoots, T. W. Dibblee, Jr., and Frank B. Tolman.*

stored to something approaching normal. The groundwork was fairly well laid for a profitable marketing operation by the time the new Richfield began business.

By the end of 1937, Richfield's administrative problems had smoothed out. Previously concerned about reorganization changes, employees now realized that new horizons were being opened to them. Francis S. Baer, chairman of the creditors' Reorganization Committee, and McDuffie had retired from the board. There was now a complete break with the past, and the board was in harmony with the new policy of boldness and courage. Its members well realized that the company could no longer maintain its splendid market position and outstanding public acceptance without building a broad base. The policy of maintaining a holding position had been changed on March 13, 1937, to one of aggressive competition and building for the long term.

By the end of 1938, Richfield had made achievements of great significance. In October the new Watson refinery had been completed and brought onstream. Except for tankage, it was new from the ground up, the most modern facility of its kind in the world. A vigorous merchandising and advertising campaign extolling the virtues and qualities of the new and improved products had been inaugurated and had been handsomely rewarded by widespread customer acceptance. Kai Jorgensen, an early employee of the old Richfield company, formed a new advertising agency which handled the advertising throughout the lifetime of the new Richfield.

At this point a brief account of the Richfield trademark is appropriate. The "Richfield Eagle" first appeared in the early 1920's, perched on a sign advertising "The Gasoline of Power" in the Richfield shield. This slogan was continued on each succeeding eagle shield. During the period of the receivership the eagle took a flying position with the shield in its claws. Then, in 1937, the reorganized Richfield proudly introduced a more aggressive eagle and announced to its dealers:

Richfield's new Eagle will raise its glorious wings on our station pumps, lube decals, advertising, outdoor boards—in fact, at every point where Richfield's products are displayed and sold. Our

186

*Richfield's refinery at Watson upon its completion in 1938, the most modern combination topping and cracking plant in the United States. Signal Hill Field is in the background at the right.*

dealers' attention is called to the tremendous dramatic power which the new design exemplifies. This great bird, with its keen eye on the future, is poised and ready to take off with one great sweep of his powerful wings. Keen . . . dominant . . . alert . . . this new and modern design harmonizes perfectly with the new spirit of Richfield. Pride in past accomplishments and great assurance for the future are the dominant motives so clearly expressed.

The eagle was on its feet. All it needed for flight was a great new oil discovery.

187

*The Richfield Eagles*
*Top left: 1920's; top right: 1931; below: 1937*

188

## 26. NORTH COLES LEVEE

BY 1938, Richfield's oil seekers were concentrating on an area near Elk Hills, in southern San Joaquin Valley, California. The region was known as Coles Levee, named for an early-day dike on the Kern River and for a local rancher who had operated a ferry over the slough created by the levee. The sector, called South Coles Levee, was being drilled by the Ohio Oil Company, and Richfield was one of four other companies also holding leases there. Richfield was the sole operator in the North Coles Levee sector, on five thousand acres leased from the largest landowner in southern San Joaquin Valley, the Kern County Land Company, whose headquarters were in San Francisco. For some time this area had shown promise to geologists. Standard of California had drilled a well in the middle of the North Coles Levee but had abandoned it at more than eight thousand feet—a deep well for that day. North Coles Levee had been condemned as barren.

Rollin P. Eckis, of Richfield's exploration department, still believed in the area, however. After discussions between Frank Morgan and others, we engaged United Geophysical Company, owned by Herbert Hoover, Jr., to run seismographic tests. By mid-1938, North Coles Levee was rumbling with Hoover's seismic shots. His results showed an anomaly in the area—that is, a difference in seismic response that can mean a formation suitable for an oil deposit. When we examined Hoover's seismic maps, we agreed with Eckis' conclusion: "This picture justifies another well —a deeper well."

Hoover's maps fairly well delineated the favorable area of North Coles Levee. After we completed leasing arrangements with the Kern County Land Company, Eckis went up to locate the test well. At that time the old levee was still holding back a half-foot of stagnant water. Through this swamp, fighting clouds of mosquitoes, Eckis tramped to drive the stake for our first well—Tupman-Western No. 1.

Meanwhile, Ohio Oil Company was proceeding with its wildcat at South Coles Levee. The company struck oil on November 11, 1938, an achievement which naturally gave Richfield added hope of a discovery at North Coles Levee. Two weeks later, on November 27, 1938, Richfield's management was on hand to see the Tupman-Western well brought in. The hole was down to 8,677 feet, not much deeper than Standard's earlier dry hole. After several hours of swabbing, the well was still refusing to release anything, and the guests were growing uncomfortable in the sharp afternoon wind. Then the first gas began to appear, bringing the crowd to the edge of the well in anticipation. Abruptly the oil and gas condensate came thundering up from the earth and into the sump. But at the same time something created a spark, which instantly ignited the gas and enveloped the well structure in flames. Just as quickly the spectators scrambled back from the blaze. Someone turned the control valves at the wellhead and stopped

*Rollin P. Eckis (above) joined Richfield in 1937 and shared responsibility for discovering several major oil fields that were a prime factor in the company's success. President of Richfield at the time of the merger with Atlantic Refining Company in 1966, Eckis became vice-president of Atlantic Richfield in 1966 and in 1969 vice-chairman of the Board of Directors.*

191

*Company executives turn out in force to watch the drillers bring in Tupman-Western No. 1, the discovery well at North Coles Levee, in November, 1938.*

the flow. The visitors watched the flame go out and then gathered cautiously as the valves were carefully turned on again.

At first it appeared that gas alone comprised the flow, but soon the oil gauge showed a rate of 3,752 barrels of oil a day. The first oil was a condensate and could scarcely be seen.

Amid the jubilation the geologists and drillers were especially

192

*Members of Richfield's management on hand on November 27, 1938,
to watch Tupman-Western No. 1 brought in. Left to right: W. T. Dinkins, vice-president; M. R. Gross, treasurer; M. E. Norris, production
superintendent; C. R. McKay, in charge of refinery operations; W. T.
Autrey, comptroller; H. H. Kelly, purchasing agent; R. W. Ragland,
attorney; H. M. Gallagher, personnel manager; A. L. Donnelley, field
superintendent; H. T. Boggs, general superintendent; N. F. Simmonds,
land and lease department; A. M. Kelley, vice-president; F. A. Morgan, vice-president in charge of exploration; R. D. Montgomery, in
charge of exploitation; and R. W. Carver, in charge of the land and
lease department.*

193

congratulated for having located their new field adjacent to the company's pipeline system from Elk Hills to the Watson refinery. Up to this time that pipeline had been useless, since the adverse government decision on the Elk Hills leases had left no oil to deliver. Though we hardly realized it at the time, the North Coles Levee discovery multiplied Richfield's oil reserves by severalfold over the 35 million barrels estimated at the company's inception on March 13, 1937—and in a location that made the oil immediately available to the Watson refinery.

Thus, while 1938 was another Depression year, Richfield's sales were lower, and net profits had increased only moderately to $2 million, the board felt justified in doubling the dividend to $.50 a share in December, 1938. North Coles Levee had provided just the shot in the arm needed to propel the new company forward.

Everette L. DeGolyer has been described as one of the most successful exponents of scientific oil hunting. He once remarked: "It takes luck to find oil. Prospecting is like gin rummy. Luck enough will win but not skill alone. Best of all are luck and skill in proper proportion, but don't ask what the proportion should be. In case of doubt weigh mine with luck."[1] Fortunately, the new Richfield company had started with a large measure of luck which was to hold throughout its existence.

As Richfield developed North Coles Levee in subsequent months, it became apparent that the leasehold from Kern County Land Company encompassed the entire field. The field therefore offered an ideal opportunity to apply oil-conservation principles which many of us were aware of but which were then being pioneered in only a very few American fields. These principles involved more than the spacing of wells and control of flow that had been practiced for years in Texas and Oklahoma. They were but elementary steps to conserve the underground gas and water

1 Quoted in Ruth Sheldon Knowles, *The Greatest Gamblers: The Epic of American Oil Exploration*, New York, McGraw-Hill Book Company, Inc., 1959, 300.

*The operator of the A. M. Kelley Pump Station (one of five such stations on the main trunk line from the San Joaquin Valley to the Watson refinery) signaling to a pipeline patrol plane, 1938.*

pressures that are the driving forces of an oil field. Still more important was the concept of repressuring a field by reinjecting natural gas or water. By this means the pressure can be maintained much longer, and the end production of oil can be far greater.

But repressuring a field requires a common operation as a single unit, known as "unitization." To such a method all operators and owners in the field must agree. In effect, they must surrender some of their sovereignty in order to reap larger end benefits. Both Rio Grande and Richfield employees had seen the disastrous effects when operators and owners failed to agree and plunged into a desperate competition with each other to get the oil out before the pressure was exhausted. Midway-Sunset, Signal Hill, and Elwood were familiar examples of fields gutted before their time.

North Coles Levee provided a unique opportunity to implement unitization. Larry E. Porter, Montgomery's chief petroleum engineer, was well acquainted with repressuring methods and was eager to apply them at North Coles Levee. It was up to Richfield's management to set the stage with a unitization agreement with Kern County Land Company.

A potential obstacle to such an agreement lay in the fact that before the discovery we had negotiated two leases, each with a different type of remuneration to Kern County Land Company. The "A" lease was on a straight royalty basis, while the "B" lease called for a royalty plus a percentage of profit. But oil, like water, seeks its own level and migrates from one side of a field to another. Under a unitization program each barrel of oil produced must be treated the same; there is no way to handle the accounting on two different royalty provisions.

To solve this problem, I arranged with the officers of the Kern County Land Company to meet with me and other Richfield officials on the North Coles Levee property. There the Richfield contingent explained the benefits of unitization. We pointed out that, while early profits would be lower, the land company would reap far more in the long run. "You'll have to take it on faith," we told them, "but we'll get a damn sight more oil this way than by the depletion method."

The Kern County Land Company officers saw the point. They

196

*Being entirely company-operated, North Coles Levee was Richfield's first opportunity to apply oil-conservation practices that would vastly increase oil recovery. Shown conferring at a Christmas-tree valve system controlling the flow of a well are, left to right: Richard Montgomery, manager, exploitation; Charles S. Jones, president; Albert Kelley, vice-president, manufacturing; and Frank Morgan, vice-president, exploration.*

made an agreement with us on the spot to draw up a new lease that would cover the whole field and treat every barrel of production the same. As a result, North Coles Levee became the first California field to be unitized. Repressuring units were erected on the property to reinject natural gas into the field and to develop it in the most scientific manner possible.

The North Coles Levee was also the first field in California with wells at depths of ten thousand feet, and much research was needed to understand and control the pressures encountered at such depths. Accordingly, Richfield established a research project at

197

the California Institute of Technology to study these phenomena. (This project was later transferred to Caltech at the request of Robert A. Millikan during World War II and was converted into the institute's rocket-research program.)

By the end of 1939 the field had proved to be a prolific producer of major size. Richfield engineers estimated that under ordinary depletion practices the field would have produced about 70 million barrels of oil and would have been practically exhausted in twenty years. They also estimated that with unitization and repressuring it could yield over twice as much oil. Even this estimate proved an understatement. As of December 31, 1969, North Coles Levee has actually produced more than 138 million barrels and at the time of this writing is still in profitable operation. Comparable in size to the Elwood Field, whose production faltered at a little more than 100 million barrels, North Coles Levee demonstrated to forward-looking California oilmen the benefits of unitization and repressuring.

Acting on this example, the operators at nearby South Coles Levee agreed to unitize and repressure that field, thus adding many more millions of barrels to California's oil resources. Absolutely convinced by its own experience of the rewards of oil conservation, Richfield bent its efforts toward unitization of other fields in which it was interested. Later, finding most of this endeavor frustrated by the get-rich-quick motivation of a few holdouts in each field, Richfield turned its attention to securing an oil-conservation law in California (see Chapter 38).

# 27. TENSION AT THE TOP

WITH the discovery of the North Coles Levee Field, Harry Sinclair became restive about his inability to control Richfield. The compromise with Cities Service Company had included an understanding between Sinclair and W. Alton Jones that their investment in Richfield would continue to be equal. Their policy would be to try to provide good management for Richfield. There was also an explicit understanding, as Jones often expressed it, that they would not spend time or energy screwing each other.

But despite the gentlemen's agreement, Sinclair was not content with a mere investment position as Jones was. On the contrary, Sinclair nursed a burning ambition to control Richfield and bring it under the Sinclair banner. He had suffered what he considered a loss of face in 1932, when he had finally succeeded in taking over Prairie Oil and Gas Company and Prairie Pipe Line Company from the Rockefeller interests. A condition attached to this transaction had been that Sinclair Consolidated Oil Corporation would change its name to Consolidated Oil Corporation and that a new president acceptable to the selling interests would be selected.

The condition was met, the name of the company was changed from Sinclair Consolidated to Consolidated, and Herbert R. Gallagher, a vice-president of Shell Oil, was elected president. But Sinclair was unhappy about the conditions imposed and longed to have his name once again incorporated in the title of his company. (He succeeded some years later. Gallagher retired in 1940, and in 1943, Sinclair changed the name of Consolidated Oil Corporation to Sinclair Oil Corporation.)

In March, 1937, Sinclair's New York organization and some members of his board had turned against the Richfield deal. They believed that Richfield's oil reserves were depleted and that the properties were so badly run-down that the new enterprise could not succeed. Though they tried to dissuade him from pursuing the matter further, Sinclair brushed aside their advice, and he never forgot what he considered their lack of loyalty and enthusiasm. The objections they had raised made him all the more elated about Richfield's successes in a less than two-year period, which sharpened his appetite for control.

In December, 1938, he asked me to consider changing the name of the company from Richfield Oil Corporation to Sinclair Richfield Oil Corporation. He had gone so far as to have an artist's sketch made to show me how the name might appear in display and in print. I told him that I was sorry but that I must completely disagree—that in my judgment the name Richfield without impedimenta was more valuable than all other assets combined and that, having given him this advice years before, I felt more strongly than ever about the matter.

Sinclair asked how W. Alton Jones viewed the matter. I replied that Jones agreed with my views. After some time Sinclair dropped the idea, but this was but one of many times that I had to break a tie vote between these two "equal investors." It was a minor incident and would not be worth recording except to show the determination for control that Sinclair was to reveal seventeen months later.

As an outcome of the reorganization of Richfield by Rio Grande, Consolidated Oil and Cities Service equally owned a total of 35.78 per cent of the 4,010,000 shares outstanding. My personal relationship with Sinclair and Jones was one of neutrality. I took the position that they were both stockholders in Richfield (two of the company's total of twelve thousand stockholders) and that they would be treated with the same respect and loyalty as any of the others. At the same time I hoped that their invaluable wisdom and experience in the oil business would always be readily available and that discussion of matters important to Richfield would be a continuing process either individually or collectively. Jones was in complete harmony with this policy; Sinclair only partly. He deviated from it on several occasions, with sometimes serious results, but as with most problems they were finally resolved without lasting damage to Richfield.

Sinclair's most serious maneuver, a basic violation of the gentlemen's agreement, occurred in May, 1940, when Hitler stepped up the war in Europe by invading the Low Countries and France. Richfield stock was selling at $6 on the New York Stock Exchange, although earnings and dividends had increased 100 per cent from 1937 to 1939. Sinclair asked for and received authority from the board of Consolidated Oil Corporation to purchase 500,000 shares of Richfield stock in the open market.

I was in New York at the time and asked Sinclair whether he had told Jones about the proposed purchase. He answered, "No." Did he intend to do so? No, he was not thinking about it as a joint investment. I reminded him of his understanding with Jones for equal participation and urged him not to start a battle for control in the market. Doherty, president of Cities Service, had just died, but Sinclair would find Jones a tough, determined fighter. Cities Service would not sit idly by, and the long, bitter battle that would ensue could do great damage to Richfield's public reputation and to its organization.

201

"Well, maybe you're right," Sinclair replied. "Let's have dinner at my house tomorrow night, and we'll talk it over."

Richfield's executives, who were in New York for a meeting, plus some senior officers of Consolidated and Cities Service, including Jones, went to Sinclair's home in Great Neck, Long Island, for dinner and bridge. After dinner Sinclair, Jones, George Mac-Donald, and I gathered at a bridge table. As a director of Consolidated, MacDonald knew of the board's action. He was also a director of Cities Service and of Richfield, and so, of course, Jones knew of Consolidated's move.

The evening wore on to the early hours of morning. Small talk continued. The bridge game was indifferent; all of us were waiting for Sinclair to make his move. But he stood pat, apparently having decided against opening the subject. Finally the time came to leave. As Jones pushed his chair from the table, he pleasantly remarked, "Mr. Chairman, Richfield's stock seems very cheap—don't you think it might be a good time to buy?" Sinclair chewed on his cigar for a few moments, went through the motions of arising, and said bluntly, "I am buying it."

Thus the evening ended, and the battle was joined. The next day Jones telephoned me and said that he would be in California in a few days and hoped that I would be able to arrange time to take him over some of Richfield's properties. The tour turned out to be a rather exhaustive questioning of Richfield's key staff members about their opinions on reserves, markets, prices, ability to stand the shock of the war, and so on. They were the kinds of questions whose answers were not to be found in the usual reports.

Jones returned to New York without confiding in me any of his thoughts or plans, but I was soon to know. In the next few months Cities Service acquired about 540,000 shares of additional stock. Most of the shares sold at between $6.00 and $7.00, though the company was still buying a small number each month at $9.50 and $10.00. In the same period Sinclair acquired only about 50,000 shares.

Fortunately for Richfield, there was no publicity in the matter. But the personal relationship between the two principals, although outwardly cordial, was as cold as ice. This relationship, if it continued, could harm Richfield.

Meanwhile, Sinclair had bought a winter home in Flintridge, near Pasadena, California. In November, 1940, Jones came to California for a meeting of the American Petroleum Institute. I took the opportunity to invite both him and Sinclair to dinner at my home, which was also in Flintridge. In a relaxed moment after dinner I suggested that it was time to make up and "start laughing again."

The result was that Cities Service stopped buying and Sinclair had the market to himself. He subsequently acquired 450,000 shares at between $10 and $12 a share. The battle ended with Cities Service owning 34,396 shares more than Sinclair. His shares had cost about 40 per cent more than those purchased by Cities Service, although neither of them did badly with the added investment, which they might not have otherwise made. By the time of the Richfield merger with the Atlantic Refining Company in 1965, their annual cash dividends were almost as much as the cost of their stock.

Thus the episode ended in a standoff—although the two companies' holdings in Richfield had increased from 35.78 to 62.04 per cent. There was no further battle for stock control. With tension relaxed, we could concentrate on the main subject, oil. We were already developing another source of it in the Wilmington–Long Beach Field—the largest in California.

# 28. OF PORTS AND RAILROADS

THE great Wilmington–Long Beach Field was discovered in 1936 by General Petroleum Corporation. When the new Richfield began operating in 1937, one of its first objectives was to win a strong position in the field. Richfield's leasing department was successful in securing a total of 135 acres in small leases which turned out to be highly productive. In addition, the company owned two ocean terminals in the area which had producing wells on the property.

With attorney George Breslin acting as counsel for Procter & Gamble Manufacturing Company, we negotiated a lease for the rights to oil beneath the soap company's huge factory in Long Beach Harbor. Only a small area in one corner of the lease was available for derricks and drilling equipment, and the lease had to be developed by directional drilling. By this method wells started in a fixed location must be completed in oil sand a mile or more underground and up to a mile in various directions.

Some years previously Rio Grande had gained experience in offshore drilling in the Elwood Field and had patented some valuable contributions to the art. But the lease negotiated with Procter & Gamble presented new problems for the drillers. Long Beach Harbor had been constructed by means of dredging channels and filling in land between the channels. The harbor area had originally been an alluvial fan at the mouth of the Los Angeles River, and many small fingers of the river and estuaries of the bay had been filled in and covered over during construction of the harbor.

Relying on old maps of the area made before the harbor was dredged, the state of California claimed title to the water areas that had been filled and covered. Some of the disputed creek beds meandered through the land owned by Procter & Gamble. Our problem was to drill a well at a given location and bottom it at a producing interval several hundred yards away without trespassing on the disputed areas. This procedure meant that the underground drill holes had to follow narrow alleys and make some remarkable hairpin turns.

The lease was a classic example of combining legal and engineering skills. "Slim" Curry, Richfield's drilling superintendent, was equal to the challenge. "What a strange and changing world," he observed. "I've spent all of my adult life learning how to drill a straight hole, and now I must drill only crooked ones!"

The Union Pacific Railroad Company was the largest private owner of land in the new Wilmington–Long Beach Field. Deciding to develop its land rather than lease it, Union Pacific had to find a market for what promised to be a very large amount of crude oil. The railroad was still using steam engines, and Richfield was supplying the fuel oil for the railroad's Los Angeles division. Union Pacific also used fuel oil for its Portland division, the oil being shipped by tankship from Los Angeles to Portland, Oregon.

In 1938 we negotiated a contract with Union Pacific's president,

205

William M. Jeffers, and its vice-president, George F. Ashby, to take all the Union Pacific production in California and supply its fuel-oil requirements in the two divisions.

During the war years Union Pacific's fuel needs zoomed so high that Richfield was forced to discontinue sales to many other customers to comply with the contract. But we managed to supply everything Union Pacific needed in its two divisions for the war effort.

On March 1, 1948, Richfield received delivery of the 100-millionth barrel of crude oil purchased from Union Pacific. By the end of 1965, Richfield had purchased from the railroad over 278 million barrels of crude oil (more than 11,676,000,000 gallons). Although the railroad now uses diesel oil for its trains, the excellent dual relationship of buyer and seller continues today after nearly a third of a century.

As a customer, as well as producer, Richfield has had a large stake in the Wilmington–Long Beach Field. How we acted upon this interest during a vital public controversy will be described in Chapter 38.

# 29. "WE HAD 100-OCTANE!"

WITH its crude production and its new 50,000-barrel Watson refinery, Richfield was ready to meet the demands of World War II. As early as 1937 the war between Japan and China had created a large demand for 100-octane aviation gasoline in the Pacific. We were among the pioneers in manufacturing this history-making fuel, which provided more speed, enormous lifting power, quicker takeoff, longer range, greater maneuverability—all the qualities that meant the margin of victory in combat.

Richfield had contracted to sell the product to Japan, and by 1940 we had completed new refining facilities and begun manufacturing it. But before we made any shipments, the United States government imposed sanctions on trade with Japan (although the

British continued to supply Japan with their products). We found ourselves making 5 per cent of the free world's 100-octane—and no customers to buy it.

Thus in 1941 there were only two potential customers for 100-octane: Japan, which had been foreclosed to us, and the United States armed forces, which were not then buying from Richfield. Nonetheless, we continued to manufacture and store it.

By this time I had come to know Bernard Baruch and his alter ego, General Hugh S. Johnson, very well. I had been greatly impressed by Johnson's book, *Hell-bent for War*, and I had some understanding of the objectives of the Roosevelt administration and the drift of world events. On May 27, 1941, the President declared an unlimited national emergency. Harry Hopkins was busy abroad promoting lend-lease. Japanese ships had been tied up in our harbor for months, and I was certain that something had to give, and soon. Agreeing with the consensus of our Board of Directors that the rapidly building 100-octane fuel inventories could not forever continue, I asked for patience until the meeting of the board scheduled for January, 1942.

The petroleum industry had cooperated with Interior Secretary Harold L. Ickes in forming the Petroleum Administration for Defense, which was created by executive order on May 28, 1941. Ickes, serving as petroleum administrator and coordinator, named as his deputy Ralph K. Davies, of Standard Oil of California. Davies used his entire staff to bring pressure on the oil industry to build facilities to manufacture 100-octane gasoline with government money (which would be paid only on delivery of the product). Richfield had finished its plant in 1940 without government assistance. We had a head start in facilities, know-how, and inventory.

Members of the oil industry met with Secretary Ickes on the morning of December 8, 1941, while Congress was declaring war on Japan. The petroleum administrator for defense now became the petroleum administrator for war. He and industry representatives plunged into the task of putting the oil industry on a wartime basis. I was made chairman of the Transportation Committee of the West Coast Petroleum Administration for War, and Norman

Simmonds, Richfield's able corporate secretary (and my right arm for thirty years), did yeoman service as the committee's secretary.

Within hours after the attack on Pearl Harbor, Richfield was the apple of the air force's eye. The company increased its production of 100-octane—by 150 per cent over 1941 in 1942, by 510 per cent in 1943, and by 977 per cent in 1944. At the end of the war Richfield was producing over 700,000 gallons a day, over fifteen times its 1941 production. During the war years approximately $1 billion was spent on major refinery-equipment projects, principally for facilities directly needed for the production of 100-octane aviation gasoline. About 75 per cent of this sum was spent by the American oil industry for facilities that it owned and operated, and 25 per cent by the government in leased facilities operated by the industry. At the outset of the war Richfield produced 5 per cent of the total, increased its production 1,423 per cent, and ended with 3.5 per cent of the total, a percentage far beyond its relative size in the industry.

Without our inventory of 100-octane on the West Coast at the time of Pearl Harbor, the air force would have had almost insurmountable problems in ferrying planes to the Pacific war zones. General Brehon B. Somervell, commanding the United States Army Service Forces, summed it up in a telegram to Richfield in 1942: "Everyone in your organization should be proud of your contribution and the important part you are playing in helping us to victory."

American 100-octane also crossed the Atlantic:

> These were the days when Britain was staggering under the bombings of the Luftwaffe; when petroleum stocks on that island were so low that no man dared guess whether they would last. These were the days of which Geoffrey Lloyd of the United Kingdom's Oil Control Board spoke . . . when he voiced thanks for American oil and noted: ". . . I think that without 100-octane we should not have won the Battle of Britain. But we *had* 100-octane."[1]

1 John W. Frey and H. Chandler Ide, eds., *A History of the Petroleum Administration for War, 1941–1945*, Washington, United States Government Printing Office, 1946, 153.

# 30. BATTLING THE JAPANESE NAVY

ON the night of December 6, 1941, while the Japanese navy was positioning itself for the attack on Pearl Harbor, the Richfield tanker *Pat Doheny* completed its job of delivering a cargo of fuel oil to the United States Navy in Hawaii. The tanker steamed away from Pearl Harbor only hours before Japanese planes made it a graveyard of ships.

Two weeks later the *Larry Doheny* was cruising along the northern California coast when a Japanese submarine surfaced nearby. The sub's five-inch deck gun damaged the *Larry*'s superstructure before the tanker could heave about and escape for San Francisco.

Richfield had breathed the smoke of battle three days earlier.

210

The tanker *Agwiworld* was steaming to San Francisco from Los Angeles loaded with oil. Wallowing low in the water as she passed Santa Cruz, she made a choice target for a Japanese sub that surfaced nearby. Before the tanker's crew caught sight of the enemy, a shell from the sub's deck gun burst over their heads. The captain of the *Agwiworld* was Frederico Gonçalves, a native of Brazil, a naturalized American citizen, and a veteran of marine warfare. In World War I he had survived a U-boat attack which sank his freighter in the North Sea. He now rushed to the bridge and shouted his orders:

"Hard aport!"

The tanker heeled around until it faced the submarine.

"Ahead full!"

Without armament, the *Agwiworld* was roaring to battle the only way it could—as a ram. Amazed by this audacity, the Japanese commander frantically ordered his sub out of the way. The *Agwiworld* slid by the sub so close that a sailor later exclaimed, "If I'd had a slingshot I could have hit the damn thing!"

Missing his big chance, Gonçalves broke away, trying to hide his ship in a blanket of smoke from the funnel. The sub followed, firing its deck gun. But the sea was choppy, and the shots went wild. Cursing their lack of arms, the *Agwiworld*'s crewmen threw raw potatoes at the enemy. Finally, with seas all but washing the gun crew overboard, the sub gave up the chase. With only small damage Gonçalves scooted into the safety of Santa Cruz Harbor. Richfield was now baptized in war.

In the first days of 1942 Richfield's seven tankers were requisitioned by the government as supply ships, though the company was left in charge of operations. Richfield was now in uniform—at least on the seas.

The next engagement came from an unexpected quarter. The story of this encounter began in the late 1930's, when a Japanese tanker stopped at the Elwood Field west of Santa Barbara to take on a cargo of crude oil. The commander, Captain Kizo Nishino, came ashore and was received by a delegation of officials representing Richfield and Santa Barbara. While climbing the path from the beach, he slipped and fell into a cactus patch. Horrified,

211

Kekoskee

Huguenot

Topila

Charles S. Jones

Larry Doheny

Pat Doheny

*Six of Richfield's seven tankers requisitioned by the government as supply ships in 1942. The total capacity of all seven tankers was about 500,000 barrels; the capacity of the largest, the* Jones, *was only 100,000 barrels, a far cry from the capacity of modern tankers. The* Agwiworld *(not shown above) was similar in design to the* Pat Doheny.

we pulled him out and began picking the spines from the seat of his trousers. But crewmen at one of the nearby oil derricks, unaware of the delicate diplomatic crisis, roared with laughter. Captain Nishino vowed that he would not forget Elwood. On February 23, 1942, he visited the same coast as captain of Submarine I-17 of the Imperial Japanese Navy. A few minutes before sunset the sub surfaced off Elwood. Crewmen scrambled up the hatch and prepared the five-inch deck gun for action. Below, Captain Nishino directed their fire through the periscope.

The gun boomed, and the first shell landed near the oil field, spraying dirt skyward as it exploded but doing no damage. Six employees of Richfield and Barnsdall scrambled for safety. A Japanese report later noted: "There was evidence of panic onshore. Air raid sirens were sounded."

As the sub leisurely cruised along the coast, clearly visible in the gathering twilight, it sent some twenty-five rounds against Elwood. One round whistled a few feet over Richfield's main gasoline storage tank and plowed into a hill beyond without exploding. Another caromed off an asphalt road and landed fifty feet below the same tank, where it dented a pipeline. Still another glanced off the board planks of a pier and ricocheted into an oil-well rig, where it peeled off part of the pump-house roof and shattered some timbers. It was the only hit in the bombardment—doing about $500 worth of damage.

In little more than fifteen minutes American coastal defenses were rushing to the scene. Believing that he would be stretching his luck to stay longer, Captain Nishino ordered his sub back to sea. One of his superiors later reported: "I-17 retired at high speed on the surface. En route she met an enemy destroyer hurrying to the scene of action but slipped by unnoticed."

Quickly the southern California coast—expecting anything, including a possible invasion—reacted. All radio stations stopped broadcasting. Thirty miles of coastline were blacked out. In Santa Barbara air-raid sirens moaned. Coast Guard ships crisscrossed the water, shooting off flares. Into Elwood roared army trucks, disgorging troops who blockaded the whole field. In Japan the im-

214

*On the evening of February 23, 1942, a Japanese submarine shelled Richfield's installations at Elwood Field (see text). One of the shells from the submarine landed fifty feet short of the main gasoline storage tank (above). Courtesy Eliot Elisofon,* Life Magazine© *Time, Inc.*

*Caroming off the boardwalk, another Japanese shell crashed into the rig, blowing some iron siding off the roof of the pump house and splintering some timbers in the walkway overhead. Courtesy Eliot Elisofon,* Life Magazine© *Time, Inc.*

216

*Splintered planks on the pier show where the Japanese gunners' only successful shot struck. Courtesy Eliot Elisofon,* Life Magazine© Time, *Inc.*

217

perial headquarters announced: "The raid proved to be a great military success."

But though Captain Nishino had avenged himself against Elwood, the most he had accomplished was to upstage President Franklin D. Roosevelt, who was holding one of his radio fireside chats when the attack occurred. The next morning Captain Nishino's sub pushed the President from the lead columns of the front pages.

Nishino also had the unintended effect of alerting Americans on the West Coast to the need for tightening defenses. Nerves reached the breaking point two nights later, when an American barrage balloon escaped its moorings and drifted over Los Angeles. Immediately antiaircraft crews opened up, pouring more than fourteen hundred rounds into the sky, while Angelenos rushed to their windows to watch. With this kind of excitement more than one coastal family foresaw a Japanese invasion and moved to the Middle West.

So it was that Richfield was the first victim of an attack by a foreign power on American soil since the War of 1812. The attack was, save for a salvo against a coastal target in Oregon, the only enemy action against the continental United States in World War II.

So far Richfield had escaped casualties, but with seven tankers running the gauntlet of enemy subs, the danger was obvious. On the night of October 4, 1942, the *Larry Doheny* was moving northward opposite Eureka, north of San Francisco, with a cargo of oil. Suddenly the night was shattered by a blast amidships. An incendiary-tipped torpedo from a Japanese submarine had struck forward of the bridge, igniting the oil in the tank and enveloping the superstructure in flames. Two navy gunners were killed almost instantly in the blast and fire. The third mate, who was standing watch at the bow, ran along the catwalk trying to get back to the bridge, but was burned to death in the flames.

Many of the crewmen jumped overboard to escape the fire, only to find themselves swimming in a burning sea of oil. Members of the crew stationed aft were able to lower lifeboats and rescue those swimming in the fiery water, some of whom were seriously burned.

218

The hero of the occasion was a boatswain's mate, also in the water, who burst into song and shouted encouragement to the flounderers during the rescue operations. The chief engineer risked his life to gather up his tools before leaving the ship. Strapping them around his waist, he started down the rope ladder to a lifeboat but lost his footing and fell into the sea. The weight of the tools carried him to the bottom.

Altogether, thirty-eight men—nearly all of the crew—were safe in the lifeboats when the flaming *Larry Doheny* sank from sight. Unmolested by the submarine, the men made their way to shore at Eureka.

I was in San Francisco when the disaster occurred. Chartering a bus, I hurried to Eureka. Red Cross workers were already on the scene, doing what they could to help the victims. We put the wounded and the victims of exposure aboard the bus and rushed them to hospitals in San Francisco. During the night the boatswain's mate again kept up the men's spirits by leading them in song. What might have been a sad ride turned out to be a rousing trip, in spite of everything.

The rest of Richfield's coastal fleet escaped such excitement for the rest of the war, but the faster and much larger *Charles S. Jones*—a 100,000-barrel tanker built at Sparrows Point, Maryland, in 1941—was commandeered by the government and sent to the South Pacific war zone. Richfield had a contract to supply refined products—mostly gasoline—to Australian Motorists Petrol, Ltd. That firm had been awarded a 10 per cent interest in the total automotive-fuel market of the Australian gasoline cartel. It was a sizable market which Richfield had been supplying for years. Ironically enough, after the *Jones* was put in uniform, she made only two trips from California to Australia. After that the government put her in the trade between the Persian Gulf and Australia and proceeded to supply Richfield's account down under with Middle East oil of another American-owned company. To an oilman this was pure outrage.

The *Jones* entered the Battle of the Pacific early in 1942. Too lowly to be honored with escort vessels, she relied on speed, evasive action, and unlimited nerve. She carried twenty-two navy gunners

*The tanker* Charles S. Jones

who manned four 50-caliber machine guns, four 20-millimeter antiaircraft guns, a 3-inch artillery piece forward, and a 4-inch piece aft. Her captain, Svend Nilsen, was a veteran skipper, whose coolness under fire was still another asset.

By the spring of 1942 the Japanese had swept through the South Pacific and were threatening Australia. The last obstacle was New Guinea, at the eastern end of which the Allies held a foothold. But the Japanese were pressing the attack, and Allied planes stationed on New Guinea were out of fuel. It was at this critical moment that the *Jones*, steering through continuous enemy attack, reached Port Moresby. Fueling up with aviation gasoline, Allied planes successfully fought off the enemy and enabled the ground forces to strengthen their hold on New Guinea.

Early in 1943 the *Jones* was in the South Pacific again, rolling heavily in the water with California aviation gasoline. After unloading half the cargo at Brisbane, she headed north along the Australian coast to discharge the rest at Townsville, in northern Queensland. Traveling abreast of her was a Liberty ship carrying supplies to Townsville. Commanding the navy gunnery crew on the voyage was Lieutenant (jg.) Harrison Chandler, of the Los Angeles newspaper family.

220

With her tanks half-filled with aviation gasoline and half with vapor, the *Jones* was a volatile target for Japanese torpedoes as she approached the southern end of the Great Barrier Reef, which flanks Australia's northeastern coast. According to the prevailing traffic rules, northbound vessels sailed outside the reef, while southbound ships ran inside the reef, where the water was generally too shallow for submarines. The northbound *Jones* was preparing to move into the dangerous waters outside the reef when her lookouts spotted two Japanese subs, one on each side.

At the sound of general quarters crewmen rushed to their battle stations. Captain Nilsen and the skipper of the Liberty ship ordered full power ahead to try to evade the attack. Two torpedoes were hurtling toward the *Jones*, one on the starboard side and one on the port side.

Lieutenant Chandler ordered his artillery to aim in the direction from which the torpedoes were coming. Seven shots were fired as the ship slid ahead of the torpedoes. Chandler has recalled that, "as they crossed the wake of the ship, porpoiselike, we could see their warheads glistening in the sun."

The torpedoes missed the tanker by about fifty feet, but one of them almost scraped the stern of the nearby Liberty ship. The two vessels then pulled away from the subs, which never surfaced to give chase. But the narrow escape called for new sailing strategy. Instead of going outside the Great Barrier Reef with the rest of the northbound traffic, they might take a chance on sailing against the southbound ships in the safer waters inside.

"What do you think about going inside the reef?" Captain Nilsen asked Chandler.

At that moment neither man was much concerned about the niceties of navigation rules.

"Let's get in there," Chandler was quick to reply.

Captain Nilsen thereupon swung his ship behind the Great Barrier Reef and sailed safely to Townsville.

By late 1943 the tide was turning in Southeast Asia, although the Allies were still short of supplies and manpower. The British recaptured Chittagong, a strategic point on the coast of India near the border of Burma. From there the British prepared to extend

221

their offensive along the Burma coast. But in February, 1944, the Japanese counterattacked and surrounded Chittagong. The British supplied their beleaguered forces with food, water, and ammunition by airlift. But they were running desperately short of fuel. Again the *Jones* steamed to the rescue with a cargo of gasoline. Japanese war planes tried repeatedly to sink her. As the *Jones*'s radio operator wrote in his log:

"The enemy has tried desperately to get us. They sent fourteen planes after us today, but the British intercepted and knocked down nine."

Somehow the tanker reached Chittagong and began unloading gasoline. But in the midst of the operation the Japanese struck again in an air raid on the harbor. With bombs dropping in every direction, the crew quickly completed the task and steamed out of Chittagong. With the help of the *Jones* and their own airlift the British fighters broke the Japanese siege and resumed their offensive.

Heading across the Bay of Bengal for Ceylon, the tanker ran the gamut of enemy subs. At one point the lookout saw a submarine periscope off the side of the ship and sent a warning to the bridge. Instantly Captain Nilsen gave the order:

"Come about!"

At the helmsman's touch the great ship heeled over and swung slowly around, to present a narrower target. Then the captain and crew saw two torpedoes darting at them just under the surface. They rushed to the rail and watched. The *Jones* continued to roll about as the torpedoes slid past—one of them scarcely a yard from the stem of the ship. Then the tanker steamed off on a zigzag course, evading further attack.

Arriving at Colombo, Ceylon, the crew believed themselves safe, at least for a time. But as the tanker pulled out of the harbor a few days later, it steamed through the middle of a mine field laid down to protect Colombo. By the time the frantic Ceylonese could warn the ship, she had miraculously passed through the underwater explosives without harm. By now the crewmen were wondering whether their ship was protected by some mysterious charm. Later still another Japanese sub attacked the *Jones* and

222

inflicted minor damage to the hull. But the crew fought back with a salvo of depth charges that brought the sub's wreckage to the surface.

Proudly the tanker continued to ply southern waters with her dangerous cargo, running past Japanese subs and airplanes, until peace brought her valiant combat career to an end. Then the scarred old veteran and her tank-fleet partners again took up their intended role as carriers of peacetime petroleum products.

Ironically, Richfield never regained its Australian account, for by the war's end Middle East oil could be delivered to Australia cheaper than California oil. The 1942 setback was compounded by the economics of 1945. And, as a final touch of irony, in 1960 the *Jones* was sold to the Mitsubishi Company, of Osaka, Japan.

# 31. BATTLING THE UNITED STATES NAVY

WHILE the war was raging, Richfield suddenly found itself in a different kind of battle to retain North Coles Levee, its prize oil field east of Elk Hills and Naval Petroleum Reserve No. 1, in California's San Joaquin Valley. As early as 1940, Admiral H. A. Stuart, director of naval petroleum reserves, began hatching a plan to condemn North Coles Levee. His objective was to add the field to Naval Petroleum Reserve No. 1 and make it part of the agreement with Standard Oil of California to operate the field.

Stuart's first move was to borrow geologist R. W. Richards from the United States Geological Survey and send him to California to study the terrain. After a few weeks Richards reported that North Coles Levee, wholly owned by Richfield, and South Coles Levee,

224

one-fourth of which was owned by Richfield, were part of the Elk Hills Field and should be added to Naval Petroleum Reserve No. 1. Of course, the Coles Levee fields were separate oil fields, well delineated by seismic studies, and were not in any manner connected with the Elk Hills Field; But Richards' report became a cornerstone of Stuart's plan.

The admiral's next move was to prepare a letter from Secretary of the Navy Frank Knox asking President Roosevelt for authority to evaluate and acquire lands belonging to others, principally Standard Oil of California, inside the exterior boundaries of Naval Petroleum Reserve No. 1. The letter was dated February 23, 1942, in the early dark days of the war, and Stuart felt sure of his ground.

Whether Stuart also drafted President Roosevelt's reply is not clear from the record, but despite the attorney general's subsequent ruling that it had no foundation in law, the letter became a charter for the plan:

The White House
Washington
March 21, 1942

The Honorable the Secretary of the Navy,

My dear Mr. Secretary:

I am in hearty agreement with the recommendation in your letter to me of February 23, 1942, that we proceed to acquire at the earliest possible date the privately owned lands lying within the Naval Petroleum Reserve No. 1 in California. However, I question the advisability of drilling the proposed test wells, and feel that the need for the acquisition of these lands as quickly as possible is so great that the delay incident to the drilling of such wells should not be permitted. In order to protect the oil within the reserve, I think that not only privately owned lands lying within the limits of the reserve but also contiguous lands lying within the same geologic structure should be acquired in order to afford permanent protection.

Accordingly, you are authorized to proceed immediately with negotiations toward the purchase, if possible, of all lands lying within the geologic structure in which Naval Petroleum Reserve

225

No. 1 is located. In this connection, I suggest the advisability of arranging for paying for such lands through the years on a royalty basis over and above a minimum price based on their lowest estimated yield. If satisfactory arrangements cannot be promptly concluded with the owners, then you are authorized to institute condemnation proceedings through the Department of Justice. You are also authorized to submit to the Director of the Bureau of the Budget estimates for such funds as may be necessary to accomplish this objective.

Sincerely yours,
FRANKLIN D. ROOSEVELT[1]

The real objective of the navy's move—to secure lands outside the Naval Reserve—was now apparent. But since North Coles Levee was several miles east of the reserve, we were not yet aware that it was the navy's main target. That became clear, however, on October 15, 1942, when the President signed Executive Order 9257 extending the east boundary of Naval Petroleum Reserve No. 1 several miles farther eastward, to the boundaries of our leases at North Coles Levee.

The effect of the order was to raise the question that a small finger edge of our oil field might now lie within the boundary of the newly extended reserve area. Even if that were true, the area could not have exceeded 100 acres of edge production of our 5,000-acre lease block. Yet, having taken the questionable small acreage, the navy now claimed that our field was draining the land it had acquired, thus giving it the right to condemn the field.

The clever twists and turns that went into the navy plan were now fully revealed. Admiral Stuart could claim that the move was a war measure, thus putting a private company at an extreme disadvantage in defending itself. Not only were we faced with losing title to the field, which would have been a death blow to the new Richfield, but Standard Oil's contract with the navy provided that if the navy succeeded in getting possession of the field it would be added to that contract. We would even be deprived of buying any oil that Standard and the navy might produce.

[1] Reginald W. Ragland, *A History of the Naval Petroleum Reserves and of the Development of the Present National Policy Respecting Them*, Los Angeles, privately printed, 1944, 172–73.

We later learned that the navy was advised that the North and South Coles Levee fields were separate structures and were not draining and could not drain Naval Petroleum Reserve No. 1, but the advice was not heeded or wanted.

At the same time, as though to add insult to injury, the navy also moved against Richfield's operations inside Elk Hills. The company had been producing 2,800 barrels of oil a day in Elk Hills under three navy leases, which had expired in 1941. The navy had declined to renew them except with 90-day cancellation privileges. This had seemed a strange provision at a time when the nation's entry into the war was imminent. But the navy owned the land and had every legal right to lease or not to lease.

On December 1, 1942, the navy canceled the three leases and added them to the Standard Oil contract. This act deprived Richfield of 2,800 barrels of oil a day at a critical time; earlier in 1942 the War Production Board had issued Order M-68, which severely restricted the drilling of wells in proven areas. Thus it became impossible for Richfield to offset the loss by accelerated development of our proven lands.

But while this blow was delivered according to the rules, the larger scheme was not. Knowing that law and equity were on our side, we plunged into nearly two years of battles and congressional hearings in Washington—time that could have been much better spent in the war effort instead of defending ourselves from naval attack. The first hearing opened in 1943 with the introduction of H.R. Bill 2596, entitled "To Protect Naval Petroleum Reserve No. 1." Throughout 1943 and until June, 1944, intermittent hearings were held by the House Committee of Public Lands, of which Representative Harden Peterson of Florida was chairman. The record of those hearings is the basis for this account.

Owing to the congressional investigation the original bill was shelved and another was introduced in the House by the Naval Affairs Committee, chaired by Representative Carl Vinson of Georgia. The new bill would deny the navy the right to condemn lands outside the reserve unless they were in fact part of the same geologic structure and were in fact substantially draining the reserve.

227

Together with Rollin Eckis and Reginald W. Ragland, our general counsel (and later vice-president of Richfield), I spent the better part of four months of 1944 in Washington testifying before the committee and gathering the information which helped the committee formulate the second bill. I shall be forever grateful to my late friend Speaker of the House of Representatives Sam J. Rayburn, for his patience in explaining to Chairman Vinson the details of the navy's plan. The result was that the House Committee on Naval Affairs reported favorably on the bill to thwart the navy. In doing so, Chairman Vinson declared:

> In summary it may be said that there are six separate hurdles over which Navy must pass before it may exercise the right of condemnation granted by the bill. These hurdles are as follows:
>
> 1. The land sought to be condemned must, as a fact, be located on the same geological structure as the lands in the Elk Hills Reserve.
>
> 2. The land sought to be condemned must as a fact be draining Government oil from under the lands in the Elk Hills Reserve.
>
> 3. The Secretary must have made a good faith attempt to enter into a unit contract for the purpose of protecting the Government oil.
>
> 4. The Secretary must have the approval of the President.
>
> 5. Before taking any steps whatsoever in the direction of condemnation, the Secretary must consult with the Naval Affairs Committee of the Congress.
>
> 6. Finally, the Secretary must receive an appropriation of the necessary funds before the lands can be acquired by the Government.[2]

On June 17, 1944, this legislation became law. It effectively blocked the navy, since it could not even begin to cross Carl Vinson's "six hurdles." Richfield's principal source of crude had been saved by the rule of reason.

---

[2] U.S. House Committee on Naval Affairs, *Report to Accompany H.R. 4771*, 78th Cong., 2d sess., 1944, H. Rept. 1529, pp. 16–17.

228

# 32. RICHFIELD AND SMOG CONTROL

IN 1946 the route from my house to the Richfield offices took me on the Pasadena Freeway. On the way I passed an old gas plant, converted during the war to make butadiene for synthetic rubber. I was offended by the smog created by the plant. At that time none of us yet understood the phenomenon of unburned hydrocarbons exposed to sunlight in a condition of extreme temperature inversion—the true cause of the Los Angeles smog. Not realizing that the offending plant was at most a very minor contributor to pollution, I reacted strongly against it. So did the public, which found a militant leader in Warren M. Dorn, mayor of Pasadena (and later county supervisor). But to my chagrin and disbelief he accused the oil refineries of being the chief architects of the evil. So did many of my uninformed friends.

The refineries, including ours, were situated twenty-five miles south of Pasadena and Los Angeles. I had never seen smog near any of them. Neither had Dorn, but soon the oil industry was joined in a fight with powerful political enemies. The *Los Angeles Times* bitterly condemned the refineries. When the California legislature created the Los Angeles County Air Pollution Control District with autonomous power to battle smog, the *Times* took full credit for it.

Louis McCabe, chief of the Coal Division in the United States Bureau of Mines, became the head of the new agency. In September, 1948, he announced that sulfur dioxide from the oil refineries was the chief cause of smog. At the time all the refineries but one were shut down by a labor strike, and the smog was worse than ever. But on the strength of his pronouncement all the blame for smog was focused on the refineries. Special police guards were deployed at them, and the inadvertent burning of a few oil-impregnated fence posts brought a quick indictment, an inordinate fine, and a front-page castigation in the *Times*. The oil industry, including Richfield, spent millions of dollars to clean up the refineries. Ours was new and almost "clean" from the beginning, and we made it an example of cleanliness. Still the smog over Los Angeles continued to grow worse.

In the meantime, at the California Institute of Technology, A. J. Haagen-Smit had been conducting experiments in the causes of smog. The results were surprising to the critics. Eye-smarting smog —the worst kind—was caused not by sulfur dioxide but by the combination of unburned hydrocarbons and sunlight. About that time McCabe quit and was replaced by Gordon P. Larson.

Once again, however, the refineries were named the villains. They were asked to install new equipment to reduce the emission of hydrocarbons. Generally speaking, the oil industry was ahead of the public agency, voluntarily seeking to eliminate every possible source of hydrocarbons. Evaporation losses from storage tanks, truck-loading racks, and other sources were curbed. Emissions during the refining process were also controlled.

230

By 1955 the California oil industry had spent $27.5 million on smog research and equipment to control it. Richfield had spent $4 million and later invested another $3 million in antismog equipment when it enlarged and modernized its Watson refinery. Ulrich Bray, technical consultant to the Air Pollution Control District, testified that "the oil industry as a whole is to be congratulated for its voluntary cooperation in this matter."

Then another remarkable development occurred. Beginning in 1953 a number of research studies by the district and other agencies proved that the principal source of hydrocarbons was not the oil industry but the automobile. Among these studies was an authoritative report by a distinguished panel chosen by Governor Goodwin J. Knight, headed by Arnold O. Beckman, and including Haagen-Smit. After further experiments Haagen-Smit concluded that automobiles, not refineries, were the real villains. One study showed that during an unendurable day of smog not one iota of refinery effluent—or for that matter any effluent from the industrial district—had reached Pasadena or Los Angeles. Now there was nowhere to place the blame but Detroit. In the confusion Larson was fired. Smog was still with us, confirming what the members of the oil industry had learned.

Eager to do something about the problem, I went to Detroit and delivered a copy of one of the reports to the chief engineer of research and design of Chrysler Corporation. Nothing came of my do-gooding. Later I learned that William L. Stewart of Union Oil Company, also motivated by a spirit of public service, went to Detroit to inform General Motors and Ford about the results of the studies. Stewart told me that he had the same cold reception, with one addition: the car manufacturers told him that they would "research in front of the engine and not behind it." Yet it was behind the engine that the trouble lay. A large percentage of gasoline was exhausted through the tailpipe as unburned hydrocarbons—the prime cause of smog. Today, nearly twenty-five years later, the problem is greatly intensified. In southern California we have far more trucks and buses than ever before, and one auto for every two people. We can put everybody in the front seat.

In recent years the American people appear to have become

231

greatly concerned about the environment. The problem of smog has been recognized nationally, and Detroit is under great pressure from lawmakers and molders of public opinion to solve it. Over a third of a century ago tetraethyl lead was introduced as a gasoline additive to prevent premature ignition, and the oil industry now makes a 100-octane-plus motor fuel which has enabled Detroit to develop powerful high-compression engines. General Motors is now asking the oil industry to make gasoline without lead and thus help it develop afterburners that will completely oxidize the unburned hydrocarbons escaping through the tailpipe. Earlier catalytic afterburners developed by Eugene J. Houdry and others failed because of lead poisoning of the catalyst (which was usually platinum). Rio Grande and Richfield were among the first companies to use lead (and as an afternote, Atlantic Richfield was one of the first to announce, in March, 1970, that they would make a leadless product to match the motors which Detroit might produce).

In time Detroit will probably solve the problem, or most of it. Even when no more unburned hydrocarbons escape out the tailpipe, there will still be oxides of nitrogen which will cause some smog. But at least by that time the auto industry will have done its part. Big bodies move slowly.

## 33. THE RETREAT FROM TEXAS

THE next chapter in Richfield's history was a jurisdictional dispute revolving around Harry Sinclair. It had its origin in the wartime income-tax laws, which were extremely unkind to Richfield. Under those laws, if a company had had a high earnings record on invested capital before 1938 it was permitted to continue those earnings without undue excess-profits-tax penalties. But the new Richfield, reorganized and taken out of receivership in 1937, had no historic earnings base. As a result it was heavily penalized tax-wise for its remarkable record in discovering and producing new oil areas and for its contribution to the war effort.

A comparison of Richfield's earnings and total tax liability with those of two of its competitors shows the inequity. In the five years

233

from 1941 to 1945, Richfield reported an income of $27,362,000 and taxes of $8,602,000. Competitor A reported an income of $48,791,000 and taxes of $11,612,000, and competitor B reported an income of $27,937,000 and taxes of $1,630,000. Moreover, the well-established companies enjoyed large lease holdings and great flexibility in searching for oil and thus could use development and exploratory costs to reduce or eliminate excess-profits taxes. They used the tax savings to expand greatly their producing capabilities and potential without net cost to the stockholders.

Not having a broad land base and facing heavy excess-profits taxes, Richfield decided on a program of expansion outside California. From the outset Harry Sinclair was opposed to the idea, and, of course, to implement the expansion, board approval was necessary. Sinclair was unimpressed by the potential tax savings and objected to expansion on two grounds.

First, he was deeply hostile to the market-demand conservation laws of Texas, New Mexico, and elsewhere outside California (the word "proration" was anathema to him). These laws, he was convinced, would mean that in the future crude oil could be purchased for less cost than it could be produced. Consequently, he had forbidden Sinclair Consolidated to expand its production research materially. Instead, he had insisted on weighting its budgets heavily in favor of refinery and service-station expansion. He brought the same attitude to Richfield's deliberations.

Second, but no less important to Sinclair, he objected to Richfield's exploring for oil in the midcontinent area, which he considered Sinclair territory.

I brought the issue to a head by asking Richfield's board to approve domiciling the company's exploration department in Wyoming, Colorado, New Mexico, and Texas, with district offices in Midland and Denver. Sinclair objected strongly to the move but after a time agreed to exploration in New Mexico and a limited area of West Texas adjoining the New Mexico border. It was in this area, incidentally, that we already had marketing outlets originated by Rio Grande Oil Company.

We started with dispatch to begin leasing in the area, but when the board formally took up the question of domiciling the company in New Mexico and Texas, Sinclair said that he had changed his mind about Texas. The matter was resolved when Richfield's management agreed not to expand the Texas operation further but to administer only the lands already leased.

With offices in Midland, Texas, we continued an aggressive campaign in New Mexico. By the end of 1947 we had acquired 372,-192 acres of leases in that state, at a cost of less than $2 an acre. In West Texas we retained our small lease position of 66,469 acres, which had cost about $3 an acre. By that time about $3 million in geological and exploration costs had been written off against the excess-profits-tax brackets. But our efforts to explore the West Texas area now met with stiffening resistance from Sinclair. He finally demanded that we materially limit our budget for production research and embark on a crash program of building service stations similar to the program he had initiated in the Sinclair company. This expansion would require the borrowing of huge sums. We objected strongly to the policy, but he was adamant. By early 1948 the matter had become a *cause célèbre* and very nearly resulted in a change in Richfield's management.

Sinclair apparently wanted to follow the Rockefeller formula of the early days: "Control refining and marketing and buy crude oil." I favored Andrew Mellon's approach "Control the crude oil and ask no man's leave." In my judgment, Sinclair's policy could not help but make Richfield a second-rate company in the long run, while a balanced budget and a strong production-research program could not help but result in a first-class and eminently profitable company.

On April 28, 1948, the board met to decide the issue. For the first and only time during his long association with Richfield, W. Alton Jones had agreed to vote with Sinclair on a matter not in Richfield's best interests. The board, controlled by Sinclair and Cities Service representatives, ordered the crash program and approved $25 million in financing, most of the money earmarked for service stations and real estate.

In May, 1948, Sinclair followed up this victory by insisting that we confine our production operations to California and dispose

235

of our lands and leases outside the state. When we declined to do so, he dispatched a Sinclair employee to Los Angeles to observe and report daily on our production activities. Hearing of this, Jones immediately said, "Me, too," and Cities Service also sent a production man to Richfield to observe and report. Richfield's owners were, in effect, spying on their own management. It is difficult to describe the effect on the morale of dedicated workers when behavior of this kind takes place at the top.

Later in May, Jones informed me that he preferred not to do battle with Sinclair at the time and that, if the matter of withdrawing from New Mexico and Texas came before the board, he would support Sinclair. I decided that, before allowing that to happen, I would bring an antitrust suit against the two major stockholders and try to stop them. I retained counsel for this purpose, and for the next several weeks the lawyers and principals argued back and forth in Delaware, New York, and Los Angeles. No fundamental change occurred in the position of either side.

In June, 1948, in the midst of the controversy, we discovered the great oil field in Cuyama Valley, California (see Chapter 34). Cuyama promised to strain our production budgets. We put ten strings of tools to work and were soon finishing wells every few days. In one 180-day period we put 60 wells into production. A new major pipeline had to be built from the field to the Watson refinery. In short, we had all the production we could handle in California, and the need to explore elsewhere was temporarily relieved.

Fortunately, at that time I alone of the management team had contact with the board, and the responsible operating executives had been spared all the arguments—the heat and lightning. I was convinced that if the fight should break into the open it would turn a close-knit, hard-working, loyal work force into a shocked, dismayed, and frustrated group. The potential damage to the company and to its stockholders would far outweigh the monetary losses we would suffer if we withdrew to California and confined our operations to the Pacific Coast.

I therefore decided that, in view of the Cuyama strike, it would be best to go along with Sinclair, at least for the time being. I tried to rationalize the retrenchment with our senior staff members by pointing out that the Cuyama discovery would keep everyone busy for some time. It would give us all of the oil we needed for the short term, and the development costs should fairly well offset the excess-profits tax for two or three years. I am sure that it was a rather poor selling job, but Cuyama developed so fast and well that the blow of retrenchment was somewhat softened.

Thus the fight was dropped, in the belief that this would serve the short-term interests of the stockholders and that, given time, the policies could be changed and thus serve their long-term interests. (Some years later the policies were changed, but by that time the opportunities in New Mexico and West Texas were almost gone.) On September 2, 1948, the board passed the following resolution: "Resolved, that all lands, leaseholds and other interests in lands held by the Corporation in the States of Texas and New Mexico be disposed of prior to December 31, 1948, and as expeditiously as practicable in the exercise of good judgment." At the same time the board rescinded the freeze order on budget allocation that had prevented adequate production research. This action made it possible to operate the company once again on a normal basis.

While this struggle was going on behind the scenes, Richfield was otherwise making great strides. By the war's end 20 per cent of the crude oil we were refining was being converted to 100-octane aviation gasoline, which put us in an outstandingly strong position to compete in the domestic market. Detroit began manufacturing automobile engines to use the new high-quality gasoline, and we were in a better position than anyone else in the industry to supply high-quality products to our domestic customers.

Thus in 1946 our stockholders at last began to benefit from the many major improvements in our position. Employee morale was high, and the ever-increasing momentum was evident in all departments. The year 1947 was a banner year. Earnings had jumped from $.74 a share in 1945 to $2.96, and dividends had doubled from $.75 a share to $1.50. But the critical year in Richfield Oil Corporation's history was 1948—a year in which acute management tensions were finally relaxed, in which we provided outstand-

237

ing service to the government and to our domestic customers, and in which we achieved extraordinary success in exploration. It was, in fact, the year in which Richfield matured into a well-balanced major company.

In 1948 sales increased $30 million over 1947, under the able leadership of W. T. Dinkins, vice-president in charge of marketing; net profits jumped to $4.19 a share; and the dividend was increased to $2.00. Richfield again became important to the armed services. We supplied 32 per cent of the Pacific Coast's contribution of 100-octane gasoline to the Berlin airlift. (It was in this critical period that some of our very largest competitors refused to supply 100-octane to the airlift because to do so would weaken their competitive position in domestic gasoline sales.)

But the outstanding achievement of 1948—and the turning point in Richfield's history—was the discovery of oil in commercial quantities in Cuyama Valley, California.

# 34. THE RUSH TO CUYAMA

THE story of Cuyama (an Indian word for the prehistoric clam-shells which abound on the valley's slopes) is a story of faultless teamwork by a group of thoroughly dedicated men of high morale and unquestioned integrity. It is also a story of how a well-conceived organizational system proved itself in rugged practice.

It was the practice at Richfield to hold formal organization meetings once a week to hear and discuss reports from all departments. In this way we made certain that everyone concerned was aware of progress and problems—the good and the bad. Suggestions from one department to another were expected and welcomed. Working under one roof, we could assemble in a matter of minutes to discuss and deal with any matter which a line officer felt needed consideration. Thus we were able to make important and far-reaching decisions on short notice—decisions that some companies, organized along more complex lines, could not make in weeks or even months. All departments, including the service departments, reported directly to the president; and while this procedure appeared rather formidable on an organization chart, in practice each line officer had such a high degree of autonomy that the result was a smoothly operating machine.

When we started the new company in 1937, I added another management technique that was to help us succeed. PBX operators manned the telephones around the clock seven days a week to answer calls from the outside or from members of the organization, who in turn agreed to keep the operators posted on their whereabouts. The system worked well and paid for itself many times over—especially on New Year's Eve, 1947.

For several years Richfield had been geologizing Cuyama Valley, which lies between the Caliente Range and the Sierre Madre, west of Bakersfield. In 1947 we decided to explore there, though all the literature denied the possibility of oil in the area. We had long thought that Cuyama was a "sleeper," although geologists had explored the region for a quarter of a century without success. Probably a dozen independent oil companies had drilled in the area, which had been rejected by two major firms, without getting a showing.

Frank Morgan was Richfield's vice-president in charge of exploration. Rollin Eckis and Mason Hill were the leading geologists. Under their direction Richfield geologists were assigned to the valley and started a careful on-the-ground survey. Eckis and Hill also assigned an old-school geologist named Tom Dibblee to study the region. Rejecting newfangled seismic methods, Dibblee went over the ground on foot. His procedure was to drop out of sight for a week or so and scramble over the rocks, making precise drawings and notes from which geologic charts could be prepared. Daily life on one of his jaunts can only be described as primitive. After one such trip he turned in an expense account of $14.92. Rollin Eckis was incredulous: "Tom, you couldn't even get enough to eat for $14.92!"

240

"Oh," drawled Tom, "I find lots of things I like to eat up in the hills."

Tom's work at Cuyama proved that the day of the leather-skinned geologist had not yet passed. Meanwhile, the company organization routinely started mapping, searching out ownership of land, and building geological maps based on all extant data. To these maps were added the on-site findings of our geologists. Our budget meetings in the fall of 1947 provided for a test well in 1948. A few leases, including a small area of the Russell Ranch, owned by Hubbard S. ("Hub") Russell, were obtained in 1947.

There was a tract of oil seepage at Chalk Mountain, at the head of Cuyama Valley. Norris Oil Company, an independent operator, had commenced a well at the seepage, and as a matter of routine we had assigned our scouts to cover the well. In 1947, New Year's Eve arrived on a Wednesday, and oil-industry executives, including Richfield's, were enthusiastic about the possibilities of a long, pleasant weekend—the Parade of Roses in Pasadena, the Rose Bowl Game, and other pastimes dear to their hearts. Late on New Year's Eve, after the offices had closed, our scouts flashed a message that the Norris well had discovered a small amount of low-gravity oil. Our telephone operators went to work finding the members of the staff and summoning them back to the office.

After working through the night and all day and night New Year's Day, the company's land men (under Frank McPhillips and A. J. West), lawyers, and technicians started moving at daybreak on January 2. Richfield owned a twin-engine Beechcraft airplane, piloted by Joe Brown and Charles Calvin. That morning flying conditions were poor, and at 7:00 A.M. visibility at the Lockheed airport was zero-zero. But Brown and the tower operator had been buddies during the war, and somehow Brown talked the operator into letting him take off through the soup. When the United States Land Office in Sacramento opened its doors later that morning, the first men to enter were Richfield's land men, who filed on selected federal leases. As for private ownership, it seemed that most of the valley, however, was owned by nonresident landlords from New York to San Francisco. The plane landed in

241

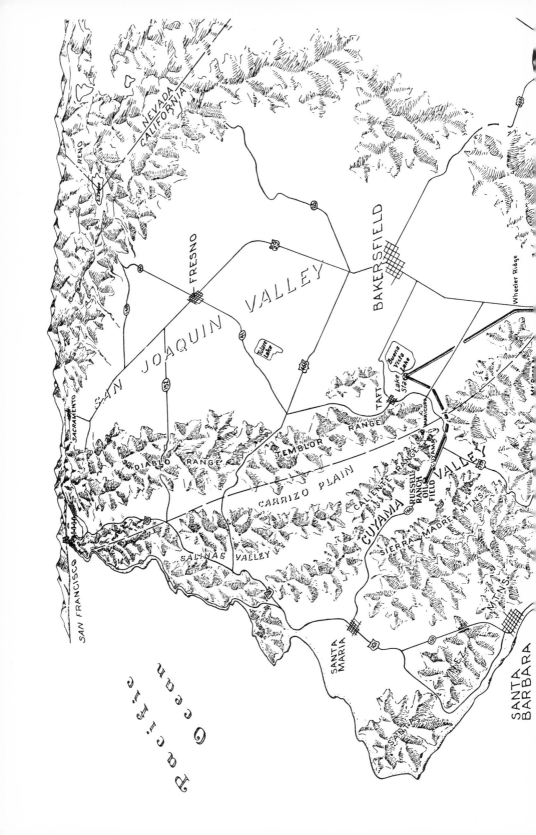

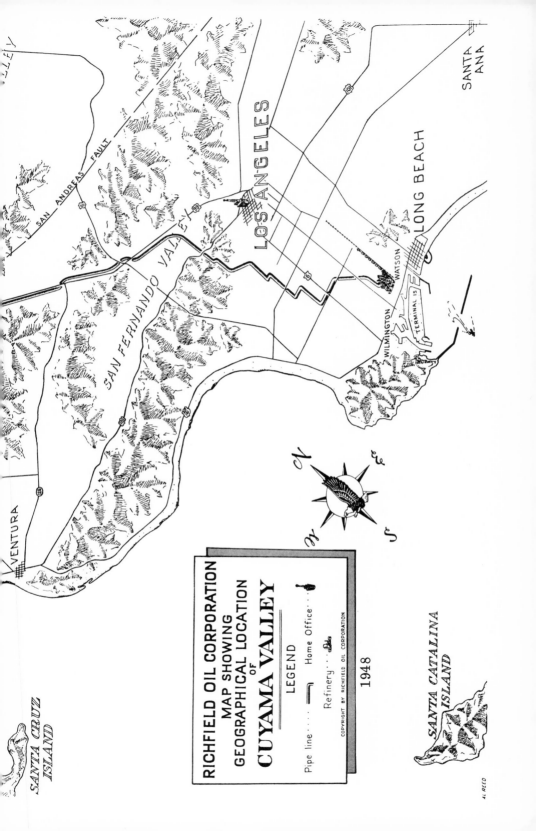

RICHFIELD OIL CORPORATION
MAP SHOWING
GEOGRAPHICAL LOCATION
OF
CUYAMA VALLEY

LEGEND

Pipe line · · · · · Home Office · · · ·

Refinery · · · ·

COPYRIGHT BY RICHFIELD OIL CORPORATION

1948

SANTA CRUZ ISLAND

SANTA CATALINA ISLAND

VENTURA

SAN FERNANDO VALLEY

SAN ANDREAS FAULT

LOS ANGELES

LONG BEACH

SANTA ANA

WILMINGTON

WATSON

TERMINAL IS.

AL REED

five different towns during the day and continued to hop about day after day as Richfield signed up Cuyama Valley leases.

To speed the process, we shifted salesmen experienced in meeting people and negotiating contracts from their regular duties to the leasing group. When the long holiday was over on January 5 and the oil-industry offices reopened, competitors started dusting off maps and old reports. But we already had a broad land base and by the middle of January had acquired over 150,000 acres of land in the valley. Subsequent developments proved that we had acquired over 87 per cent of the potential production in the valley. The other leases in the area were acquired by independent operators who could make quick decisions. None of the major companies had acquired any interest in the valley.

Altogether, the boldness and imagination of our exploration executives was superb. The few days of holiday campaigning had cost us over $3 million of nonbudgeted funds. But Frank Morgan, Eckis, and I believed that the odds were with us, and we staked our reputation and future on the proposition that Cuyama Valley would be a producing province. We had one helpful advantage. Just twenty years before, Frank had located the Elwood Field. Cuyama was exactly forty miles north of Elwood, and the potential producing geologic formations were of Vaqueros age, exactly the same age as those at Elwood. Thus we had some awareness of what to expect.

One can imagine the necessity for calm nerves in locating the first well and awaiting the reports from the drillers. The first good news came barely four months after the blitz leasing campaign. On May 11, 1948, the well cored excellent oil sand at approximately 3,000 feet. The following press release was issued on June 8, 1948:

> Richfield Oil Corporation today announced that its Cuyama Valley Wildcat Well, Russell No. 1, has discovered a substantial body of oil sand at approximately 3,000 feet which the Company believes will be commercially productive. Casing is being set in the well at this time and production tests will be made early next week.
> If a successful producer, the well will mark the first commercial production in this region and will be of great importance to Richfield and to the future of California production. The Cuyama Val-

*Russell No. 1, the discovery well at the Russell Ranch Field, Cuyama Valley, California, 1948.*

ley is a large sedimentary basin approximately 50 miles long and 15 miles wide located about midway between the San Joaquin Valley and the Coastal region, each of which is a major oil producing district of California.

Richfield has spent some four years geologizing this area and has acquired approximately 150,000 acres of leases based upon its geological studies. Richfield's first test well, Russell No. 1, is located on Mr. H. S. Russell's Cuyama Ranch.

If the Cuyama wildcat is successful it will be the third oil discovery by Richfield so far this year. The first one being its Miller & Lux well 78-24 which proved a substantial extension to the Paloma Field. The second discovery was the opening of a new field known as Coal Oil Canyon in the Wheeler Ridge area.

On June 13, Richfield's executives were on hand at the Russell Ranch to observe the first production test of the well. Hub Russell, the valley's leading cattleman and one of the West's veteran

*Happy men after the discovery of oil in June, 1948, on H. S. ("Hub") Russell's ranch in Cuyama Valley. Left to right: Richard Montgomery, manager, exploitation; Hub Russell; Frank Hess, an employee of Russell's; and Frank Morgan, vice-president, exploration.*

ranchers, was standing beside me near the sump into which the oil, if any, would flow. The well came in with some force and splattered us with what proved to be an excellent 38-gravity oil. For me, an oilman, there could be no finer cologne. But Russell was somewhat dubious and perplexed.

"What does this mean?" he asked.

"Mr. Russell," I replied, "it means that you are a very rich man."

Russell thought about this for a moment and said, "Well, in that case I can buy me a good ranch." Many times I have wondered what his definition of a good ranch was. My own definition would

246

*Drilling in Cuyama Valley. The wells shown here are in the White Rock Bluff area of the Russell Ranch Field, on the rugged slopes of the Caliente Range.*

be one exactly like Russell's: 50,000 acres of fee land with the Cuyama River running through it and a major oil field in the middle of it.

At last Richfield had a land position large enough to justify rapid development and to reduce our painful excess-profits taxes. Vice-President Dick Montgomery, in charge of the exploitation

247

*Two views of Homan No. 81-35, the discovery well of South Cuyama Field, on the date of completion, May 4, 1949.*

248

*The first well on the Perkins lease in the South Cuyama Field.*

*On hand in July, 1949, to witness the discovery of oil on the Perkins lease in South Cuyama were, left to right: Frank A. Morgan, Mr. and Mrs. F. K. Perkins, and Mr. and Mrs. Charles S. Jones.*

department, immediately put eight strings of tools to work drilling the area on a ten-acre spacing, and within a month we were completing a well every four days. By the spring of 1949, seventy-two wells had been completed in the Russell Ranch Field.

Still, that was not the largest Cuyama strike. One of our other important leases had been secured from the Perkins family, the heirs of Senator George Clement Perkins. I called on Russell in Cuyama in April, 1949, and met Mrs. F. K. Perkins, who was visiting him. After a gracious luncheon, as I was preparing to leave, Mrs. Perkins called me aside and said confidentially, "Mr. Jones, we just have to have some oil." Just as confidentially and very seriously I said, "My dear lady, just a little more time, please. I promise you a nice big oil well on your land." On May 4, 1949, our wildcat well, Homan No. 81-35, came in, discovering the South Cuyama Field. In July we brought in the first well for Mrs. Perkins in the middle of the large Perkins lease in the South Cuyama Field, which turned out to be bigger than our first strike at North Cuyama.

250

# 35. THE LABOR STRIKE OF 1948

DURING the first excitement over Cuyama we were beset by another kind of strike—a serious labor stoppage. It was a particularly distressing conflict, since the agreements negotiated with the Oil Workers International Union in 1937, and amended from time to time, had worked very well indeed for over ten years. There had been no strike or threat of strike, our employees' wages were generally higher than industry averages, and our employees were happy—one could visit any department or division of the company and be cordially greeted by smiling, busy people secure in their jobs and their future with a growing company. Grievances were few and were handled promptly and fairly by both sides.

During that period the OWIU functioned under a policy of

intelligent negotiation and persuasion. Committees of employees sat down with representatives of management and union negotiators in a cooperative atmosphere. Discussions were based not only on concern for employee welfare but also on the recognition that company and employees were dependent on each other.

After World War II, the OWIU management changed, and its policy switched to one of militancy—the company be damned. We realized that we would soon have to meet this situation head on and negotiate not with our employees but with militant new union leaders. Remembering the bitterness of the oil strike of 1921, when the Industrial Workers of the World was active, we decided to take the lead in preparing the California oil industry for what was to my mind an inevitable general strike by the OWIU.

Our efforts were well received by responsible industry leaders, and on February 7, 1946, six oil companies joined forces to form the Pacific Oil Institute. The stated purpose of the POI was to "aid members in forming sound and desirable labor policies and harmonious industrial relations between employee and employer in this great Western industry" and to achieve that goal through consultation and exchange of information. Many unions represented the employees of these six companies, including the OWIU, craft, machinists', maritime, and company unions, and the Teamsters Union.

The POI was managed by a board of governors. The first governors were Sidney Belither, Shell Oil; Samuel J. Dickey, General Petroleum; R. Gwin Follis, Standard of California; William F. Humphrey, Tide Water Associated Oil; Reese H. Taylor, Union Oil. I represented Richfield. Humphrey was the first chairman of the board, and the chairmanship rotated quarterly among the governors under an agreed system.

We hired a staff and established a library, and the institute began its research. In short order the staff members had at their fingertips the data needed by the governors in their deliberations.

In December, 1946, less than a year after the institute was formed and only a few months after it began functioning, dark clouds began to form. Pointing to the rapid rise in living costs, the unions, led by the OWIU, began demanding substantial wage

252

increases. The oil companies were agreeable but, believing that the recent postwar rises in prices and living costs might be temporary, contended that any wage increase should be provisional and limited to a term of six or nine months, subject to renegotiation. On the West Coast the offer was an increase of $35 a month for a period of six months, which was comparable to offers elsewhere in the country.

Practically all the unions accepted the limited offers without serious protest. The OWIU, however, insisted that it would not permit employers to establish the precedent of temporary increases. Choosing the West Coast for its battleground, the union began taking strike votes, advertising the results as overwhelmingly in favor of a walkout. On February 15, 1947, the union announced its intention to strike all major oil companies at 10:00 A.M. on February 20.

The lines were clearly drawn, and no conciliatory attitude was discernible on either side. Just before the strike deadline, however, the parties compromised by moving up the contract opening date from December 31, 1947, to September 1, 1947, enlarging the period of the wage increase from six to nine months. The union accepted the industry offer and called off the strike.

Obviously, the POI was functioning well. The governors were learning to consult each other without joint bargaining and without surrendering their individual prerogatives in managing their own companies. Each firm bargained individually and for itself alone.

But the major test was to come in 1948—an epochal year for Richfield, for the Pacific Oil Institute, and for the California oil industry as a whole. The unions reopened their contracts in July of that year and made unusually large and inordinate retroactive wage demands which they never expected to gain. The companies countered with a smaller offer than they were willing to pay, and the usual bargaining routine followed. The union reduced its demand to an increase of 25 cents an hour, and the companies increased their offer to 12.5 cents an hour.

Toward the end of August the OWIU became increasingly belligerent and began taking strike votes. O. A. Knight, president of the OWIU, assured his members in a press interview that it would take but a short strike in California to win a wage increase of 17.5 to 18 cents an hour. He argued that petroleum products were in short supply and the companies probably would not want to risk a long strike.

By September 1 the OWIU was going from company to company threatening to strike and pressing for further concessions. The union suggested that it would accept an hourly increase of 21 cents. The companies replied that they still believed 12.5 cents to be a fair and reasonable offer. At 12:01 A.M. on September 4 the union struck the refineries and oil fields.

The California State Conciliation Service proposed a statewide conference to air the arguments. The usual myriad of well-meaning but uninformed do-gooders got into the act: ministers, professors, and politicians offered their advice without facts. To the Conciliation Service and the do-gooders the industry made one reply: "We are willing at all times to sit down with legally certified representatives of our employees for the purpose of collective bargaining. We do not see that any benefit will be derived from the adoption of your suggestions."

Of the seven major company refineries in California only General Petroleum was not struck. Their contract carried a no-strike clause. Standard of California was able to continue operations, owing to a diversity of unions—OWIU had only a small representation among Standard's employees. Richfield and the other major company refineries were shut down, but as soon as additional equipment and supplies could be moved into the plants, management and supervisory personnel took over operations. Shortly afterward the refineries and the fields were producing at about 90 per cent of capacity.

The unions assured their members that such operations could continue only a few days. The refineries became scenes of mass picketing and violence. At night organized gangs prowled in automobiles, attacking employees suspected of working in the struck refineries, stoning houses, smashing windows, and hurling cans of paint and creosote through windows.

Such violence and brutality, plus the OWIU's picket affiliation

254

with the International Longshoremen's Union, cost the OWIU whatever chance of public support it might otherwise have had. Employees, many of whom had walked out halfheartedly, became disillusioned.

The OWIU also suffered an unexpected blow. In 1947, Congress had passed the Taft Anti-Inflation Act (Public Law 395). Its purpose was to relieve inflationary stresses on commodities in scarce supply by stabilizing the economy, especially prices, through voluntary action by the industries concerned. Such a plan for the oil industry was drawn up by the Department of the Interior, to extend from February 28, 1948, to January 23, 1949. Shortly after the strike was called, the National Petroleum Council put this plan into effect on the Pacific Coast.

In the process an advisory committee was appointed, consisting of twenty-five members representing a cross section of the West Coast oil industry. The duty of the committee was to allocate petroleum products among West Coast states to alleviate shortages of products at the retail level. The committee was also authorized to approve exchanges and loans of products and thereby pool the equipment and services of both struck and nonstruck companies. In other words, the oil companies were exempted from certain restrictive provisions of the Sherman Antitrust Act for the period of the emergency. By and large, the public was well served.

Despite these countermeasures the union continued its strike. But employees who had walked out were returning daily (the companies rehired those who had not engaged in violence). On November 2 a tentative settlement was reached with the union. The OWIU agreed to end the strike and accept the terms that had been offered before the strike began nine weeks earlier.

The strike was expensive for both the companies and the union. Some of the companies, however, found that they could operate their refineries with a much smaller number of employees, and for them the strike proved advantageous in the long run.

With the exception of this incident Richfield Oil Corporation enjoyed a cordial and harmonious relationship with its employees, union and nonunion alike, from its beginning in 1937 until its merger with Atlantic Refining Company.

255

## 36. TAMING THE CUYAMA

AS though releasing the pent-up frustration of the retreat from Texas and New Mexico, Richfield developed its Cuyama fields with remarkable speed. By the end of 1949, 147 producing wells had been completed in Cuyama Valley—109 in the Russell Ranch Field and 38 in the new South Cuyama Field.

Handling the growing production from these fields became a new but happy kind of problem for Richfield. There was a severe shortage of steel pipe in 1948, when Russell Ranch Field was discovered. To meet the emergency, Richfield bought thirty miles of battered and dented secondhand 6-inch steel invasion pipe. The pipe, designed by S. S. ("Syd") Smith, of Shell Oil Company, had been used by the army to string a surface pipeline across Europe to supply George Patton's fast-moving tanks. With this makeshift line Richfield was able to start moving oil to market almost immediately, by means of San Joaquin pipeline connections. In April, 1949, this temporary arrangement was replaced with a permanent 8⅝-inch conventional pipeline. In 1950, to service the added production, a new 14-inch main trunk line from the San Joaquin Valley to the Watson refinery was completed and integrated with the existing lines.

Much natural gas was being produced with the oil. Richfield decided not to sell the gas from the Cuyama Valley fields immediately but to return it to the producing sands and thus maintain the formation pressures. Our experience at North Coles Levee had taught us that in this manner we could greatly increase the production of oil from the field. Such waste prevention we believed to be good stewardship of natural resources and, although initially expensive, intelligent conservation practice that would prove beneficial in the long run. The gas would be available for sale at a later time when it had served its purpose in the conservation of oil.

In the early stages of developing an oil field, it is extremely difficult and sometimes impossible to return all the dry gas to the oil formation. Pumping gas under high pressure requires large compressors and other facilities. Good engineering takes time; it is necessary to understand the size and characteristics of the field to plan intelligently and execute a repressuring program. For this reason some of the early gas production had to be delivered to the gas company to prevent its being blown into the air and wasted. There was only one customer for the gas: Pacific Lighting Corporation, which supplies most of southern California.

We explained to a Pacific executive how Richfield intended to use the Cuyama Valley gas—first to return it to the ground and then later to sell it to the company when it was no longer needed. We asked Pacific to build a gas line from Cuyama to connect with its facilities in San Joaquin Valley and to buy such gas as we would not need during the early stages of development. Pacific refused to do so unless we dedicated and currently delivered to it all our gas. Although ultimately it would have bought all the gas on its own terms, Pacific declined to cooperate in our conservation effort.

257

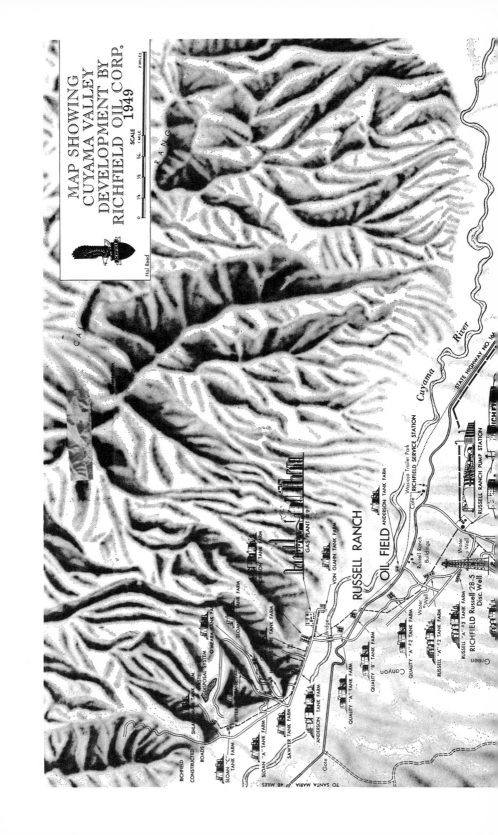

MAP SHOWING
CUYAMA VALLEY
DEVELOPMENT BY
RICHFIELD OIL CORP.
1949

SCALE

0   ¼   ½   ¾   1 MILE        2 MILES

Hal Reed

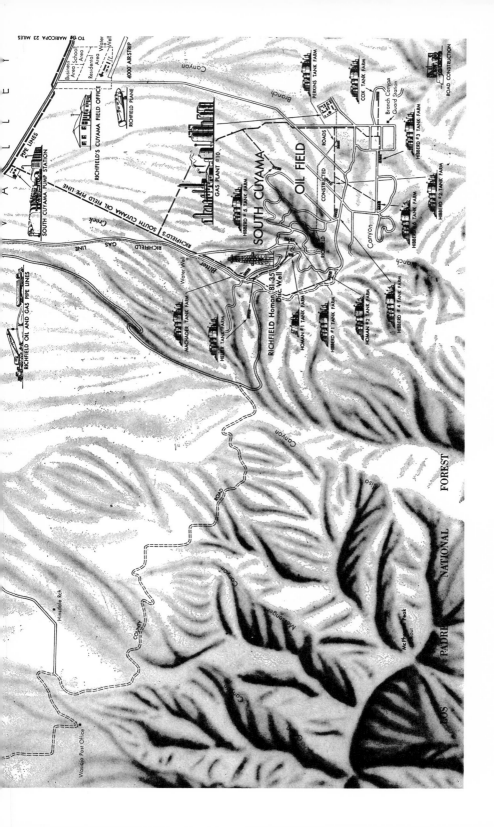

*The new 14-inch main trunk line from San Joaquin Valley to the Watson refinery, completed in 1950. The line has a capacity of 75,000 barrels a day.*

Thus, to avoid wasting gas into the air, we were forced to build a gas line from Cuyama to the North Coles Levee Field in the San Joaquin Valley and pump the gas into that field. This episode laid the foundation for an all-out legal battle with Pacific Lighting Corporation. That battle will be described in Chapter 42.

By the end of 1950, 264 producing wells had been completed in the Cuyama Valley, and by the end of the year total gross crude-oil and condensate reserves were certified at approximately 407 million barrels. Profits had risen from $5.12 a share in 1949 to $6.02. Over the three-year period from 1948 to 1950 net sales and other operating revenue had increased over 76 per cent to $155 million. Total profits in 1950 were $24 million, compared with $12 million in 1947.

At the same time we were able to meet some large financial requirements. In the three years from 1948 to 1950 capital expenditures were $85.5 million; cash flow was $96 million; $30 million was disbursed to stockholders; and $30 million was added to surplus. To help ease the company's growing pains, a ten-year bank loan for $25 million at 1.85 per cent and a twenty-five-year insurance loan for $25 million at 2.85 per cent were arranged.

These problems and their solutions were only a prelude to the more complex one of taming the Cuyama Field. Increasing the yield of an oil field through repressuring was not new to the industry, especially in states with conservation laws. Our success in maintaining pressures in North Coles Levee by reinjecting gas, thus substantially increasing the producible oil reserves and maintaining a fairly even production rate over a long period, had proved beyond any doubt that the ideal way to produce the Cuyama oil was by gas injection.

Fortunately, North Coles Levee was wholly owned by Richfield. We did not have to deal with any competitive producers. The engineering and production policy was a matter of agreement between Richfield as lessee and Kern County Land Company as lessor. But the Cuyama story was different. Competitive leases on the South Cuyama structure had been obtained by Superior Oil Company and Bell Petroleum Company, and one of Richfield's lessors, Glenn J. Homan, had sold most of his royalty before the discovery well came in. The Homan royalty group, excluding Homan himself, banded together, and thus we had three important interests to deal with when we set about unitizing South Cuyama.

As we had learned at North Coles Levee, unitization is necessary to reinject the gas and produce the field in accordance with the best engineering practices. According to our own experience, it would assure the highest possible recovery of oil and maximum profitability. On the other hand, in the absence of a conservation law in California it is not too difficult for a 5 per cent owner to rape a field, blow off gas pressure, and reduce the ultimate recovery of oil by 50 per cent or more. In fact, such a situation enables a few operators to make a fast buck by producing quickly more oil than that lying under their own leases by causing pressures

261

262

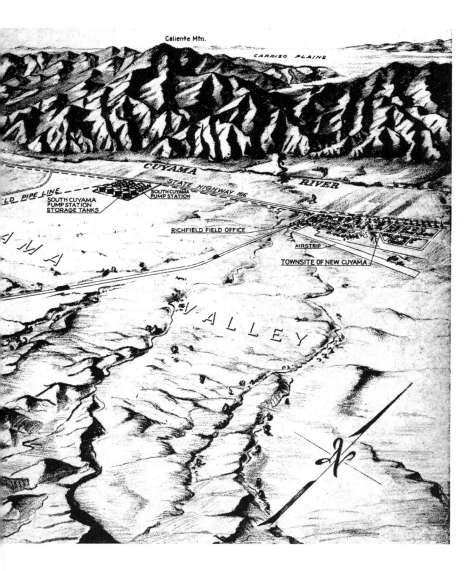

*Operations of Richfield Oil Corporation in Cuyama Valley, 1950.*

263

under their own leases to drop and additional oil to migrate from adjoining lands to their own. If the adjoining owners drill more wells and produce more oil to try to prevent these losses, the net effect is a drop of pressure in the whole field. Most of the oil originally in place will never be produced. The field will be water-flooded, and irreparable damage will result.

If this archaic method of producing oil had no end consequence except a division of dollars between the competing oil operators, the public would have no real interest in the matter. But the public does have a very great interest, because the end result is the destruction of vast quantities of an irreplaceable natural resource. Moreover, about 99 per cent of the time the fast-buck operators make far less from their venture than they would if they produced for the long pull, using the best engineering and conservation practices known. Sound conservation practice in oil production has the happy effect of producing the most oil for the public good and the most money for the owners and operators.

There were, of course, many examples of unbelievably bad production practices in California. Richfield decided that South Cuyama would not be among them but would be known for its outstanding excellence in production performance. There would be no more Elwoods if we could prevent it, and we believed we could. We therefore took the initiative in developing the unit plan. Engineering consultants determined the relative values and equities. We prepared a unit and conservation agreement, allocating each party its proper share. The United States Department of the Interior, owner of one parcel of land, found the engineering data correct and signed the agreement. Homan, as lessor, and his lawyer, who held a royalty interest, also signed the agreement, as in time did the other, smaller lessors.

The remaining Homan royalty interests threatened to sue, certain that we would pay handsomely for their signatures. We decided to let them sue. We felt that it would be interesting to learn how a court would judge the matter. The Homan group finally became convinced that we were prepared to litigate and signed the agreement without suit.

264

Superior Oil Company brought suit claiming a portion of our leases on which were several excellent producing wells. After a long, expensive court battle, which we won, the company signed the agreement. Bell Petroleum Company signed only after we agreed to participate with it in some other leases of questionable value.

Thus everyone has been well repaid, and a great natural resource has been managed for maximum public benefit. If we had not maintained pressures and produced Cuyama as a unit, our engineers estimated that, instead of remaining a producing field today, Cuyama would long since have been depleted and millions of barrels of oil would have been lost for all time. By ordinary depletion methods South Cuyama would have produced about 130 million barrels—25 per cent of the oil in place. As of April 1, 1969, the field had produced 196 million barrels—66 million barrels more—valued at $191 million. It was still earning over $30,000 a day, twenty years after discovery.

Frank T. Lloyd was transferred to the headquarters of the Northern Division after the Cuyama strike and became the able steward of Richfield's reserves. At the time of the merger with Atlantic Refining Company he was Richfield's chief production and valuation engineer.

Cuyama confirmed Richfield's position among the strongest majors on the Pacific Coast. The annual report for 1951, concluding the fifteenth year of business for Richfield Oil Corporation, gave management an opportunity to tell the story in figures. Starting with 35 million barrels of oil reserves in early 1937, the company had discovered 530,964,000 barrels and had produced 180,864,000 barrels, with remaining reserves of 385,100,000 barrels. "Without buying any properties already developed," read the Letter to Stockholders, "the Corporation has become one of the leading producers of crude oil in California." In the years since early 1937 capital expenditure put into the business totaled $231,-264,000, approximately 97 per cent of which was made from cash earnings. Pipeline capacity had more than tripled. Refinery runs and sales had risen from 40,000 to 100,000 barrels a day.

The corporation had paid $58,902,000 in federal taxes and $38,-818,000 in direct taxes. It had paid $184,157,000 in wages, salaries, and so on, and $72 million to the stockholders in dividends.

It could be said with truth that Richfield had come a long way in the fifteen years since its rebirth in 1937.

# 37. THE EGYPTIAN AFFAIR

DESPITE its successes Richfield's management had no time to bask in yesterday's sunshine. In the early 1950's population and car registrations on the West Coast were increasing at astronomical rates. California's oil reserves were declining and demand was increasing by the hour.

Richfield's position was comfortable, much better than that of the industry as a whole. But a forward look revealed a great challenge: maintain and increase this magnificent market position and find more crude oil to supply it. In short, we had to increase our oil reserves in order to maintain our vigorous growth curve. By now Cuyama was fairly well drilled up, and while it continued to be a good producer, we were confronted with a declining produc-

267

tion curve. Although encouraging originally, the failure of the Eocene sand to produce commercially at North Coles Levee was disappointing, and we had no clues where to look for new oil provinces in California. There had been nothing new since Cuyama; indeed, as of this writing there has been nothing new since Cuyama.

Our two principal stockholders had withdrawn their objection to exploration research outside California, and we began planning to expand our hunt for oil. By 1954 we had acquired potential oil-land holdings in the states of Colorado, Montana, North Dakota, Nevada, Oregon, South Dakota, Utah, Washington, and Wyoming and had filed applications on approximately 70,000 acres of federally owned lands on the Kenai Peninsula of Alaska.

We had also moved overseas, to Egypt, where we had 22.5 per cent of a 72,000-square-mile concession held under a joint arrangement with Cities Service, Continental, and Marathon Oil Company (formerly the Ohio Oil Company). It was a major undertaking, and under Continental's management a large-scale exploration program was begun and drilling commenced in 1955. On September 27, 1955, we were startled by news that Gamal Abdel Nasser, prime minister (and later president) of Egypt, had made a deal with the Soviet Union for a supply of arms. W. Alton Jones and I left at once for Cairo.

Jefferson Caffery, the former ambassador to Egypt, whom we had come to know and rely on for advice, was living in Rome while continuing his study of Egyptian archaeology. We stopped in Rome to discuss the new development with him. As usual, his advice was sound. He suggested that, after we had seen Ambassador Henry Byroade, the current ambassador to Egypt, and before we called on Nasser, we arrange a meeting with Muhammad Hassanein Heikal, editor of the newspaper *Al Ahram*. Caffery explained that Heikal was Nasser's closest friend and had worked in the underground while Nasser was in the trenches during an early war with Israel.

We found Ambassador Byroade very tired and deeply concerned. The strain of the preceding few weeks climaxed by the arms deal with the Soviet Union had left its mark. He told us an interesting but distressing story.

According to Byroade, sometime after the Israeli raid on the Gaza Strip in February, 1955, Nasser asked the United States government to sell Egypt some arms. The junta which had assisted Nasser in the coup that made him the head of state was insisting on arms, and only by procuring them could Nasser avoid a countercoup.

The United States agreed to sell arms to Egypt, and the Pentagon negotiated a list of items which both parties found satisfactory. Later the State Department decided that the amount was too great, and the list of items was renegotiated downward by more than half to a total of $30 to $35 million, roughly 15 million Egyptian pounds. In agreeing to the smaller figure, Nasser had said that he was not interested in any great quantity of arms—only enough to display to his people and to satisfy a group of army officers, primarily the junta.

The question then arose about the method of payment. Nasser offered cotton or Egyptian pounds. Early each year the United States government had been announcing a support price for American cotton but for some reason had delayed the announcement in 1955. Although Egypt had a bumper cotton crop, it could not be sold or evaluated until the United States announced its base prices. Ambassador Byroade was shocked when word came that the United States wanted gold in payment for the arms and would settle for nothing less. Since Egypt had no gold or dollars, the demand was equivalent to saying "No sale."

Nasser then sent for the Soviet ambassador and asked him whether Russia would sell him arms, and on what terms. The Russian replied that he did not know but would try to give Nasser a prompt answer. The answer was not long in coming. The Russians said yes. They would arrange for Czechoslovakia to sell such arms as Nasser wished, and the seller would take Egyptian cotton in payment.

Within a matter of hours after the United States government learned of this development, the British ambassador informed

269

Nasser that any purchase of arms from the Soviet Union would be considered by Britain an unfriendly act. (Apparently the State Department was keeping the British well informed.) In September, Byroade cabled his superiors that he was certain that Nasser would sign with the Russians within a few days if he could not deal with the United States. Day by day Byroade waited for the government to act, unwilling to believe that Washington would ignore his advice and force Nasser to complete the deal with Russia. But no word came, and, as Byroade had predicted, Nasser took the step which brought the Soviet Union into the Middle East.

Ambassador Byroade, a onetime army officer turned career diplomat, was of course a highly disciplined public servant. This quality probably accounted for much of his frustration. Whether a maverick ambassador might have lifted the phone to call Washington and raise hell or called a special press conference and thus achieved a different result will never be known.

In the evening of the same day of our meeting with Byroade, we dined with Heikal. His story agreed in every detail with Byroade's. We had already begun drilling an exploratory well near Alexandria. Nasser had a summer home nearby. Heikal told us that one evening he and Nasser had looked at the derrick by moonlight from Nasser's home. Nasser had commented: "If only this dream could come true. My people need so much."

On the next day Prime Minister Nasser received us. He asked the purpose of our visit. We explained that we had embarked on a program that would necessitate spending many millions of dollars of our stockholders' money in Egypt and that we took a dim view of investments in a nation that might become Communist-controlled. Nasser replied that Egypt was not going to be Communist-controlled—or for that matter British- or American-controlled. He added that for centuries the Egyptians had been under the control of Turkey, had only very recently been relieved of British troops, and were not about to be controlled by anyone. Surely we must realize, he said, that neither he nor his people would have any future under communism. He then launched into a long account of his attempts to establish friendly relations with the United States and the events leading up to the deal with the Soviet

Union. His account agreed in every detail with those of Byroade and Heikal.

Being laymen, Jones and I were not, of course, privy to all the facts or to the position of our policy makers in Washington. But to us it seemed impossible for all the stories to agree unless they were substantially true. We left Nasser's office with the strong impression that there was still a chance to correct what seemed to us a truly grievous blunder. As far as payment for arms was concerned, the group of oil companies of which Richfield was a member was spending more dollars in Egypt than the arms deal required and could easily buy Egyptian pounds in advance, thus providing Nasser with the gold the State Department demanded.

We hurried back to the States, and I went directly to Washington. President Eisenhower was in Denver recuperating from a heart attack. Secretary of State John Foster Dulles was in the South Pacific bolstering SEATO. Undersecretary of State Herbert Hoover, Jr., was on an obscure mission to Brazil.

Time being of the essence, I flew to Bonham, Texas, and visited Speaker of the House Sam Rayburn at his farm home. I hoped to get some idea from him where our story could be heard promptly, but he had no advice except to wait for Secretary Dulles or Undersecretary Hoover to return.

In the meantime, Jones had told our story to former Governor Thomas E. Dewey (who had returned to his private law practice), and finally we sent a detailed letter to President Eisenhower. We did not expect the President to see it but hoped that the White House staff would promptly place the letter in the right hands.

When Undersecretary Hoover returned to Washington, I told him the story, and he read our letter to the President. Sometime later he told me that he had checked the story and found it accurate. The important fact he discovered was that Byroade's cable had reached the department but had never been delivered to his office or Secretary Dulles' office or the office of any responsible assistant secretary.

Whether the decision not to act was made because of Israeli influence, British influence, ineptness on the part of the American government, or a combination of all three will probably never be

271

known. But today's headlines telling about strife in the Middle East, as well as America's relatively eroded position in that area, stem from this 1955 decision.

The significance of the arms deal to Richfield was that we decided against further operations in Egypt after the group's initial expenditure of some $30 million. Only time will judge the wisdom of that decision.

In the meantime, continuing our overseas efforts, we had joined with Cities Service on a fifty-fifty basis in explorations in Peru and in the province of Dhofar in the sultanate of Muscat and Oman, South Arabia. We had also begun to look toward an untapped source of California oil—the additional underground supply that could be recovered by proper conservation methods. This project would require a state conservation law, and that effort would move Richfield beyond the familiar realm of petroleum engineering and marketing into the thickets of California politics. At the time, such a move did not seem too formidable for a team of eagles.

# 38. THE CONSERVATION CRUSADE

BY the early 1950's our experience with advanced conservation methods in North Coles Levee and Cuyama, plus the results of pressure maintenance and unitized projects in states with conservation laws, had convinced us that a vast amount of additional oil could be recovered by such methods in other fields in California. The producer, the landowner, the tax collector, and the public at large would benefit if California would enact a conservation law.

As a first step we commissioned William Horner, of Core Laboratories, Inc., to make a study of unitized oil-field conservation projects in the United States. His study reinforced our conviction that recoverable oil reserves in California could be increased by several billion barrels through widespread unit operation. About a dozen California fields had already been unitized voluntarily, and Horner's research indicated that those fields alone would produce nearly a billion barrels of additional oil. At prevailing prices the value would exceed $3 billion.

Richfield had a large interest in the town-lot area of Signal Hill, where nothing could be done to produce more oil without unitization. We also had a substantial position in Long Beach. There, too, unitization could materially increase our productive potential. Opportunities also existed in many older fields to acquire leases or to make contracts with present lessees for a participating interest.

Oil production in the town-lot area of Long Beach had caused an unusual problem of subsidence. By 1955 the surface of the land had sunk 21.5 feet at the epicenter of the subsidence area (about 10 square miles), creating a sunken basin and causing serious damage to existing facilities. Much of the area, including harbor facilities and the naval base, was protected from inundation by the sea only at great expense. Unitization and repressuring of the area could halt the subsidence and at the same time result in greater production.

Altogether, the economic potential of a law that would make possible all this added production to the oil industry, including Richfield, seemed so desirable and logical as to be beyond debate. Certainly several billion barrels more oil from fields not yet unitized seemed to be such a worthwhile objective that industry and government alike would have a compelling incentive to achieve it.

Funds were needed, of course, to frame and promote a conservation law. The search for new reserves required substantial expenditures for geological research, as well as large outlays for exploratory drilling. But in the conservation program we were dealing with known producing oil fields, and none of these exploratory-risk expenditures would be required. Thus it seemed more than reasonable to spend a substantial amount of money in attempting to bring into being the legal basis for oil conservation.

Two previous attempts—in 1932 and 1939—to obtain a conservation law in California had failed. In both years bills passed the legislature but were defeated by popular referendum. Both contained clauses relating oil production to market demand, and it was those clauses which were believed to be the reason they were opposed by a small group of enormously rich and politically powerful independent oilmen. (Actually, market-demand clauses have been determined by the Supreme Court to be sound conservation measures.)

Early in 1953, when Richfield began its public program to achieve a conservation law, we decided to eliminate the market-demand clauses and to take the issue directly to the people with an initiative measure. We believed that, by carrying on a well-organized educational program over a long period, we might win the public and industry support necessary to place California among the conservation states. A staff was set up at Richfield to carry out a program of education in oil conservation.

We found it no easy task to explain to laymen the technical aspects of oil-field operation—such as the meaning of MER (maximum efficient rate), efficient gas-oil ratios, the law of capture ("the law of the jungle"), and the function of pressures and pressure maintenance in the production of oil.

Long before, Oklahoma and Texas had enacted sound conservation laws. In each instance martial law had been declared and the militia had controlled the principal oil fields while the legislatures worked out the laws. The blessings of oil in those states had spread far and wide among farmers and urbanites, while in California the immediate blessings were mostly limited to the large landowners. Thus, while California was and has continued to be one of the most important oil-producing areas, even today the average citizen of the state is aware of petroleum only at the service-station pump. The state of California, by reason of its paramount interest in Long Beach Harbor, has become an important beneficiary of oil, but the average citizen does not know of its significance.

Our educational program included three color films, *California's Buried Treasure* and *The Conservation Dollar*, both written by Erick Strutt, and *The Conservation Story*, by Donald Culross Peattie and Louise Redfield Peattie; a working model of an oil field, designed by Herman H. Kaveler; and a series of speeches and lectures. *California's Buried Treasure* was exhibited at Disneyland and by 1956 had reached an audience of 650,000 persons. It was also shown to about 280,000 persons at fourteen county fairs. About 225,000 pamphlets were also distributed at the fairs. The response was so good that the film was booked at 980 meetings of various clubs throughout the state. Kaveler's oil-field model, showing the manner in which oil is produced through modern conservation techniques, was exhibited by Richfield's engineers, scientists, and lawyers at 173 dinner meetings throughout the state. The exhibit was seen by more than 13,500 opinion leaders in nearly all the towns in California with populations of 5,000 or more.

On December 8, 1953, David Faville, of Stanford University, spoke before the San Francisco Rotary Club. In his talk, which received a good deal of space in Bay-area newspapers, he brought the subject of oil imports into the picture. He spoke out against the wasting of oil deposits by "some producers" at a time when California had become an importing state.

The "bankers' view" of conservation was presented in June, 1954, at a meeting of about 300 banking executives of southern California. In a speech at the meeting Hugo A. Anderson, vice-president of the First National Bank of Chicago, declared that oil-conservation laws provided assurance to the banker that oil reserves on which the bank loaned money would be wisely used. Richfield reprinted Anderson's speech in pamphlet form and distributed it widely.

In the fall of 1954, Richfield launched a speakers' bureau to take its conservation story to the people through programs for service clubs and other organizations. Using the films and the model field, as well as calling upon the services of Richfield's attorneys, engineers, and employees of other departments who volunteered to undertake speaking engagements, the bureau was able to offer six programs of varying lengths and formats.

By the fall of 1955 all the major oil firms operating in California except Union Oil Company had indicated their interest in supporting a conservation measure. Union Oil was the one major company that displayed active opposition. No other really formidable opposition was apparent. Many of the independents also

276

agreed to support the proposed legislation, although several had declared their opposition. In late October, 1955, the chances of passage were appraised as better than even, and we decided to draft an initiative measure for the voters. On November 4, 1955, we mailed copies of the draft, along with a letter soliciting comments and suggestions, to interested organizations and individuals both in the oil industry and in conservation fields.

Almost immediately, substantially the same small group of independent oilmen who had destroyed the legislation passed in 1932 and 1939—now joined by Union Oil and assisted by Gulf Oil—formed an association to defeat the initiative measure. Some newspapers and politicians who had previously supported it now cautiously backed up to determine how their pocketbook interests might best be served.

On January 3, 1956, the measure was filed with the state. On Friday, January 13, over the strenuous objection of lobbyists for the opposition, the California attorney general issued the official Title and Summary of the measure:

> "Oil and Gas Conservation, Initiative" (*a*) prohibits waste, defined as production methods which reduce maximum economic quantity of oil and gas ultimately recoverable by good engineering practices; (*b*) provides for unit operation of pools to increase ultimate recovery on agreement of lessors and lessees of three-fourths of the pool; (*c*) creates California Oil and Gas Conservation Commission to prevent waste by any necessary or proper orders, including orders limiting production only to the extent necessary to prevent waste; (*d*) provides for well spacing. Provides for pooling of spacing units in the pools; and (*e*) provides for enforcement and administration.

The Declaration of Intent stated:

> It is hereby declared to be the intent of this Act to encourage and promote conservation in the production of oil and gas in the State of California; to protect the public interest in waste in the production of oil and gas; and to encourage production practices designed to increase the ultimate recovery of oil and gas.[1]

The battle was joined. The power, wealth, and influence of the

[1] From title and summary of "Oil and Gas Conservation Act: Initiative Measure to be Submitted Directly to the Electors."

277

opponents were everywhere in evidence. If a college professor spoke favorably for conservation, both he and his college felt their wrath. Many newspapers who had formerly supported the proposal were subjected to heavy attack and were either neutralized or converted to the opposition. The major companies supporting the measure were scornfully referred to as "International Oil Companies" and were accused of buying and using slaves in the production of oil in foreign lands (the opposition's charges were directed at the major companies; no mention was made of the many independent companies supporting the measure). Billboards and newspaper ads carried pictures of public slave markets and claims that "slave Arab oil" would drown the independent companies. The real issues were ignored. A director of one of the independent groups prophesied: "This is going to be a dirty, all-out fight. The independents have been holding off intentionally with the idea of blasting them [the supporters of the measure] now."

By the time the opposition's campaign had moved into high gear, our conservation efforts had passed the point of no return. We had to keep faith with our supporters and conservation-minded allies. While we realized that in all probability we would be unable to secure the necessary votes, to fail to do our best would be unfair to the conservation effort. Despite all our education efforts we were unable to overcome the vilification of such slogans as "Arab Slave Markets," "Sharks Eating Minnows," "Standard Oil Monopoly," and "$1.00 Gasoline." We were defeated at the polls on November 6, 1956.

In 1957, Erich W. Zimmermann, in his *Conservation in the Production of Petroleum* (New Haven, Yale University Press), had this to say:

> Of late, interest in conservation laws in California seems to be focusing on secondary recovery. That is due mainly to the fact that California finds it increasingly difficult to meet the demand of the area for petroleum products. Since 1938, very few major fields have been found. Older ones are playing out. Population and industry are growing by leaps and bounds. California was the logical source of supply for the Korean theater of war. So it looks as if California is going to depend on imports of both oil and gas—not

necessarily all the time but much of the time. A deficit state should be keenly interested in conservation, manifested in part by its carefully planned unitized or cooperative scientific development programs, including secondary recovery, cycling, pressure maintenance, repressuring, and other types of secondary recovery operations, but it need not be much concerned with fixing statewide allowables so that excessive production will be avoided.

In line with this shift in general attitude was the recent move on the part of the Richfield Oil Corporation to initiate a new oil law in California. A vital feature of the new law was a provision which would allow an oil pool to be put under unit operation through an agreement of 75 per cent of the operating and royalty interests in the field. The law was to have been enforced by a three-man commission which would also have authority to establish well-spacing patterns in pools discovered after the law went into effect. Regulation of production was to be on the basis of MER and not of market demand.[1] Richfield's move had the support of other large oil companies but was fought by the same interests that defeated earlier efforts to bring conservation to California. The enemies of conservation won again in 1956, as they had in 1932 and 1939.

[1] *Petroleum Week*, Vol. II, No. 2 (January 13, 1956), 9.

Though the noble effort had failed, it was not without some benefit. It had educated the California legislature to the value of unitization and repressuring. On July 2, 1957—less than eight months after the defeat of the initiative—the legislature passed a similar law affecting state-owned lands, and on April 10, 1958, it extended the law to city- and county-owned lands. The legislature could not, however, find the courage to include private lands, and so the private owner has been denied the protection and benefit of the conservation laws.

The new laws made possible the protection, unitization, and repressuring of the large East Wilmington Field, in which the state of California had a paramount interest. No move was made by the industry to unitize and repressure the field, however. Meanwhile, subsidence was continuing in both that field and the adjacent Long Beach Field.

On August 10, 1955, to further our conservation effort, I had addressed the Rotary Club of Long Beach, California, and pointed

279

the way to unitization, repressuring, and an end to subsidence. Printed and distributed in pamphlet form, this speech awakened the federal government to the fact that it had cause for damage against the oil operators in the area. In August, 1958, the Department of Justice brought suit for damages and asked for an injunction to prevent further damage. The wording of the suit incorporated much of the speech I had delivered in Long Beach. I had talked with Perry W. Morton, the head of the Justice Department's Land and Natural Resources Division, and William Gray, a Los Angeles attorney who had been chosen by the Justice Department to bring the action. I had urged that the action be one of injunctive relief, but they chose to ask for both damages and the injunction.

The case was not settled until September, 1963, at which time the oil companies agreed to pay $6 million in damages and accepted the injunction. Of course, as one of the producers in the area, Richfield had to pay its share. In the meantime, the companies had unitized the area, and repressuring had stopped the subsidence.

After the case was settled, the state and the oil companies joined forces to unitize the East Wilmington Field, and the unit in which Richfield owned a small interest is now being operated by a group of responsible companies. It is conservatively estimated that the state will collect for its share more than $3 billion during the life of the field.

In these responsible acts, California gained at least one victory. The state saved not only an oil field but also a great harbor and naval base.

## 39. NORTH TO ALASKA

IN the mid-1950's, Richfield turned its attention to Alaska as a potential new source of crude oil. We little guessed that this activity would lead to the largest oil discovery in North America, or that the discovery would be made in a context of corporate mergers that would create a new nationwide company and a major power in American oil. Our concern was an immediate one: the higher purchasing costs of crude oil that were a factor in reducing Richfield's earnings (down from $30.8 million in 1951 to $27.3 million in 1956). Convinced of the absolute need to discover more new reserves, we went north to Alaska.

Richfield's interest in Alaska had begun in the late 1930's, following some exploration activity by others on Iniskin Peninsula, on the west side of Cook Inlet. Our research had been suspended in 1941 because of the federal conversion to a moose preserve of one important area in which we were interested (see below) and the onset of World War II and the attendant limitations on costly exploration.

After the war we resumed our research. Our geologists joined naval operations in Naval Petroleum Reserve No. 4, at the extreme northern tip of Alaska, and made geological reconnaissance of many areas. Then, in 1954, Secretary of the Interior Douglas McKay decided that multiple use of withdrawn federal lands was in the best interests of the people of Alaska and of the United States. This ruling opened the possibility of operations in lands previously foreclosed to us. Richfield's vice-president in charge of exploration, Rollin Eckis, recommended four areas of interest, listed below in order of priority:

1. The Arctic Slope north of Brooks Range, in northern Alaska
2. The Kenai Peninsula, in southern Alaska
3. Wide Bay, on the Alaska Peninsula
4. The Katalla–Yakataga region, on the coast east of Kenai and south of the Chugach Mountains

The federal government had not yet opened the Arctic Slope for filing, and so we were barred from our first choice. As for the Kenai Peninsula, as mentioned above, President Roosevelt had in 1941 signed a withdrawal order converting a large part of the peninsula to a refuge and breeding ground for moose, thereby providing moose hunters with a range where they could be reasonably sure of securing specimen antlers. Richfield's area of interest in the Kenai Peninsula fell within the boundaries of the Moose Range, but we believed that oil exploration and production constituted a proper multiple use of federal lands and would not adversely affect the welfare of the moose. We filed on 70,000 acres of land in the range, about 40 miles southwest of Anchorage.

In 1955 the United States Senate Committee on Interior and Insular Affairs held hearings on our application. The results were favorable, and we negotiated and signed a development agreement with the Department of the Interior. By agreement among owners

284

and operators, the lands were unitized and Richfield held an 89.5 per cent interest in them.

We commenced geological and geophysical studies in the same year and began drilling in 1956. In 1957 we discovered the Swanson River Field, the first commercial oil field in Alaska. Our first well was completed on September 29 at a depth below 11,000 feet, and it was soon producing at a rate of over 900 barrels a day. We promptly drilled a second well two miles south to confirm the all-important discovery. It produced from the same depth, as well as at a lower level.

By the time the second well was finished, heated opposition to oil development had arisen among conservationists in the "Lower Forty-eight" (the Alaskans' term for the forty-eight states). They argued that oil development was incompatible with conservation of moose. Suddenly Secretary of the Interior Fred A. Seaton, reacting to heavy political pressure from conservation organizations, stopped the issuance of leases and closed down existing oil operations. While we waited for him to issue new regulations for leasing and development, we were at a standstill in proving out the Swanson River Field. Strangely—and, we hoped, temporarily—we found ourselves on the other side of the table from our conservationist colleagues.

After thoroughly investigating all aspects of the Kenai Moose Range issue, Secretary Seaton became convinced that no harm would be done to the moose by oil development. To settle the question, he suggested to his close friend Theodore W. Braun, Richfield's public-affairs adviser, that I be asked to select a group of oilmen to meet with Seaton and a group of conservationists to be chosen by Seaton.

The members of the conference from the oil industry were Morgan J. Davis, president, Humble Oil & Refining Company, representing Texas Mid-Continent Oil and Gas Association; R. G. Follis, chairman of the board, Standard Oil Company of California, representing Western Oil and Gas Association; Charles S. Jones, president, Richfield Oil Corporation, representing Western Oil and Gas Association; Theodore W. Braun, Braun & Company, public-relations adviser to Richfield; W. C. Whaley, president,

*Alaska's first commercial oil well, Richfield's Swanson River No. 1 discovery well, on the Kenai Peninsula, completed September 29, 1957.*

Sunray Mid-Continent Oil Company, representing Mid-Continent Oil and Gas Association; James C. Donnell II, president, Ohio Oil Company, representing Rocky Mountain Oil and Gas Association; L. F. McCollum, president, Continental Oil Company, representing Mid-Continent Oil and Gas Association; Paul Endacott, presi-

286

dent, Phillips Petroleum Company, representing Louisiana-Arkansas Division, Mid-Continent Oil and Gas Association.

The members representing the conservation organizations were John Baker, president, National Audubon Society; David R. Brower, chairman, Natural Resources Council of America; Ira N. Gabrielson, president, Wildlife Management Institute; Paul A. Herbert, president and vice-chairman, Board of Directors, National Wildlife Federation; Max McGraw, president, North American Wildlife Foundation; John M. Olin, Olin Mathieson Chemical Corporation; Roger Hale, vice-president, Conservation Foundation; William H. Pringle, president, Izaak Walton League of America.

Members from the Department of the Interior were Secretary Seaton and Ross Leffler, assistant secretary for conservation matters.

When those of us from the oil industry entered Seaton's conference room, the conservationists were already present. All of them were known to us, and several were good friends of mine. Secretary Seaton said, "I will ask the conservationists to sit on this side of the table." I remarked, "Mr. Secretary, how do you tell the difference?" From the ripple of laughter I judged that at least some of my conservationist friends understood my point.

Not long after the conference opened, everyone present realized that we had no basic differences and that, by working together, we could make substantial contributions to conservation causes and greatly improve the public's understanding of the issues. As an outgrowth of the conference, the American Petroleum Institute set up a permanent staff to serve as a means of liaison with the conservation groups, and the result has been a great deal of constructive accomplishment. Secretary Seaton was given due credit for his wise statesmanship. We were able to proceed with oil development in the Kenai, taking care to observe precautions recommended by the conservationists.

This enlightened approach was in sharp contrast to that of 1941, when the President withdrew the Kenai Moose Range. The industry had catalogued the area as potential oil land, based on data issued by the United States Geological Survey. On the eve of our

287

entry into World War II, the United States Navy needed depend-able oil supplies in Alaska probably more than at any other point on earth (General Brehon Somervell was busy spending $150 million on construction of a tiny pipeline from Norman Wells to White Horse, hoping to pump 3,000 barrels of aviation gasoline daily to armed forces in Alaska).

With the advantage of over twenty-five years' hindsight, it could be suggested to the federal government that it might at least consult the oil industry before withdrawing potential oil lands which might mean the difference between success and failure in national defense during some future crisis.

Discover a major new oil field, and litigious-minded people are legion. That had been our experience for over forty years, ever since the discovery of Elwood, and Alaska proved no different. Titles to leases issued to Richfield and others were attacked in *Tallman et al.* v. *Secretary of the Interior.* We were not parties to the suit and knew nothing about it until September, 1963. When the United States Court of Appeals for the District of Columbia decided in favor of the plaintiffs, the small amount of land leased by Richfield that was directly involved in the suit was nonproduc-tive and unimportant. But in rendering the decision the court gratuitously added, "The leases issued to parties other than these appellants were a nullity."

By then six years had passed since the discovery of oil in Alaska, and the young oil industry there had invested many millions in exploration of leases that the court had nullified. Sometimes oil-men generate more adrenalin from uninformed American court decisions than they do from the acts of foreign landowners. We at Richfield promptly joined forces with Standard of California, Marathon Oil, Union Oil, and many other lessees and set about the business of overthrowing the court's decision. Some wanted the United States Congress to clear the title, but the better decision was made to proceed through the courts and avoid getting involved in politics.

During the eighteen months of litigation that followed, no one could predict the future of Alaskan oil. Fortunately, the industry

*Swanson River No. 23-3, one of the many Alaskan wells in which Richfield had an interest. The vast acres of timberland shown in this aerial view refute the common belief that the Alaskan landscape is composed of nothing but ice and snow.*

had the faith—and the courage—to continue its vigorous growth during these months of suspense. In March, 1965, that faith was rewarded when the United States Supreme Court decided in our favor, thus opening the way to vigorous development of the Alaskan oil industry.

By 1961 our four-year-old Swanson River Field had matured

into a major field and was producing about 30,000 barrels a day. A terminal for tanker loading was completed, and Richfield commenced moving oil by tanker from Alaska to California. At the same time federal legislation was enacted to open the offshore waters of Cook Inlet to oil development, and in 1961 we began bidding on and acquiring leases with other companies. In September, 1963, we participated in the first important discovery in Cook Inlet, the second major oil-field discovery in Alaska.

Meanwhile, despite opposition from various quarters, Alaska itself had benefited enormously from oil development. In 1957, the year in which Richfield discovered Alaska's first commercial oil, on the Kenai Peninsula, Alaska received $314,000 in bonuses, rentals, and so on, from the industry. By the end of 1963, Alaska had received over $84 million in bonuses, royalties, and rentals, in addition to a substantial sum levied as ad valorem taxes. Alaska also benefited from the large capital outlay and expenditures for operating costs which the industry had incurred and was increasing year by year. This proved to be but the beginning, as Richfield and other companies continued to open still more and larger oil deposits in Alaska.

When Congress was considering the question of statehood for Alaska, we were optimistic in our forecasts of the revenue to be derived by the proposed state from royalties, bonuses, employment, and income from the Alaskan oil industry. This optimism, fully shared by the late Senator E. L. ("Bob") Bartlett of Alaska, has been more than justified. Without question, the Kenai oil discovery by Richfield in 1957 accelerated the addition of the forty-ninth star to the American flag in 1959.

## 40. THE SUEZ CRISIS

WHILE Richfield was discovering oil in Alaska, the company's main activities continued to center in California, where a serious marketing problem had developed. From its inception to the early 1950's the California oil industry had been a separate and well-protected entity. Unrelated geologically to the rest of the United States, the industry was self-contained. It produced enough for its own market (except for short periods caused by two world wars). In 1948, demand was 970,000 barrels a day, and production was 1 million barrels a day.

But by 1955 demand had climbed to 1,290,000 barrels a day and production only to 1,060,000 barrels a day. The remainder was shipped principally from the Rocky Mountain area and from fields in Sumatra, the Persian Gulf, and Venezuela. California was no longer self-sufficient but was dependent on foreign oil to supplement its production.

Then, in October, 1956, Egypt closed the Suez Canal, and the oil lines from the Middle East to the Mediterranean were shut down. The shock to the oil industry was felt around the world. A flood of foreign oil started pouring into California late in 1956 and by 1957 had reached 263,000 barrels a day. Prices broke sharply, and inventories became unmanageable.

The situation was aggravated by the fact that the United States government had asked domestic companies to increase production to help supply nations affected by closing of the canal. The industry adjusted rapidly to the situation, building larger tankers and sailing them around the Cape of Good Hope and also putting the pipelines back into operation. But after the worldwide shortage was alleviated, American companies continued to produce at the accelerated pace, thus adding to the flood of foreign oil continuing into California.

On December 12, 1957, the Department of the Interior instituted a voluntary oil-import program for California. The program was separate from that instituted for the rest of the United States and provided for a limitation of imports in the first half of 1958. Along with a few other companies, Richfield substantially reduced its own production and strictly observed the guidelines of the program. But by and large the program was observed in the breach. Stability did not begin returning to the industry in California until 1959, when President Eisenhower signed the law making the import program mandatory and prohibiting any oil imports beyond the quotas set by the Department of the Interior.

Because of this import debacle, from a profit standpoint the years 1956 to 1958 were unhappy ones for Richfield. By 1958 profits had dropped to $21 million, or $5.20 a share, the lowest in ten years. In the meantime, however, Richfield had continued to improve its position in refining and marketing, headed by Vice-President for Manufacturing David E. Day and Vice-President for Marketing W. G. King, Jr. We continued to be active in production as well, and of the $162 million plowed into capital expenditures

*Two Richfield tankships, leased under long-term charter. Above: the* Cuyama Valley, *delivered in 1958. Below: the* Kenai Peninsula, *delivered in 1959. Each weighs 45,000 tons and has a capacity of 400,-000 barrels.*

for 1957 to 1959 a substantial portion was dedicated to oil exploration. Our adventures in Egypt and the sultanate of Muscat and Oman had come to naught, but in Alaska we had expanded our explorations to the Wide Bay and Katalla–Yakataga areas, and we had also become interested in several areas of Alberta, Canada.

By 1960, owing to the Kenai discovery and growth in other activities, we had recovered. In that year sales and other operating revenues reached $368 million, production achieved a new high, and earnings were $7.14 a share. In 1959 we became the second-largest crude-oil producer in California—no small feat for a company that had come out of receivership only twenty-two years before. We were braced for the decade of the 1960's, which was to bring some monumental triumphs, problems, and opportunities —and would see the end of Richfield's history as a separate company.

## 41. THE PROMISE OF NUCLEAR RECOVERY

ONE of the long-range opportunities presented to Richfield even before the 1960's—and still unseized at this writing—was that of the Athabasca bituminous-sands region in Alberta, Canada, the largest known tar-sand deposit in the world. In 1956, Richfield acquired reservations and permits from the Alberta provincial government on about a million acres of the sands. Various techniques were employed in unsuccessful efforts to extract and convert the tar to liquid form, thereby opening a whole new source of petroleum products.

In September, 1957, the Atomic Energy Commission detonated a nuclear device of the Hiroshima type at a depth of 790 feet at a test site called Rainier, northwest of Las Vegas, Nevada. The re-

294

sults of the test were made public by Gerald W. Johnson, of the Lawrence Radiation Laboratory at the University of California. We calculated that, by detonating the same device at a selected location at a depth of 1,400 feet, slightly below the tar sand, we could heat enough tar-sand oil to make the production of synthetic crude-oil profitable. By 1958, Richfield had acquired reservations and permits on more than two million acres in the Athabasca region, and we applied to the provincial government for permission to make experiments to prove our theory. We had the support of the Atomic Energy Commission and the "Plowshare" (atoms-for-peace) group, including Edward Teller and Gerald Johnson.

Because of the magnitude of the project Richfield invited Cities Service, Sinclair, and Imperial Oil, Ltd., to participate as equal partners. Cities and Imperial accepted; Sinclair did not. In the approximately 1,236,000 acres in which the tar sands lie at depths too great for surface mining but which might respond to nuclear heating or some other *in situ* process, the three equal participants were Richfield (the operator), Cities Service, and Imperial.

The Alberta provincial government and the Canadian government appointed committees to study the feasibility of recovering oil from the tar sands along the lines of the Rainier test. The Alberta government filed a favorable report, but the committee appointed by the Canadian government withheld its report. Then, in 1960, Canada joined the United States, Russia, and other countries in a moratorium on the testing of nuclear devices. While the proposed research was not in any way related to the testing of nuclear devices as defined in the moratorium, the Canadian government considered it a sensitive subject, and the matter was tabled.

Our physicists and engineers believed the idea to be simple, workable, perfectly safe, and economically practical, but there was no way to prove or disprove their conclusions without experimentation. We could only hope that the political climate would someday enable the Canadians to let us continue our research and prove beyond doubt the feasibility of the plan. The significance of a successful test to Canada and the free world would be tremendous.

In addition to the proposed research on producing the tar sands by thermonuclear heating, we were investigating the possibility of

295

*The Athabasca bituminous-sands region in Alberta, Canada, the largest-known tar-sand deposit in the world. Shown above is the pilot plant at Mildred Lake for mining surface sands which was operated by Cities Service Athabasca, Inc., for the four-company group now known as Syncrude Canada, Ltd.*

*The miniature replica of Krupp's famous mining wheel, built for pilot studies at Mildred Lake, Canada, to determine the commercial feasibility of extracting hydrocarbons from the Athabasca tar sands at or near the surface.*

297

mining a portion of the Athabasca sands in a large area where the sands are either exposed or are shallow enough for strip mining. The participants in this project were Richfield (30 per cent), Imperial (30 per cent), Cities Service (30 per cent), and Gulf Oil Canada, Ltd. (10 per cent). The four companies held leases or permits on 287,000 acres.

The research involved three phases: (1) the mining and recovery of the tar sand, (2) the separation of the tar from the sands, and (3) the processing of the recovered hydrocarbon into a usable synthetic crude oil for further refining into petroleum products. For phase 1 we commissioned the Krupp Works to build a miniature replica of their famous mining wheel that was used to mine the lignite coal beds of Germany. The wheel was armed with huge teeth for digging and cutting the highly viscous sands. Buckets were placed under each set of teeth to catch the cuttings. The wheel was installed at Mildred Lake, near Fort McMurray, Canada, where a model separation plant and a distillation plant were constructed and put into operation. The research plant had a capacity of 3,000 barrels a day.

The research proved that the recovery of tar from the oil sands is commercially feasible, and the Canadian government has recently granted an application to build a commercial plant. Other companies are working in the area, and it is expected that over the years enormous additional reserves of oil will be recovered from it.

# 42. DOUBLING IN GAS

WE had greater success in our efforts to utilize another resource—natural gas. As mentioned earlier, in 1948 the Pacific Lighting Corporation, the gas utility company holding the monopoly on natural gas in most of southern California, refused to buy dry gas from Richfield on a temporary basis. We then built a gas line from South Cuyama to North Coles Levee and commenced using our dry gas for repressuring in the conservation program at the latter field.

From 1948 to 1959, Richfield repressured its North Coles Levee and South Cuyama fields by injecting into the producing zones gas produced from those and other fields. This procedure was a sound oil-conservation measure, since natural gas is one of the chief sources of energy for moving oil underground to the producing wells. It has resulted in the production of much more oil from those two fields than would otherwise have been possible. It also resulted in the largest reserves of uncommitted gas in the state of California—amounting to approximately 1 trillion cubic feet. The accumulation of these reserves, plus the discovery in 1958 of additional oil-and-gas fields, enabled Richfield to commence selling gas without detriment to its oil-conservation program.

At that time the gas utility was paying 14.5 cents a thousand cubic feet to the oil producers in California and was paying other gas utilities 45 cents a thousand cubic feet for gas delivered to the California border. We had enough gas to enable us to deal independently with any large consumer and not be at the mercy of the monopoly.

Accordingly, we entered into a contract with Southern California Edison Company for the sale of 500 billion cubic feet over a period of twenty-five years, for use as fuel in Edison's Mandalay Generating Plant near Ventura, California. The beginning price for gas delivered under the contract was 34.5 cents a thousand cubic feet, which was the average price Edison paid to the gas-utility company for gas in 1959. Edison had never been able to secure gas from the utility company on an assured annual basis, but under its contract with Richfield, Edison was to receive daily deliveries.

To deliver the gas to Edison, it was necessary for us to construct a twenty-inch pipeline fifty-nine miles long from the Cuyama fields to the Mandalay plant. Pacific Lighting Corporation instituted proceedings before the Public Utilities Commission of California to prevent Richfield from building the pipeline. As far as costs went, the interests of California consumers were not involved because Edison paid no more to Richfield than to Pacific. The issue was solely whether Edison and Richfield could deal with each other directly or whether Pacific had to be given a middleman's commission without providing Edison the service it required. The commission to Pacific would be $100 million, and we thought it best to oppose the legal action brought against us. We retained attorneys Joseph Ball and Clark Heggeness to defend us.

*The pipeline from the Cuyama fields to Edison's Mandalay plant*

Pacific pulled out all the stops in its effort to prevent us from building the line, but we built it anyway. In the end the Supreme Court of California decided that we were right, and the Supreme Court of the United States concurred.

The entire oil industry benefited from our success. Pacific raised the schedules of prices it paid to California gas producers by about 100 per cent, which was still less than it had to pay for gas imported from Texas. We calculated the value to the California producers to be about $1.5 billion, based on the 1959 California dry-gas reserves.

301

## 43. JUSTICE REARS ITS HEAD

BY 1962, Richfield had solved its crude-oil shortages through discoveries in Alaska and elsewhere. A quarter-century after its rebirth it was moving confidently ahead toward new opportunities. But in October of that year the United States Department of Justice struck a fateful blow that is best described in the following excerpt from Richfield's stockholders' report for 1962:

### ANTITRUST LITIGATION

Stockholders familiar with the history of Richfield know that it came into being as the result of a plan of reorganization of the former Richfield Oil Company of California and its subsidiary, Pan American Petroleum Company, pursuant to what was then known as "Section 77B" of the National Bankruptcy Act. The old

302

Richfield company had gone into receivership in January, 1931, and the Pan American Company in March, 1932. All efforts to work out their financial difficulties failed, and they faced forced sale of their assets and complete liquidation. If this had happened they would, of course, have disappeared from the competitive oil industry on the Pacific Coast. Instead, the business was reorganized into a new enterprise (Richfield Oil Corporation) under an order approving the plan of reorganization made by the U. S. District Court for the Southern District of California in Los Angeles on December 23, 1936. The new Corporation began business in March, 1937, and has been a strong competitive factor on the Pacific Coast ever since.

The plan of reorganization was made possible by two companies, Sinclair Oil Corporation and Cities Service Company. These two companies furnished the financial support necessary for the success of the new company and each received approximately 18 per cent of the stock of the new company. Each also provided directors for the new company. All of this was approved not only by the U. S. District Court but by the U. S. Circuit Court of Appeals of the 9th Circuit, which refused to review the judgment of the District Court. It was also approved by a Congressional Committee— the "House Select Committee to Investigate Bondholders' Reorganizations" (the so-called "Sabath Committee").

Notwithstanding these approvals and the continued competition by Richfield on the West Coast, the U.S. Department of Justice in October, 1962, filed an action in the District Court in Los Angeles against Richfield Oil Corporation, Cities Service Company and Sinclair Oil Corporation, and the persons who were directors of both Richfield and Cities Service and the persons who were directors of both Richfield and Sinclair, alleging violation of the Federal antitrust laws, in that (1) Cities Service and Sinclair do not compete with Richfield in the six-state area consisting of California, Oregon, Washington, Idaho, Nevada and Arizona and that Richfield does not compete with Cities and Sinclair outside of such area; (2) since 1936, Cities and Sinclair have owned and presently own substantial amounts of stock in Richfield; and (3) directors of Cities and Sinclair have been directors of Richfield.

The complaint asks the court to declare unlawful the acquisition of stock in Richfield by Cities and Sinclair and that those companies be required to divest themselves of Richfield stock and that persons who are directors of Cities and Sinclair be ordered to resign as directors of Richfield.

This action brought after 25 years against Richfield, Cities and

303

Sinclair completely ignores the original approval by the Government of the acts now complained of and the continued acquiescence through 25 years of the same things. Stockholders may be assured that the action will be vigorously opposed by the management.

Counsel for Richfield, for Sinclair, for Cities and for the directors named as defendants have expressed the opinion that the charges by the Government are completely unfounded, that there has been no violation of the antitrust laws, and that the case will be successfully defended.

Little did anyone realize the far-reaching effects of the government's action. Within a matter of hours after the suit was filed, I began receiving telephone calls, letters, and visits from bankers, brokers, oil companies, and large investors, all making a play for ownership or control of the company at the quoted price of the stock. To each of them I made the same reply: "Not interested—we plan to win the suit."

I had believed up to then that I was fairly well acquainted with Wall Street (and I use the name generically), but I found that my postgraduate work lay ahead. Make the numbers big enough, and the entrepreneurs do their homework. The skill and finesse with which I was constantly presented the most flattering personal offers would be good material for a textbook for advanced business colleges. Add to these activities the fast-buck operators and the seekers of inside knowledge, and you come face to face with some hard facts of life about which the courts have recently started doing something and which probably will also receive legislative action.

At the time of the Justice Department's action in 1962, Rollin Eckis, now president of Richfield (I had become chairman of the board), and other top executives had been with the company since its formation in 1937. They included Cleve B. Bonner, vice-president and treasurer; David E. Day, vice-president in charge of projects for diversification; W. G. King, Jr., vice-president in charge of marketing; R. W. Ragland, vice-president and general counsel; Stender Sweeney, vice-president in charge of personnel and industrial relations; W. J. Travers, vice-president in charge of production; Norman F. Simmonds, secretary; and W. W. Gamel, comptroller. Some of these men had worked for Richfield's pre-

304

decessors, Rio Grande and Richfield of California. Another, John W. Gendron, vice-president in charge of manufacturing and transportation, had joined the company in 1959. Dedicated, hard-working, intelligent, and extremely happy in their work, they were deeply shocked by the government's attack. All of us realized that our first obligation was to preserve the morale of Richfield's employees, most of whom owned stock under the company's stock-purchase plan, and to reassure our stockholders about their investments.

Richfield retained the law firm of Ball, Hunt & Hart in Los Angeles and Arnold, Fortas & Porter as our Washington counsel. Sinclair and Cities Service retained their own counsel. The legal representatives set up committees to mount the defense against the antitrust action, and we made it clear that we intended to fight it.

Meanwhile, management carried on with the problems of continuing the company's growth, keeping employee morale high, maintaining a constructive stockholder relationship, and, above all, nourishing and preserving the superlative customer acceptance of Richfield products. Budgets were increased, and the organization was soon too busy building Richfield's long-term competitive position to worry about lawsuits.

The Antitrust Division's demands for records and for answers to interrogatories going back for a third of a century were as insatiable as they were burdensome. There were times when we wondered whether we could continue to divert staff members from their regular duties to searching files and answering the government's questions and still maintain a competitive oil company. The struggle for position in the oil industry is a vigorous and never-ending battle. Epitaphs are carved and ready for any company that weakens, gets tired, or lowers its guard.

From the beginning of the action, I insisted to the lawyers that we must bring the case to trial at the earliest possible moment. If we could win it, I maintained, then we should win it and get on with our business. I insisted that we must be finished with the litigation in no more than two years. The lawyers were seasoned antitrust specialists with reputations for winning such suits. They took a very different view and insisted that five years would be a reasonable minimum and that we might resolve the case in no more than six years. Of all those living at the time the suit was filed in October, 1962, I alone knew all the facts about the company from its inception. Having helped create it and manage it from the beginning, I knew that without my help and interpretation of its operations the chances of winning would be lessened. I was then sixty-seven years old—two years past normal retirement and a few months past the average life expectancy of males. The five- or six-year forecast seemed to me interminable and unrealistic.

The weight of the suit became more oppressive with each passing month. I became convinced that if the government had five years to continue fishing it would undoubtedly discover one or more instances in which Harry Sinclair, with Cities Service's acquiescence, had tried to insist on a division of territory (until the late evening of his life Sinclair could not rid himself of the conviction that Richfield was a Sinclair subsidiary). I knew of instances which, seen by themselves, would have made the case difficult to defend. I vividly remembered when, fourteen years earlier, Sinclair had insisted on Richfield's retreat from Texas and New Mexico—a move that had led to my retaining counsel and strongly considering just the action which the government had now brought. But these events were in the past, and for some years preceding 1962 there had been no interference with management by the controlling stockholders.

By the spring of 1964 our chances of winning were somewhat brightened, but still the lawyers counseled patience. In April, I reluctantly concluded that, if our 14,000 stockholders, large and small, were to be protected, we would have to liquidate the company or make a favorable merger that would eliminate Sinclair's and Cities Service's control. The stock was selling for $48 a share, and in my judgment the liquidation value would be at least $80. Four more years of oppressive litigation and probably another two years in the higher courts could very well bring deterioration in the company's position and values and, most serious of all, deterioration in its management team. A weaker management could very well mean retrogression into a "holding position" reminiscent of the 1931–37 receivership. In my judgment that would be fatal even if we won the suit. And if we lost the suit, then certainly all the stockholders would be badly hurt. A forced liquidation would be equivalent to placing the company's assets on the auction block.

As harsh as this may sound, I believed that the government apparently intended just that outcome when it filed the suit. The Justice Department had gone out of its way to give the suit wide publicity. Convinced of this fact, I had to lay it before our principal stockholders. P. C. Spencer and Burl S. Watson, of Sinclair and Cities Service, respectively, were invited to join me—with our wives—for a long weekend at my vacation home at Las Cruces, in Baja California, Mexico. There we could discuss the problem and, if we agreed on the idea of merger or sale, determine a procedure.

During that weekend we reached full agreement. I was to seek out prospective purchasers or merger partners. We also agreed upon absolute secrecy. To my thinking there could be nothing worse than sending the shock wave of this decision through the Richfield organization. Our employees would start speculating about their futures, lose their splendid verve, and hurt not only the company but themselves as well. They had trusted me these many years, and I was not about to let them down now.

Time proved this decision to be sound, because a merger was not effected until late the following year, 1965, and some of Richfield's most important business decisions were made in the intervening months. One, for instance, was the acquisition of a major position on the Arctic Slope of Alaska, including the great Prudhoe Bay structure, which established the company at a new level of strength and prosperity.

307

## 44. THE MERGER WITH ATLANTIC

AFTER we made the decision to try to effect a merger, my first move was to go to London to visit my friend Sir Maurice R. Bridgeman, chairman of British Petroleum. While his company was very much interested in entering the United States market, British Petroleum needed government approval to use dollars, and Sir Maurice thought the market value of British Petroleum shares too low for an advantageous exchange of stock. The matter was left in abeyance until either party desired to explore it further.

The next step was to look over the list of presently known suitors and select one which might be acceptable to us and to the Antitrust Division of the Justice Department. Phillips Petroleum was the first choice. I met K. S. ("Boots") Adams, chairman of the board

of Phillips, at Santa Fe, New Mexico. I had set a price of $80 a
share—the liquidation value—on Richfield stock. Boots was interested but wanted to trade on the relative market prices of Phillips
and Richfield shares. There seemed to be no real enthusiasm on
Adams' part, but the matter was left open.

The next choice was Standard of Indiana. John E. Swearingen,
chairman of Standard's board, had spoken to me at a meeting of
the American Petroleum Institute earlier in the year. As the site of
initial talks we selected Railroad Ranch on the Snake River (a
good trout stream) in southeastern Idaho. Railroad Ranch belongs
principally to E. Roland Harriman, and I had a cabin there.

In retrospect, I am sure that I could have made a recording of
one of these merger negotiations and saved a lot of energy merely
by playing it, asking whether anyone wished to make any changes,
and, if not, adjourning the meeting. The script would go something
like this:

> SUITOR: Now my stock is selling for X, and yours is selling for
> Y. Mine is worth a great deal more and in six months should be
> selling for its real worth. So what do you think about three-
> quarters of a share of mine for one share of yours?
> MAIDEN: Oh, no! Mine is worth a great deal more than the $80
> I am asking, and you are offered a real bargain.
> SUITOR: Oh, my gracious, my board would never agree to using
> our stock at the market price to pay you $80 for yours. The dilu-
> tion would be unjustified—that's entirely too much.
> MAIDEN: Well, then, save your stock and pay cash for our shares.
> SUITOR: That adds up to a great deal of cash, and we just
> couldn't do that unless we could find the same kind of cash or
> equivalent in your vaults when we take you over.
> MAIDEN: Well, I think we can't do business. You seem to want
> to have me without paying me.

The negotiations with Standard of Indiana continued over a
period of time. I supplied Swearingen with all pertinent Richfield
data, and his staff made an in-depth study of the company, but he
could not bring himself to meet the $80-a-share figure.

By this time it was the summer of 1965, Richfield stock had
moved up to 71, and rumors of a possible merger were rife. At no
time had I mentioned to our organization anything whatever about

309

plans or negotiations, but there were leaks in financial circles. I had, of course, kept Spencer and Watson advised about negotiations, and one leak was revealed in an unusual way. Swearingen's financial advisers were the investment bankers at Morgan, Stanley & Company. I reported to Watson about a meeting I had had with Swearingen, and Watson briefed his board of directors about it. Thereupon a member of Watson's organization, who was also a board member, got in touch with a member of Morgan, Stanley and gave him the news. I had another meeting with Swearingen later in the day and learned that the story had already been reported back to him.

Later I came into possession of an almost verbatim memo on the Richfield merger situation. It had been circulated privately by the head of one of the important companies that furnished advisory services. Obviously his clients had retained him to obtain information about Richfield. A short time later he barged into my office in Los Angeles and announced that he represented 165,000 shares of Richfield stock and wanted full details on the status of our merger negotiations, the price being considered, and so on. I told him that I represented 9.8 million shares, including the ones he represented, and that I was not about to give him information of any kind or answer his questions. He was a very skillful questioner and must indeed have been well paid for his ability to secure inside information. In this instance, however, he had to be satisfied with the published reports to our stockholders and general news releases.

These incidents are not related in a critical vein but only to offer a brief glimpse of how the game was played and what powerful incentives and mechanisms were utilized by the operators. They also demonstrate how extremely difficult it can be for an executive to protect the morale of his organization, keep his company competing vigorously, and at the same time protect his company's stockholders from the depredations of outsiders who are professionally organized to secure inside information.

With the increase in the market value of Richfield shares came a revival of interest by some of the latent suitors, and some new suitors also threw their hats in the ring. Among the latter was Robert O. Anderson, who had recently assumed the chairmanship

310

*Robert O. Anderson, chairman of Atlantic Refining Company at the time of the merger with Richfield Oil Corporation in 1965 and at the time of this writing chairman of Atlantic Richfield Company.*

of Atlantic Refining Company of Philadelphia. Bob held a substantial stock interest in Atlantic. I had known his father, Hugo A.
Anderson, for many years and had also become acquainted with
Bob when he lived in Los Angeles ten years earlier. We now met
again in Los Angeles, and I told Bob that the price was $80 each
for the Richfield shares. I had just about decided, I added, that a
cash deal would be better because of the seeming reluctance of
timid executives to pay an appropriate amount in stock. Anderson
argued against a sale of assets and preferred a stock deal. But, of
course, he was trading and showed no particular enthusiasm for
the $80 figure.

I had some private misgivings about a deal with Atlantic because
of the geographical locations of the two companies. Atlantic Refining Company was an integrated company operating on the
Atlantic Coast. Richfield was an integrated company operating on
the Pacific Coast. In between lay a vast region of the United States
in which neither company had interests. There seemed nothing to
integrate. My misgivings were based on precedent. Twenty-nine
years before, I had seen the merger of Associated Oil Company of
California with Tide Water Oil Company of New York. They covered the two coasts, with nothing in the middle. It was not a particularly happy marriage. There was, however, one fundamental
difference in the two situations, and that was Bob Anderson. Bob
was a man who knew where he was going and why. He was young
and had made a great success of his life. I had profound respect for
him and for his abilities as an oilman. His decisiveness and confidence had been proved after he took over the management of
Atlantic.

Our next meeting was in August, 1965, at Railroad Ranch. The
weather and the trout fishing are both good there in August, and
I have found that one thinks more clearly about important matters
in the quiet serenity of such surroundings. Anderson's visit came
to an end without agreement, but we understood each other better.

I returned to Los Angeles to continue discussions with other
interested companies. I had set up special offices in the Biltmore
Hotel and had pressed our auditing firm, Price Waterhouse & Co.,
into service to give prospective suitors all the pertinent data on

312

Richfield and to secure necessary information from them. Several of the smaller companies, among them Tenneco, Inc., and Sunray DX Oil Company, were actively interested. Gardiner Symonds, chairman of Tenneco, and Paul Taliaferro, of Sunray, came to Los Angeles to study our operations. Each decided that Richfield was too much for them. I had believed this from the beginning, but they were both able men, and I wanted them to have their chance.

During the first half of September, 1965, our stock was rather strong, and that fact apparently triggered the interest of still more suitors. During this period Boots Adams of Phillips called to say that he would like an appointment to talk further and seriously about a deal. I made an appointment to see him the following week. Morgan Davis of Humble also expressed interest.

Then a curious event occurred. One of our Washington lawyers called to tell me that a Mr. Cladouhos, an Antitrust Division lawyer assigned to the case, had suggested that Richfield settle the suit by merging with Atlantic Refining Company. The division had earlier suggested a merger, but this was the first time it had named a partner. The suggestion seemed most unusual, but I concluded that Bob Anderson's lawyers had probably been exploring the Justice Department's attitude toward a merger with Richfield and had thus given Cladouhos this particular inspiration.

As far back as 1959, when W. Alton Jones was still living, we had made a study of the possibility of merging Richfield, Sinclair, and Cities Service to form a national company strong enough to compete with the international majors. There was always the imponderable of the Justice Department's attitude, but we decided that we would never know the reaction until we tried. During the discussions both Cities Service and Sinclair had favored the idea of merging with Richfield, each excluding the other company, but each had taken such a dim view of the possibility that the other might win the prize that no serious proposals resulted. With the passing of Jones in March, 1962, and the elevation of E. L. Steiniger to chairmanship of the board of Sinclair, the two companies had dropped the matter.

But in September, 1965, the chairman of Cities Service, Burl Watson, informed me that he wanted to make an offer for Rich-

313

field. Cities Service already owned about 30 per cent of Richfield, and this was a logical offer on his part. I told Burl that I would be happy to receive an offer but that it would have to be for no less than $80 a share. He knew, of course, about my discussions with others and had undoubtedly considered the price, but I felt it best to place the figure in the record. I also told Burl that I was going to New York the following day to brief him and the Sinclair people on my recent discussions with other potential buyers. He said that he would "look forward to seeing me." By itself, of course, the phrase was a platitude, but taken in context, it might mean that he would have an offer ready when he saw me. Within an hour Bob Anderson telephoned from Philadelphia—he must have been prescient, because his timing was perfect. A day later, and there would probably have been no merger of Atlantic and Richfield.

Bob began the conversation with the usual trading talk: "Price too high," and so on.

"I think you should just forget the matter," I said.

"Well," he responded, "I'd like to talk to you, and I'll come to Los Angeles."

"Sorry, but I'm leaving tomorrow morning for New York." This did not deter Bob, and I agreed to see him at my hotel on my arrival in New York the next evening, September 15.

This time Bob came prepared to try to conclude the business. At our meeting in Idaho I had given him a draft of a tentative merger agreement. Complete except for the terms, it was a succinct piece of craftsmanship. Upon meeting with me in New York, Anderson handed me the identical merger agreement with only one minor change. His merger proposal was set forth in detail.

As I studied the proposal, I realized that he was making a sincere try for an agreement (putting the offer in the context of the form which I had given him and which I could quote verbatim was a superb bit of psychology on Bob's part).

In sum, the offer was to give Richfield's stockholders one share of a new $3 Atlantic convertible preference stock for each share of Richfield. Each share of the preference would be convertible into 85/100 of a share of Atlantic common stock. Of course, the value of the offer would have to be judged by a financial expert, but

314

my own judgment was that the security would sell in the market place for $80.

"Bob," I said, "you might have yourself a deal."

The following morning the financial experts gathered in my hotel room. Francis Kernan and others of White, Weld & Company represented Richfield, while a contingent from Smith, Barney & Company, led by Ernest B. Schwarzenbach, represented Atlantic. With the pertinent data of both companies at hand they certified the value of Anderson's offer to be a minimum of $79. Anderson and I shook hands on the deal. Thornton F. Bradshaw, president of Atlantic, was present to give us his blessing. Later the same day Burl Watson of Cities Service, and Steiniger and Spencer of Sinclair came to the hotel and agreed with Anderson to vote their companies' stock (approximately 60 per cent) for the merger.

With the merger assured, Anderson and I prepared to sign the agreement. We agreed to release the information immediately afterward, which meant that we would have to wait until after the stock exchanges closed for the day. I called Eckis in Los Angeles and asked him to gather the organization together and stand by until the Pacific Coast Stock Exchange in Los Angeles closed at 2:30 P.M., Pacific time. At 5:30 P.M., New York time, on September 16, 1965, Anderson and I signed the agreement. A minute later I relayed the deal to Eckis and to the organization. Like the good soldier he was, Eckis' comment was, "A hell of a surprise and a mutually good deal."

315

## 45. TO THE NORTH SLOPE

BEFORE it merged with Atlantic, Richfield had one more goal to achieve. It proved to be one of the biggest oil bonanzas the world had ever seen—a fitting curtain performance for a great company drama.

Despite all the antitrust litigation and merger negotiations, Richfield's primary business remained that of producing, refining, and marketing petroleum. During the oppressive years from 1962 to 1965 its management concentrated on this primary business. Profits, however, slipped materially, from $31 million in 1962 to $24 million in 1965, owing primarily to vicious price wars that began in 1963 and to a decline in net production.

The lead time necessary to mature a new discovery also grew

316

much longer. The offshore wells in Cook Inlet had to be drilled from platforms. Although Richfield was maintaining first place in Alaskan production, the buildup of daily production was slow. Bob Anderson knew all this when he made his offer. He knew that Richfield would report earnings of less than $3 a share for 1965, but that did not deter him from offering us a convertible preference stock with a $3 dividend. He had learned everything there was to know about the company. He understood the basic values of Richfield and knew that the profit decline was temporary. Throughout history, I imagine, it has been this kind of basic intelligence that has produced the boldness that has separated the men from the boys and has been primarily responsible for creative enterprise.

But Bob was not aware of Richfield's current decisions, which were soon to have a profound impact not only on Atlantic Richfield stockholders but on the worldwide oil industry as well. I have already related the story of Richfield's discovery of the first commercial oil field in Alaska—the Swanson River Field—which resulted in the development of a vigorous young oil industry. I have also described the first major discovery in the Cook Inlet (the second discovery in Alaska) by the joint adventurers Richfield, Shell, and Standard of California.

But the area of greatest interest to Richfield was the Arctic Slope, lying north of the Brooks Range. It was a vast basin with a tremendously thick deposit of marine sediments. A large area of the North Slope had been withdrawn by the federal government to create Naval Petroleum Reserve No. 4. We knew, from drilling done under navy auspices, that these sediments contained both oil and gas. We also knew, from surface geology and seismic work, that there were large structures favorable to the accumulation of oil.

The North Slope was a remote region, at that time accessible by sea at Point Barrow for only a few weeks each year and accessible only by air at other times. An exploration program would require opening an overland supply route from the end of the Alaska Railroad near Fairbanks.

Our first step was to support the Frontier Contractors Company in moving the first caterpillar train from Dunbar Siding, near Fair-

317

banks, northwest to Bettles, in the Yukon drainage, then through Anaktuvuk Pass, a low-altitude gap through Brooks Range, to the Arctic Slope. This historic expedition brought the first overland freight cargo across Brooks Range and proved the feasibility of the Anaktuvuk Pass route in supplying the North Slope. The route made surface transportation possible for seven months of the year.

By 1964, Richfield had acquired from the federal and state governments leases and development contracts (in whole or in part interest) covering more than 2.5 million acres of land, of which 800,000 acres were on the North Slope. Alaska was planning to advertise for bids on various lands, including the large Prudhoe Bay structure, 200 miles east of Point Barrow, in which we were also interested.

Exploration in the rugged Arctic frontier had proved extremely costly. Rather than try to finance the venture alone, we decided to invite Humble Oil & Refining Company to share a portion of our holdings and the future of the North Slope with us. Since we had done a comprehensive job of geologizing the area and Humble had done practically none, it was a logical partnership. With this arrangement completed, Richfield was faced with perhaps the most important decision of its history: How much to bid on the Prudhoe Bay structure?

We knew that the navy had spent perhaps $100 million in the area without success. We believed that any oil discovery would have to be of a magnitude to justify building a pipeline from the Arctic south to the Gulf of Alaska, which would cost at least $1 billion. Additionally, an enormous outlay of money would be required for ships and for shore facilities to move the oil to the continental United States. We also knew that Sinclair and British Petroleum had drilled six dry holes on the North Slope in the two preceding years. But what was equally important, we knew that this vast basin remained practically unexplored.

What we did not know was whether the structures in question contained the favorable reservoir conditions essential for the truly major accumulations of oil that would make the whole venture worthwhile. The surface area of the Prudhoe Bay structure was over 200,000 acres. If the reservoir conditions were favorable, it

318

was almost too large to comprehend. The possibility that conditions might not be favorable made it a gamble of giant proportions.

And so the question was: How much to bid?

When it came to open bidding on public lands or private negotiations for domestic or foreign lands, Richfield had a unique management problem. The board was controlled by executives of Sinclair and Cities Service. Until the death of W. Alton Jones in 1962 all our foreign ventures were made in partnership with Cities Service. Sinclair was always invited but only twice accepted—both times in Canada. Whenever Richfield and Cities Service were partners in a venture, enough directors were involved to ratify budgets and expenditures, although the board was never notified in advance. The Sinclair company had usually been interested in the same opportunities, but in separate operations, and had joined British Petroleum in both international and Alaskan exploration. Therefore, we could not disclose our plans to their board members who also served on Richfield's board.

Jones was a good friend of Richfield's, but after his death Cities Service preferred to go it alone or with other partners. Thus Richfield's management had the unique problem of being without a board of directors when it came to bidding or negotiating on new oil properties. To discuss these matters with the board even in general terms was tantamount to giving our competitor directors a look at our proposed bid. Such information was so well guarded in the company that usually only one executive, and never more than two, knew of it.

In the past the board had raised no question about our judgment on various matters and had ratified our actions without criticism. But in the past the largest items had entailed a financial outlay of a few million dollars at most. Now we were thinking in much larger terms. A wildcat on Prudhoe Bay could cost $25 million or more.

Even so, Eckis and I decided that, because of the need for maintaining competitive secrecy, we would not discuss this question with the board. Eckis wanted especially to explore this structure, and so we decided to concentrate on means of keeping the cost within the limits of prudence. Of course, we had the assistance of

*All this drilling equipment and more was put into the belly of the Lockheed Hercules C-130 airfreighter and flown from Fairbanks, Alaska, to a drilling location on the North Slope.*

Humble, which was now our partner. A joint decision was made on bids of some $15 million; together with the wildcat well, that would mean a cover charge of over $20 million each.

As it turned out, we were high bidders on about two-thirds of

320

*The Hercules C-130 airfreighter supplying rig and drilling equipment for the Prudhoe Bay well in the background.*

the structure at a cost of over $9 million; unfortunately we did not bid on enough land. British Petroleum won most of the balance of the structure, with a few scattered leases going to others.

At the time of the merger with Atlantic we had shipped a complete set of drilling equipment—some 3,000 tons of rigs, camps, pipe, and so on—by rail to Fairbanks. We had also chartered from Lockheed Aircraft Corporation a four-engine turboprop Hercules C-130 airfreighter to fly the equipment to a drilling location on the North Slope, where a deep test well was planned. Without knowing it at the time he signed the merger agreement, Bob Anderson had a new bonanza under his feet.

# 46. "THE PERILS OF RICHFIELD"

THE merger agreement signed on September 16, 1965, was tentative and required ratification by the board, approval by the stockholders, the agreement of the Department of Justice, settlement of the antitrust suit, and agreement by the Internal Revenue Service that the merger would be tax-free to Richfield's stockholders. These were the normal provisions, and there was no question in our minds that such approvals would be routine.

According to the tentative agreement, the merger would become effective on December 31, and stockholder meetings of both companies were set for simultaneous approvals at 12:00 noon, Eastern Standard Time, on December 30, 1965. Richfield's meeting was to be held in Wilmington, Delaware, and Atlantic's in

322

Philadelphia. The organizations of both companies concentrated on finalizing the definitive merger agreement, and the respective board approvals were given simultaneously on November 1, 1965.

The only remaining matters were the various government approvals and agreements. Lawyers representing the companies involved—Richfield, Atlantic, Sinclair, and Cities Service—were in Washington working with the Justice Department and the Internal Revenue Service. It was past mid-December, with the stockholders' meetings only two weeks away, when we were amazed to learn from our attorneys that the Internal Revenue Service had refused a tax-free clearance. This most unusual decision meant a penalty that destroyed the terms of the merger.

The trouble was that the Justice Department, in agreeing to the merger and dismissing the antitrust suit, had imposed a condition that Sinclair and Cities Service dispose of the stock they would receive in Atlantic Richfield within seven years. But an Internal Revenue Service regulation stated that if, at the time of the merger, the recipient of stock in a merged company intended to sell his shares, the transaction would be taxable. Thus we were caught between the upper and nether millstones. Justice forced Sinclair and Cities Service to agree to sell; the Internal Revenue Service said they would be taxed for it.

The impasse between the two agencies, with us in the middle, was most vexing. I went to Washington at once to solicit support from members of Congress whom I knew well. My assistant, Rodney W. Rood, joined me in Washington a few days later and provided valuable help and counsel. Certainly an attempt to break a stalemate between two government agencies could not be construed as lobbying. My hotel rooms became headquarters for the lawyers of the four companies. Morning and afternoon sessions were held daily at which we conferred and reported progress—or rather the lack of it.

December 30 was the deadline for the stockholders' meeting, and if the deal was not then finalized, the stockholders could not vote on the merger. The issue would have to await a special later meeting, and by then conditions—including the relative stock values—could change enough to kill the deal, even if we obtained a favorable tax ruling. Richfield would then be at the mercy of the Justice Department's suit. Someone in government would certainly be blamed for all this, but that could not restore the merger deal with Atlantic.

As the days dragged on without news from the IRS, our attorneys began taking a dim view of our chances. But I refused to believe that the IRS would not find a way to grant the tax clearance. Failure to do so would be the height of folly, and certainly someone's head would roll. I did not think that the agency would care to face the political and public heat that would be generated by a clear failure of duty. A way had to be found. On December 20 we started a countdown: ten days, nine, eight, seven, six. The melodrama of the situation reminded me of *The Perils of Pauline*, an early weekly movie serial. Christmas Day came and went; we had four days to go. Earlier the Washington office of Braun & Company, our public relations advisers, had been alerted. If the merger failed, there was a lot of explaining to do, and the team was already at work preparing for the worst. I continued to believe that the clearance would be forthcoming, but it seemed prudent to be prepared for the worst.

The melodrama continued. Our heroine was still bound to the railroad track, and the onrushing train was drawing very near. Some executives of our large-stockholder companies had practically given up, and there was some surliness among them. One man who did not lose his cool or his faith was Bob Anderson. With two and a half days to go and the Internal Revenue Service still silent, Anderson came to Washington from Philadelphia to see me. He had been constantly briefed by his lawyers. I told him that I was now more certain than ever that the clearance would be forthcoming, because the very silence of IRS indicated that the agency was trying to solve the problem. It was inconceivable that it would say nothing or would say no at one minute to 12:00 noon. Anderson agreed with my reasoning. We had a laugh about the melodrama, and he returned to Philadelphia without any sign of misgivings.

About 5:30 P.M. on the following and last day, December 29, all of us who were working on the problem assembled in my hotel room. Victor H. Kramer, of Arnold & Porter, our Washington

counsel, handed me a scribbled note that he had just taken down
by telephone from the IRS. It was a proposed new ruling approved
by the various branches of the agency and by Commissioner Sheldon S. Cohen. Now known as the "Richfield Rule," it stated that
"recipients of new company stock shall have no *present arrangements* to sell the stock." The old rule had said that "recipients shall
have no *present intention* of selling the stock" (italics added). IRS
said that it would publish the rule at once and that the written
clearance would be forthcoming under the new rule on the following morning, December 30.

Early the next morning I drove to Wilmington, Delaware, where
the stockholders' meeting was called for 12:00 noon. The Atlantic
meeting in Philadelphia was to be convened at the same time so
that we could take simultaneous action. Direct telephone connections had been opened between the two cities. At 11:30 A.M. our
lawyers called from Washington and relayed the definitive IRS
rule. Our lawyers in attendance at the meeting pronounced it satisfactory at about ten minutes before noon.

At 12:00 noon exactly, I convened the meeting, performing my
last official act as chairman of Richfield and thus ending nearly
fifty years of an active and happy career with Richfield and its
predecessor companies. I explained to the assembled stockholders
that, while we would have very much preferred to continue Richfield as a separate company, I felt that its greatest days lay ahead.
I explained that the government's antitrust suit had forced us to
decide that a merger with Atlantic Refining Company would be in
the best interest of all our stockholders. Because of the geographical location of the operations of the companies it would also be in
the best interest of our loyal employees. Richfield was not over-
staffed, and the new company would surely grow and open new
opportunities for all.

For all our stockholders, I continued, the $3-a-share Atlantic
preference dividend would be an immediate improvement on their
present Richfield dividend income of $1.80 a share. I expressed
the hope that our stockholders would continue to have the faith,
patience, and confidence in their new Atlantic Richfield investment that they had had with Richfield stock, which many had held

325

for nearly thirty years and which had performed very well for them. I therefore recommended that they vote affirmatively on the merger proposition. The vote approving the merger equaled 87.5 per cent of the outstanding stock.

The merger was now a fact. Documents were filed in Wilmington and Philadelphia, and the merger became effective on January 3, 1966.

In *The Perils of Pauline*, the film always stopped flickering an instant before the train reached Pauline, who would then be rescued in the first scene of the next Saturday's serial. It had been the same for Richfield. Others have told me that such a melodrama is not uncommon in Washington. It certainly causes a lot of wear and tear on its victim, but no event could be better designed to convince the victim that his lawyers, who pull him from the tracks in the nick of time, can be anything less than supermen.

## 47. THE BIGGEST BONANZA

A logical date to end this account of the highlights of Richfield's history would be January 3, 1966, on which day Richfield was officially merged with Atlantic and ceased to exist as a corporate entity. One subsequent development, however, has been too closely interwoven with Richfield's story to be excluded.

That has been the continuing exploration—begun by Richfield and now pursued by Atlantic Richfield—of Richfield's lands on Alaska's North Slope. In this effort the major movement of drilling equipment and material from Fairbanks to the Arctic did not begin until February, 1966. But that effort, led by E. M. ("Mo") Benson, former general manager of operations for Richfield and now vice-president in charge of exploration, engineering, and production operations for Atlantic Richfield's North American Producing Division, was superb. Bob Anderson made a trip to the Arctic to become acquainted with the operation at first hand.

The tools were in place and operating before the spring thaw began. The first well was drilled on a structure called Susie No. 1, sixty miles south of Prudhoe Bay, and after ten months of drilling it was abandoned as a dry hole. After that failure I commented to Rollin Eckis, executive vice-president of Atlantic Richfield, that, with the dry holes that Sinclair had drilled in the area and our disappointment in Susie, the North Slope was beginning to look a little grim.

"Don't lose your enthusiasm for this great basin," Rollin replied. "There have been oil showings in every well drilled. The area hasn't been scratched, and research has just begun. Don't forget, we still have Prudhoe Bay."

The tools were moved from Susie No. 1 to Prudhoe Bay No. 1, and on March 13, 1968, Atlantic Richfield discovered the fabulous Prudhoe Bay Field. A second well was drilled—SAG River State No. 1—about seven miles southeast, which confirmed the discovery. On July 16, 1968, the firm of DeGolyer and MacNaughton certified that the discovery was at least 5 to 10 billion barrels. It was the largest oil field in North America—certainly more than meeting the requirement that it be rich enough to justify the high expense of opening the Arctic Slope. The reserves on the North Slope may eventually equal all the presently known reserves of the lower forty-eight states.

Alaska has already reaped a rich reward from its oil industry, which Richfield founded with its discovery of oil reserves in the Kenai Peninsula in 1957. By the end of 1967, the oil industry had paid state and local taxes in Alaska of $46.5 million and had $177 million in rents, royalties, and bonuses to the state, as well as a substantial amount to the federal government. By the end of 1967 the industry had invested $1.3 billion in Alaska—$383 million in 1967 alone—and with the Prudhoe Bay discovery, investments have been greatly accelerated. In 1969 the state conducted a land sale that brought in nearly $1 billion.

Atlantic Richfield and its associates will spend several billion

*Standing at the second well completed in the Prudhoe Bay Field on Alaska's North Slope are, left to right: Robert O. Anderson, chairman of Atlantic Richfield; Charles S. Jones; and Rollin Eckis, executive vice-president, summer, 1968.*

329

AIME ENGINEERING ACHIEVEMENT AWARD
~ ROLLIN ECKIS -- 1969 ~
IN RECOGNITION OF HIS IMAGINATIVE DIRECTION OF GEOLOGICAL EXPLORATION
WHICH HAS LED TO THE DISCOVERY OF NEW MAJOR OIL AND GAS RESERVES,
INCLUDING ALASKA'S FIRST COMMERCIAL OIL AND MORE RECENTLY THE VAST
ALASKA NORTH SLOPE PRUDHOE BAY RESERVE.

*A proud moment for Atlantic Richfield was the presentation in 1969 of this AIME Engineering Achievement Award to Rollin Eckis, vice-chairman of the board, by the American Institute of Mining, Metallurgical and Petroleum Engineers.*

330

dollars for development, pipelines, tankers, refineries, and related facilities—a large portion of it in Alaska to mature the Prudhoe Bay discovery. Oil will start moving to market when the pipeline is completed. My personal judgment would be that the North Slope will be producing no less than 2 million barrels daily by 1980 and that Alaska's income from the North Slope in royalties alone may well be over $600,000 daily. I hope that my judgment will prove accurate. I wish the Alaskans good health, long life, continued oil discoveries, and, above all, the courage and intelligence to be outstanding stewards of their fabulous good fortune.

As for Richfield, its saga had come to an end as a separate business story. It had done so with a fitting burst of excitement characteristic of its action-filled history—the discovery of the largest oil field in North America.

Lockhart, Kellogg, and Whittier would not have recognized the product they had created. But they would have recognized the adventurous spirit that still sparked the organization—a spirit that had carried it from the Rio Grande to the Arctic Ocean and had left an indelible mark on the world of oil.

*Appendices*

**APPENDIX A. The Richfield Family Tree**

1966

Richfield Oil Corporation merged into
the Atlantic Refining Company.

1937

Richfield Oil Corporation, organized in 1936,
acquired Richfield Oil Company of California,
Pan American Petroleum Company, and certain
of the assets of Rio Grande Oil Company, half of
which was owned by Sinclair Consolidated Oil
Company, and half by Cities Service
Company. A court-approved Plan of Reorganization
was made possible by Sinclair Consolidated and
Cities Service.

1935

Richfield Oil Company of New York,
organized in 1929, was sold to Sinclair
Oil Company.

1931–1932

Receiver appointed for Richfield Oil
Company of California in 1931, and
for its subsidiary, Pan American
Petroleum Company, in 1932.

1928

Richfield Oil Company of California
acquired Pan American Petroleum
Company, organized by E. L. Doheny
in 1916.

1926

Richfield Oil Company of California,
organized in 1926, acquired United
Oil Company and its subsidiary,
Richfield Oil Company.

23

nited Oil Company, organized by
F. Whittier in 1909, acquired
chfield Oil Company.

1915

Richfield Oil Company acquired Kellogg Oil
Company and Los Angeles Oil & Refining
Company; and National Petroleum Company,
organized by them in 1913.

11

rst "Richfield" company—Richfield
Company, organized by six owners
Kellogg Oil Company and Los Angeles
& Refining Company, organized in
05 and 1909, respectively.

## APPENDIX B. Chronological Record of Richfield Oil Corporation and Its Predecessors

1905  Kellogg Oil Company was organized by F. R. Kellogg, G. J. Symington, and S. R. Roseberg.

1909  Los Angeles Oil & Refining Company was organized by T. A. Winter, J. R. Jacobs, and George Gillons; and United Oil Company was organized by Colon F. Whittier.

1911  The six owners of Kellogg Oil Company and Los Angeles Oil & Refining Company organized Richfield Oil Company.

1913  The six owners of Richfield Oil Company organized National Petroleum Company.

1915  Richfield Oil Company acquired Kellogg Oil Company, Los Angeles Oil & Refining Company, and National Petroleum Company.

1915  Rio Grande Oil Company was organized by Lloyd E. Lockhart.

336

1923    United Oil Company acquired Richfield Oil Company.

1925    Pan American Western Petroleum Company was organized, and its subsidiary, Pan American Petroleum Company (in 1916), both by Edward L. Doheny.

1926    Richfield Oil Company of California was organized and at the same time acquired United Oil Company and its subsidiary, Richfield Oil Company.

1928    Richfield Oil Company of California acquired Pan American Western Petroleum Company and its subsidiary, Pan American Petroleum Company, and dissolved Pan American Western Petroleum Company (1929).

1929    Richfield Oil Corporation of New York, a subsidiary of Richfield Oil Company of California, was organized.

1931    United States district courts appointed a receiver for Richfield Oil Company of California and (in 1932) for its subsidiary, Pan American Petroleum Company, in equity proceedings.

1932    Sinclair Consolidated Oil Company acquired Rio Grande Oil Company.

1935    Cities Service Company acquired a one-half interest in Rio Grande Oil Company from Sinclair.

1935    Sinclair Oil Company, a subsidiary of Consolidated Oil Company, acquired Richfield Oil Corporation of New York.

1963    Rio Grande Oil Corporation, organized in 1936 for the purpose of carrying out the court-approved plan of reorganization made possible by Sinclair Consolidated Oil Company and Cities Service Company, acquired all the assets and business of Richfield Oil Company of California and Pan American Petroleum Company, as well as certain of the assets of Rio Grande Oil Company, in proceedings under Section 77B of the National Bankruptcy Act. At the same time the name was changed to Richfield Oil Corporation.

1966    Atlantic Refining Company acquired Richfield Oil Corporation.

# APPENDIX C. Directors and Officers, 1937 and 1965

RICHFIELD OIL CORPORATION

AT BEGINNING OF BUSINESS, MARCH 13, 1937

*Board of Directors*

| | | |
|---|---|---|
| Francis S. Baer | Charles S. Jones | William C. McDuffie |
| Frederick H. Bartlett | W. Alton Jones | P. H. O'Neil |
| F. R. Coates | Alexander Macdonald | Joseph M. Schenck |
| H. R. Gallagher | George MacDonald | H. F. Sinclair |

*Officers*

| | |
|---|---|
| H. F. Sinclair | M. Richard Gross |
| Chairman of the Board of Directors | Treasurer |
| W. Alton Jones | R. J. Pagen |
| Chairman of the Finance Committee | Comptroller |

338

DIRECTORS AND OFFICERS, 1937 AND 1965

Charles S. Jones
President
A. M. Kelley
Vice-President

Morgan W. Lowery
Secretary
E. B. Downey
Assistant Secretary-Treasurer

AT END OF BUSINESS, DECEMBER 31, 1965

*Board of Directors*

| Cleve B. Bonner | Charles S. Jones | Stender Sweeney |
| Rollin Eckis | Henry L. O'Brien | O. P. Thomas |
| John W. Gendron | P. C. Spencer | J. Ed. Warren |
| H. T. Hutchinson | E. L. Steiniger | B. S. Watson |

*Officers*

Charles S. Jones
Chairman of the Board of Directors
P. C. Spencer
Chairman of the Finance Committee
Rollin Eckis
President
Cleve B. Bonner
Vice-President and Treasurer
John W. Gendron
Vice-President
H. T. Hutchinson
Vice-President

Stender Sweeney
Vice-President
W. W. Gamel
Comptroller
Norman F. Simmonds
Secretary
R. C. Chase
Assistant Treasurer
J. P. McLaughlin
Assistant Treasurer
R. G. Nelson
Assistant Secretary
J. A. Wibalda
Assistant Secretary

# APPENDIX D. Changes in Directors and Officers, 1937 to 1965

RICHFIELD OIL CORPORATION

*Directors*

1937 Resigned: Francis S. Baer, F. R. Coates, Alexander Macdonald, and William C. McDuffie; elected: W. T. Dinkins, H. F. Sinclair, Jr., Herbert R. Straight, and Temple W. Tutwiler

1939 Resigned: P. H. O'Neil

1940 Resigned: H. R. Gallagher

1941 Elected: Cleve B. Bonner

1942 Resigned: Joseph M. Schenck; elected: E. W. Sinclair

1943 Resigned: H. F. Sinclair, Jr.; elected: M. L. Gosney

1944 Died: E. W. Sinclair

1945 Elected: Sheldon Clark

1947 Resigned: Herbert R. Straight

340

1948    Died: Frederick H. Bartlett;    resigned: Temple W. Tutwiler; elected: A. W. Ambrose and Burl S. Watson
1949    Died: W. T. Dinkins
1950    Elected: Henry L. O'Brien and P. C. Spencer
1952    Died: A. W. Ambrose and Sheldon Clark; elected: P. W. Thirtle
1953    Elected: S. B. Irelan
1956    Died: S. B. Irelan and H. F. Sinclair
1957    Elected: David E. Day, Rollin Eckis, W. G. King, Jr., and W. J. Travers
1960    Resigned: P. W. Thirtle; elected: E. L. Steiniger
1961    Died: George MacDonald
1962    Died: W. Alton Jones; elected: J. Ed. Warren and Stender Sweeney
1963    Resigned: David E. Day;    elected: John W. Gendron
1964    Resigned: M. L. Gosney;    elected: H. T. Hutchinson and O. P. Thomas; retired: W. G. King, Jr. and W. J. Travers

*Officers*

1937    Resigned: Morgan W. Lowery, secretary; and R. J. Pagen, comptroller;    elected: W. T. Dinkins, vice-president; Cleve B. Bonner, secretary; W. T. Autrey, comptroller; and Leonard Switzer, assistant secretary
1938    Elected: Frank A. Morgan, vice-president
1945    Died: A. M. Kelley, vice-president;    elected: David E. Day, vice-president
1949    Died: W. T. Dinkins, vice-president;    elected: W. G. King, Jr., vice-president
1951    Elected: R. D. Montgomery, vice-president; J. P. McLaughlin, assistant treasurer and assistant secretary; J. R. Jenks, assistant secretary
1952    Died: R. D. Montgomery, vice-president;    retired: M. Richard Gross, treasurer; elected: R. W. Ragland, vice-president; Stender Sweeney, vice-president; W. J. Travers, vice-president; and H. Safford Nye, treasurer
1954    Resigned: Frank A. Morgan, vice-president;    elected: Rollin Eckis, vice-president
1955    Elected: S. H. Rankin, assistant treasurer
1956    Died: H. F. Sinclair, chairman of the board;    resigned: H. Safford Nye, treasurer;    elected: W. Alton Jones, chairman

341

of the board; P. C. Spencer, chairman of the finance committee; Rollin Eckis, executive vice-president; Cleve B. Bonner, treasurer; and Norman F. Simmonds, secretary

1958 Elected: J. P. McLaughlin, assistant treasurer; R. G. Nelson, assistant secretary; and J. A. Wibalda, assistant secretary

1961 Elected: W. W. Gamel, assistant comptroller

1962 Died: W. Alton Jones, chairman of the board;   retired: W. T. Autrey, vice-president (elected in 1962) and comptroller; elected: Charles S. Jones, chairman of the board; Rollin Eckis, president; Cleve B. Bonner, vice-president; John W. Gendron, vice-president; and W. W. Gamel, comptroller

1963 Retired: E. B. Downey, assistant secretary-treasurer

1964 Retired: David E. Day, vice-president; W. G. King, Jr., vice-president; W. J. Travers, vice-president; and S. H. Rankin, assistant treasurer; elected: R. C. Chase, assistant treasurer

1965 Retired: R. W. Ragland, vice-president

# APPENDIX E. Net Income and Dividends Paid, 1937 to 1965

RICHFIELD OIL CORPORATION

| Year | Net income | | Dividends paid | |
| | Amount | Per share† | Amount | Per share† |
|---|---|---|---|---|
| (Mar. 13–Dec. 31) | | | | |
| 1937 | $ 1,406,456 | $0.18 | $ 996,659 | $ 0.125 |
| 1938 | 2,042,955 | 0.26 | 2,002,341 | 0.25 |
| 1939 | 2,601,926 | 0.33 | 2,003,509 | 0.25 |
| 1940 | 3,814,590 | 0.48 | 2,005,000 | 0.25 |
| 1941 | 4,323,611 | 0.54 | 2,506,269 | 0.3125 |
| 1942 | 4,017,757 | 0.50 | 2,005,000 | 0.25 |
| 1943 | 4,351,455 | 0.55 | 2,005,000 | 0.25 |

*(Continued on page 344)*

| | Net income | | Dividends paid | |
| Year | Amount | Per share† | Amount | Per share† |
|---|---|---|---|---|
| 1944 | 3,080,974 | 0.39 | 2,406,000 | 0.30 |
| 1945 | 2,985,699 | 0.38 | 3,007,500 | 0.375 |
| 1946 | 7,062,276 | 0.88 | 3,208,000 | 0.40 |
| 1947 | 11,853,397 | 1.48 | 6,015,002 | 0.75 |
| 1948 | 16,751,475 | 2.10 | 8,000,000 | 1.00 |
| 1949 | 20,434,099 | 2.56 | 10,000,000 | 1.25 |
| 1950 | 24,046,379 | 3.01 | 12,000,000 | 1.50 |
| 1951 | 30,818,281 | 3.85 | 14,000,000 | 1.75 |
| 1952 | 27,224,998 | 3.40 | 14,000,000 | 1.75 |
| 1953 | 28,875,486 | 3.61 | 14,000,000 | 1.75 |
| 1954 | 25,570,701 | 3.20 | 14,000,000 | 1.75 |
| 1955 | 30,566,073 | 3.82 | 14,000,000 | 1.75 |
| 1956 | 27,252,270 | 3.41 | 14,000,000 | 1.75 |
| 1957 | 28,340,063 | 3.54 | 14,000,000 | 1.75 |
| 1958 | 20,839,260 | 2.60 | 14,011,109 | 1.75 |
| 1959 | 28,565,886 | 3.54 | 14,132,007 | 1.75 |
| 1960 | 28,841,755 | 3.57 | 14,136,765 | 1.75 |
| 1961 | 25,350,180 | 3.13 | 14,572,793 | 1.80 |
| 1962 | 30,846,743 | 3.80 | 14,593,535 | 1.80 |
| 1963 | 27,944,349 | 3.44 | 14,641,832 | 1.80 |
| 1964 | 21,455,432 | 2.60 | 14,906,874 | 1.80 |
| 1965 | 23,945,702 | 2.82 | 15,311,948 | 1.80 |
| Totals | $515,210,228 | | $272,467,143 | $33.7625 |

Total dividends paid, per cent of total net income: 52.88

* Richfield Oil Corporation and subsidiaries consolidated, except for 1944–54, during which years the subsidiaries were not significant.

† Adjusted to give effect to the two-for-one stock split effective May 1, 1961.

344

# APPENDIX F. Gross Crude-Oil Production and Reserves

RICHFIELD OIL CORPORATION

| Gross production | Barrels* |
|---|---|
| March 13–Dec. 31 | |
| 1937 | 5,508,000 |
| 1938 | 7,720,000 |
| 1939 | 7,174,000 |
| 1940 | 7,493,000 |
| 1941 | 9,350,000 |
| 1942 | 9,260,000 |
| 1943 | 9,253,000 |

*(Continued on page 346)*

345

| Gross production | Barrels* |
|---|---|
| 1944 | 10,686,000 |
| 1945 | 10,936,000 |
| 1946 | 11,305,000 |
| 1947 | 11,959,000 |
| 1948 | 11,559,000 |
| 1949 | 17,582,000 |
| 1950 | 22,986,000 |
| 1951 | 28,093,000 |
| 1952 | 27,440,000 |
| 1953 | 26,499,000 |
| 1954 | 26,746,000 |
| 1955 | 28,223,000 |
| 1956 | 28,935,000 |
| 1957 | 30,138,000 |
| 1958 | 28,500,000 |
| 1959 | 32,974,000 |
| 1960 | 35,446,000 |
| 1961 | 37,810,000 |
| 1962 | 38,737,000 |
| 1963 | 38,608,000 |
| 1964 | 36,822,000 |
| 1965 | 36,244,000 |
| Total production—29 years | 633,986,000 |
| Reserves, December 31, 1965 | 937,939,000 |
| Total | 1,571,925,000 |
| Less reserves, March 13, 1937 | 35,000,000 |
| Crude oil discovered | 1,536,925,000 |

* Excluding natural-gas liquids and 69,887,000 barrels of crude-oil produced for the city of Long Beach, Parcel A, 1947–65, under contract.

# APPENDIX G. Consolidated Balance Sheets, 1937 and 1965

RICHFIELD OIL CORPORATION AND SUBSIDIARIES

(Prior to Merger into Atlantic Refining Company)
At December 31, 1965, and March 13, 1937

| Assets | 1965 | 1937 |
|---|---|---|
| **Current assets** | | |
| Cash and short-term securities | $ 27,127,000 | $23,010,000 |
| Accounts and notes receivable, less reserves of $1,991,000 in 1965 and $494,000 in 1937 | 75,483,000 | 3,172,000 |
| **Inventories** | | |
| Crude oil and refined products, on basis of cost determined by the annual last in first out method and, in the aggregate, below market | 36,956,000 | 9,855,000 |
| Material and supplies, at or below cost | 7,741,000 | 1,044,000 |
| Total | $147,307,000 | $37,081,000 |
| Investments and advances, at cost | $ 14,897,000 | $ 132,000 |
| **Properties, plant and equipment** | | |
| Oil-and-gas lands and leases, oil wells and equipment, refinery, marketing facilities, transportation equipment and facilities, terminals, office buildings, etc., at cost | $718,436,000 | $49,250,000 |
| Less reserves for depreciation and depletion | 390,697,000 | |
| Total | $327,739,000 | $49,250,000 |
| **Deferred charges:** | | |
| Taxes, insurance, and rents | $ 6,462,000 | $ 671,000 |
| Other | 3,215,000 | 891,000 |
| | $ 9,677,000 | $ 1,562,000 |
| Total | $499,620,000 | $88,025,000 |

| Liabilities and capital | 1965 | 1937 |
|---|---|---|
| **Current liabilities** | | |
| Accounts payable | $ 19,397,000 | $ 2,230,000 |
| Federal and foreign taxes on income | 7,135,000 | 27,000 |
| Other taxes | 14,420,000 | 991,000 |
| Installments due within one year on long-term debt | 3,094,000 | 86,000 |
| Other liabilities | 10,816,000 | 1,012,000 |
| | $ 54,862,000 | $ 4,346,000 |
| **Long-term debt (due after one year):** | | |
| Sinking-fund debentures 15-year 4%, due 1952 | | $ 7,664,000 |
| 25 year 2.85%, due 1974 | $20,000,000 | |
| 30-year 3.85%, due 1983 | 31,000,000 | |
| 4⅜% convertible subordinated, due 1983 | 39,412,000 | |
| Installment notes (4⅞%) for 1965 and (6%) for 1937 | 1,685,000 | 1,078,000 |
| Total | $92,097,000 | $ 8,742,000 |
| **Deferred income:** | | |
| Production payments sold, net of income taxes | $11,700,000 | |
| Reserve for contingencies | | $ 500,000 |
| **Stockholders' equity:** | | |
| Capital stock (after giving effect to the 2 for 1 stock split in 1961) Authorized— 15,000,000 shares without par value Issued—8,650,520 shares for 1965 and 7,973,274 shares for 1937 | $100,043,000 | $74,437,000 |
| Earnings employed in the business | 241,942,000 | |
| | $341,985,000 | $74,437,000 |
| Less treasury stock, 21,800 shares, at cost | 1,024,000 | |
| | $340,961,000 | $74,437,000 |
| Total | $499,620,000 | $88,025,000 |

347

# APPENDIX H. Income Account by Years, 1937 to 1965*

RICHFIELD OIL CORPORATION

| Year | Sales and other operating revenue | Less state and federal gasoline and oil taxes | Net sales and other operating revenue | Interest and other income (net) | Total | Costs, operating and general expenses | Taxes, excluding oil taxes | Depreciation, depletion and amortization | Dry holes and retirements | Interest on long-term debt | Total | Net income |
|---|---|---|---|---|---|---|---|---|---|---|---|---|
| 1937 (Mar. 13–Dec. 31) | $ 44,249 | $ 9,247 | $ 35,002 | $ (19) | $ 34,983 | $ 28,221 | $ 1,214 | $ 3,526 | $ 301 | $ 315 | $ 33,577 | $ 1,406 |
| 1938 | 51,243 | 10,667 | 40,576 | 85 | 40,661 | 30,665 | 1,472 | 5,168 | 894 | 419 | 38,618 | 2,043 |
| 1939 | 55,591 | 11,519 | 44,072 | 66 | 44,138 | 32,272 | 1,941 | 5,692 | 1,190 | 441 | 41,536 | 2,602 |
| 1940 | 56,581 | 12,303 | 44,278 | 379 | 44,657 | 31,095 | 2,341 | 5,866 | 1,080 | 460 | 40,842 | 3,815 |
| 1941 | 63,706 | 13,149 | 50,557 | 95 | 50,652 | 35,096 | 3,585 | 6,471 | 738 | 438 | 46,328 | 4,324 |
| 1942 | 63,981 | 10,660 | 53,321 | 613 | 53,934 | 38,192 | 4,093 | 6,560 | 850 | 221 | 49,916 | 4,018 |
| 1943 | 80,261 | 9,769 | 70,492 | 521 | 71,013 | 51,877 | 6,722 | 7,153 | 725 | 185 | 66,662 | 4,351 |
| 1944 | 90,357 | 11,343 | 79,014 | 138 | 79,152 | 57,309 | 2,326 | 13,635 | 2,668 | 133 | 76,071 | 3,081 |
| 1945 | 99,091 | 14,216 | 84,875 | 290 | 85,165 | 59,047 | 1,144 | 18,642 | 3,189 | 157 | 82,179 | 2,986 |
| 1946 | 84,334 | 15,479 | 68,855 | 342 | 69,197 | 48,391 | 4,915 | 7,224 | 1,502 | 103 | 62,135 | 7,062 |
| 1947 | 105,756 | 17,798 | 87,958 | 775 | 88,733 | 61,397 | 6,614 | 6,124 | 2,661 | 84 | 76,880 | 11,853 |
| 1948 | 138,514 | 19,743 | 118,771 | 763 | 119,534 | 83,772 | 8,152 | 6,894 | 3,745 | 220 | 102,783 | 16,751 |
| 1949 | 144,830 | 21,848 | 122,982 | 972 | 123,954 | 81,537 | 8,997 | 8,686 | 3,663 | 637 | 103,520 | 20,434 |
| 1950 | 179,364 | 24,418 | 154,946 | 585 | 155,531 | 103,702 | 14,081 | 10,428 | 2,099 | 1,175 | 131,485 | 24,046 |
| 1951 | 214,763 | 28,302 | 186,461 | 951 | 187,412 | 109,819 | 30,110 | 12,125 | 3,365 | 1,175 | 156,594 | 30,818 |
| 1952 | 215,144 | 34,316 | 180,828 | 955 | 181,783 | 110,114 | 24,907 | 12,743 | 5,619 | 1,175 | 154,558 | 27,225 |
| 1953 | 242,966 | 40,927 | 202,039 | 1,584 | 203,623 | 124,982 | 23,783 | 15,172 | 8,846 | 1,965 | 174,748 | 28,875 |
| 1954 | 270,070 | 46,759 | 223,311 | 1,417 | 224,728 | 147,736 | 20,241 | 20,634 | 7,671 | 2,875 | 199,157 | 25,571 |
| 1955 | 296,894 | 51,165 | 245,729 | 1,381 | 247,110 | 155,737 | 27,760 | 22,494 | 7,611 | 2,942 | 216,544 | 30,566 |
| 1956 | 312,929 | 58,886 | 254,043 | 1,334 | 255,377 | 166,895 | 25,695 | 23,960 | 8,705 | 2,870 | 228,125 | 27,252 |
| 1957 | 320,632 | 65,251 | 255,381 | 844 | 256,225 | 169,833 | 20,203 | 26,173 | 8,424 | 3,202 | 227,885 | 28,340 |
| 1958 | 325,444 | 67,236 | 258,208 | 1,883 | 260,091 | 180,222 | 16,943 | 26,477 | 10,678 | 4,932 | 239,252 | 20,839 |
| 1959 | 341,914 | 72,148 | 269,766 | 2,497 | 272,263 | 179,220 | 23,016 | 27,736 | 8,306 | 5,419 | 243,697 | 28,566 |
| 1960 | 368,082 | 79,109 | 288,973 | 3,444 | 292,417 | 188,407 | 30,317 | 29,617 | 9,920 | 5,314 | 263,575 | 28,842 |
| | | | | | | 200,467 | 19,859 | 28,043 | 11,575 | 5,158 | 265,102 | 25,350 |
| 1961 | 364,916 | 79,841 | 285,075 | 5,377 | 290,452 | 198,585 | 23,790 | 29,047 | 11,497 | 4,996 | 267,915 | 30,847 |
| 1962 | 381,453 | 86,673 | 294,780 | 3,982 | 298,762 | 214,910 | 20,128 | 27,981 | 10,263 | 4,819 | 278,101 | 27,944 |
| 1963 | 392,389 | 90,458 | 301,931 | 4,114 | 306,045 | 225,927 | 19,077 | 27,621 | 8,651 | 4,081 | 285,357 | 21,455 |
| 1964 | 398,939 | 97,392 | 301,547 | 5,265 | 306,812 | 232,333 | 17,938 | 28,430 | 11,709 | 3,862 | 294,272 | 23,946 |
| 1965 | 420,864 | 106,486 | 314,378 | 3,840 | 318,218 | | | | | | | |

* Richfield Oil Corporation and subsidiaries consolidated except for years 1944–1954, at which time the subsidiaries were not significant.

# APPENDIX I. Cities Service's Stock Offer, 1931

DURING Richfield's financial crisis of 1930–31, Henry L. Doherty, on behalf of Cities Service, took a hand by making this public offer to trade one share of Cities Service common stock for four shares of Richfield stock. After Richfield's receivership in 1931 this investment proved worthless to Cities Service. When Harry F. Sinclair moved to buy Richfield's assets, Cities Service countered to preserve its interest by purchasing a large block of Richfield and Pan American bonds.

January 26, 1931.

TO THE HOLDERS OF COMMON STOCK OF
RICHFIELD OIL COMPANY OF CALIFORNIA:

Cities Service Company is a holder of a substantial amount of common stock of the Richfield Oil Company of California.

We are prepared to offer to the holders of common stock of Richfield Oil Company of California common stock of Cities Service Company in exchange therefor, on the basis of one share of Cities Service Company common stock for four shares of the common stock of Richfield Oil Company of California. The shares of the Richfield Oil Company should be forwarded, duly endorsed, witnessed and guaranteed for transfer, through your banker or broker, to the undersigned.

The undersigned shall not be required to accept a total of more than five hundred thousand shares of the stock of said Richfield Oil Company under this offer (same to be accepted in the order of its receipt), nor to accept such stock after thirty days from the date hereof.

                    HENRY L. DOHERTY & COMPANY,
                        60 Wall Street,
                        New York, N. Y.

# APPENDIX J. Newspaper Articles, 1933, on Government Suit

RICHFIELD OIL CORPORATION

ONE of the chief stumbling blocks to an early end to Richfield's receivership was a federal government claim of more than nine million dollars for oil taken from canceled leases at the Elk Hills Naval Reserve by Pan American Petroleum Company, which Richfield had acquired from Edward L. Doheny in 1928. As shown in the articles from the *Wall Street Journal* for February 27, 1933 (datelined Los Angeles) and April 27, 1933 (datelined Washington), Congress had to pass a resolution authorizing acceptance of $5,001,500 as settlement of the claim. This settlement helped open the way for the reorganization of Richfield in 1937.

# PPROVAL GIVEN OIL COMPROMISE

### ill, Which Now Goes Before House, Authorizes U. S. to Take $5,000,000

#### OW PLANS ARE AFFECTED

LOS ANGELES — Another important step
vard the working out of affairs of Richfield
Co. was taken when the United States Sen-
on Saturday adopted a bill authorizing the
:orney General, with concurrence of the Sec-
ary of the Navy, to execute the terms of the
npromise of the federal claims against Pan
\erican Petroleum Co. and Richfield Oil Co.
the oil extracted from the land covered by
old Elk Hills Naval Reserve leases.
The compromise was reached in Los Angeles
gotiations some weeks ago, and while not re-
·ded as wholly obligatory, it was deemed by
vernment representatives as essential that it
·uld have congressional sanction because of
political background of the controversy.

#### House Approval Likely

The Senate bill authorizing the compromise
v goes to the House of Representatives. If
l when sanctioned by this body, an action
t is expected, it is presumed that the final
portant barrier to sale of Richfield assets will
·e been removed.
The compromise arranged is for payment of
·01,500 in cash for a $9,277,666 judgment
\inst Pan American.
The whole settlement, which will be effected
er acceptance by the House, comprises a gen-
l claim of $17,000,000, which Pan American
ght have pressed against Richfield and elim-
tes a smaller claim in excess of $1,000,000,
ich the Government might also have held
\inst Richfield.

#### Holding Up Negotiations

Pending settlement of these claims, it has
n practically impossible for the reorganiza-
a committees to determine a basis for dis-
\puting any offer which they might have ac-
·ted for Richfield.
The basis of the compromise, which was ap-
·ved by the Senate, was originally determined
Los Angeles during negotiations between
·al authorities, H. J. Crawford and Frank
rrison, special assistant attorney generals,
·resenting the Government, and legal counsel
Richfield and Pan American companies.
Pan American and Richfield bondholders' and
·ditors' committees, .he two trustees for the
\ads and the receivers for the two companies
·e all signified approval of the compromise.
tion in Washington indicates that the Gov-
·ment concurs in this opinion, and accordingly
ion of the House is expected likewise to be
·orable and is expected to be completed this
ek.

# HOUSE ACCEPTS RICHFIELD PLAN

### Action Removes Big Barrier to Negotiations for Sale of Company Properties

*Dow Jones News Service*
WASHINGTON—By a vote of 244 to 116 the
House Wednesday passed the resolution authorizing the Secretary of the Navy and the Attorney General to accept the $5,000,000 compromise
of the $9,277,000 judgment against Richfield Oil
Co. and Pan American Petroleum in connection
with oil taken from canceled Elk Hills leases.

Representative Fuller of Arkansas, who
spoke for adoption, said there was necessity for
haste or it might be impossible for the Government to collect anything. The resolution goes
back to the Senate for concurrence in minor
changes of form.

353

# INDEX

Adams, K. S. ("Boots"): 308, 313
Adeline Consolidated Road Oil
    Company: 86
Agua Prieta, Mexico: 3–4, 8
*Agwiworld* (tanker): 210
*Al Ahram* (Egyptian newspaper):
    268
Alaska Railroad: 317
Alvin H. Frank & Company: 38
Amerada Petroleum Corporation:
    152
American Expeditionary Force: 18
American International Corpora-
    tion: 53

American Petroleum Institute: 203,
    287
American Red Cross: 219
Anchorage, Alaska: 284
Anderson, Hugo A.: 276, 310
Anderson, J. C.: 138
Anderson, Robert O.: 310ff., 317,
    321, 324, 328
Andreano, Ralph L.: 159n.
Arkansas Natural Gas Corporation:
    165
Arnold, Billy: 102
Arnold, Fortas & Palmer: 305
Arnold & Porter: 324

Aronson & Company: 78
Ascot Speedway (Los Angeles): 95
Ashby, George F.: 206
Associated Oil Company of California: 40, 151–52, 312
Atchison, Topeka & Santa Fe Railroad: 27, 82, 85
Athabasca tar sands (Canada): 294ff.
Atlantic Refining Company: 103, 255, 265, 312ff., 321ff.
Atlantic Richfield Company: 85, 232, 317, 325ff.
Atlas Corporation: 171
Australian Motorists Petrol, Ltd.: 219
Autrey, W. T.: 178
Aviation, Richfield's role in: 105–17
Aviation fuel: 15, 18, 105, 207–209

Baer, Francis S.: 174, 186
Baker, John: 287
Bakersfield, Calif.: 67, 86, 93, 151, 240
Ball, Hunt & Hart: 305
Ball, Joseph: 300
Baltimore, Md.: 142
Bancamerica-Blair Corporation: 57, 62, 163
Bankland Oil Company: 50, 53
Barneson, H. J.: 57
Barnsdall, T. N.: 53
Barnsdall Oil Company of California: 41–44, 49, 214
Bartlett, E. L. ("Bob"): 290
Bartlett, Frederick H.: 171
Baruch, Bernard: 208
Bauer, Harry J.: 154
Bauer, Macdonald, Schultheis & Pettit: 172
Beckman, Arnold O.: 231
Bell Petroleum Company: 261, 265
Belridge Field (California): 151–52
Belridge Oil Company: 151
Benson, E. M. ("Mo"): 327
Berlin airlift: 238
Bettles, Alaska: 318

Blair & Company, Inc.: 144
Blyth, Witter & Company: 142
Blythe, Sam: 53
Blythe & Company: 171
Bohemian Grove, Calif.: 53
Bond, Goodwin & Tucker, Inc.: 144
Bonner, Cleve B.: 178, 304
Boston, Mass.: 143
Boston Elevated Railroad: 53
Braddy, Haldeen: 10n.
Bradshaw, Thornton F.: 315
Braun, Theodore W.: 285
Braun & Company: 285, 324
Bray, Ulrich: 231
Breslin, George: 204
Bridgeman, Sir Maurice R.: 308
Brilliant (tanker): 123
Brisbane, Australia: 220
British Petroleum Company, Ltd.: 308, 318–19, 321
Broomfield, R. A.: 42–43
Brower, David R.: 287
Brown, Joe: 241
Brush, Matthew C.: 53–54
Byroade, Henry: 268–70

Caffery, Jefferson: 268
California Institute of Technology: 198, 230
California's Buried Treasure (film): 275
California State Conciliation Service: 254
California Stock & Oil Exchange: 71
Calles, General Plutarco Elías: 3
Calvin, Charles: 241
Campbell, C. P.: 69–70
Canfield, Charles A.: 51, 81
Canon, J. Y.: 18
Carver, Roy W.: 182
C. F. Braun & Company: 180
Chamizal, Texas: 24
Chandler, Lieut. Harrison: 220–21
Charles S. Jones (tanker): 219ff.
Cheney, Mrs. Katherine Bell: 49
Cheney, Mrs. Mary Bell: 49

Cherry Hills Country Club (Denver): 38n.
Chevrolet, Gaston: 98
Chicago, Ill.: 171
Chittagong, India: 221–22
Chrysler Corporation: 231
Cisco, Texas: 24
Cities Service Corporation: 235–36, 268, 272, 295, 298, 303–304, 313–15, 319, 323; acquires Richfield stock, 158–59; strengthens interest in Richfield, 164–66; participates in Richfield reorganization, 167ff.; increases Richfield holdings, 199ff.
Ciudad Obregón, Mexico: 35
Cladouhos, Harry W.: 313
Coalinga Oil Field (California): 68
Coates, F. R.: 174
Cohen, Sheldon S.: 325
Colombo, Ceylon: 222
Columbus, N.Mex.: 8ff., 13
Connally "Hot Oil" Act: 169
*Conservation Dollar* (film): 275
Conservation Foundation: 287
Continental Oil Company: 30, 38, 268, 286
Cook Inlet, Alaska: 284, 290, 317
Cooley, Winchester: 21, 24
Cooper, Ellwood: 41
Core Laboratories, Inc.: 273
Cotten, H. H.: 154
Coulter, James C.: 179
Crary, Gordon: 58
Culiacán, Mexico: 34
Curry, "Slim": 205
Cuyama Valley Field (California): 236ff., 256ff.

Danziger, J. M.: 67, 70
Daugherty, J. M.: 18
Daum, Arnold F.: 159n.
Davies, Ralph K.: 208
Davis, Morgan J.: 285, 313
Davis, W. V.: 105
Day, David E.: 122, 180, 292, 304
DeGolyer, Everette L.: 194
DeGolyer and MacNaughton: 328

Delaney Petroleum Corporation: 131
Deming, N.Mex.: 18
Democratic Convention of 1932: 44n.
Den, Nicholas A.: 49, 51
Denni, Louis: 76
Denver, Colo.: 38, 234
DePalma, Ralph: 95, 98–100
Deterding, Sir Henry: 143, 147
Detroit, Mich.: 231–32
Dhofar, South Arabia: 272
Dibblee, Tom: 240–41
Dinkins, W. T.: 178, 182, 238
Disneyland, Calif.: 275
Doheny, Edward L.: 51, 81, 133–39, 142ff., 164–65
Doherty, Henry L.: 158, 160, 162, 164, 166–67, 201
Donnell, James C., II: 286
Dorn, Mayor Warren M.: 229–30
Douglas, Ariz.: 3
Douglas, James: 35–36
Downey, Calif.: 32
Dulles, John Foster: 271
Dunlap, W. E.: 154
Dunn, Robert: 14

Eagle Pass, Texas: 3
Eaker, Ira: 109
East Texas Field: 62
Eckis, Rollin P.: 182, 190, 228, 240, 243, 284, 304, 315, 319, 328ff.
Eisenhower, Pres. Dwight D.: 38, 271, 292
Elk Hills Field (California): 137, 165–66, 189, 194, 224ff.
El Paso and Southwestern Railway: 8
Elwood Terrace Field (California): 39ff., 52–54, 57, 142, 158, 196, 198, 205, 211, 214–18, 288
Endacott, Paul: 286
Etheridge, Fletcher H.: 41, 43, 49
Eureka, Calif.: 218–19

Fairbanks, Alaska: 317, 321, 327
Fall, Albert B.: 165

Faries, David: 49
Farmington, N.Mex.: 30
Faville, David: 276
Fellows, Calif.: 70, 90
Ferguson, W. H.: 38
Financing: 7, 18, 21, 24, 32, 87, 89,
    119, 129–31, 133–38, 144–52,
    154, 157, 159ff.
Fitzpatrick, Sam: 60
Fleishhacker, H.: 150
Flintridge, Calif.: 203
Follis, R. G.: 285
Ford Motor Company: 231
Fort Bliss, Texas: 13, 18, 24
Fort McMurray, Canada: 298
Fort Worth, Texas: 21
Fort Worth Star-Telegram: 53
Foster, A. C.: 38&n.
Frame, Fred: 102
Frey, John W.: 209n.
Frontier Contractors Company:
    317
Fuller, Clarence M.: 86–88, 90–91,
    93, 95, 109, 122, 128, 131, 148,
    151, 153–55; joins Richfield, 86;
    promotes auto racing, 95ff.; be-
    comes Richfield president, 139;
    creates Richfield of New York,
    142–43; resigns as president, 154

Gabrielson, Ira N.: 287
Gallagher, Herbert R.: 163, 171,
    200
Gamel, W. W.: 304
Garner, John Nance: 44n.
Gendron, John W.: 305
General Motors Corporation: 231–
    32
General Petroleum Corporation:
    76, 85–86, 204
Getty, J. Paul: 32
Gibbons, Floyd: 14
Gillons, George: 85, 91
Glasscock County, Texas: 38
Goebel, Arthur C.: 108
Goleta, Calif.: 40, 44, 49
Gonçalves, Capt. Frederico: 211
Grand Prix (France): 100

Gray, William: 280
Great Neck, N.Y.: 202
Gross, M. Richard: 178
Guadalajara, Mexico: 35
Guaymas, Mexico: 34
Gulf Oil Canada, Ltd.: 298
Gulf Oil Corporation: 277

Haagen-Smit, A. J.: 230–31
Hale, Roger: 287
Hanna, R. W.: 150˙
Harding, Pres. Warren G.: 165
Hartz, Harry: 102, 103
Haskins, Sam: 151
Hearne, Eddie: 97, 102
Heggeness, Clark: 300
Heikal, Muhammad Hassanein:
    268, 270
Hellman, Irving H.: 78
Hemphill, Noyes & Company: 144
Hendrick, J. B.: 70
Herbert, Paul A.: 287
Hill, Mason L.: 182, 240
Hitler, Adolph: 201
H. J. Barneson & Company: 54, 60
Hogan, Frank J.: 165
Homan, Glenn J.: 261, 264
Hoots, Harold W.: 182
Hoover, Herbert, Jr.: 190, 271
Hopkins, Harry: 208
Horner, William: 273–74
Houdry, Eugene J.: 232
Howard County, Texas: 38
Humble Oil & Refining Company:
    285, 313, 318, 320
Humphrey, William F.: 151
Hunter, Dulin & Company: 144
Huntington Beach Field (Cali-
    fornia): 31
Hutchinson, H. J.: 182
Hynes refinery (California): 122,
    180

Ickes, Harold L.: 208
Ide, H. Chandler: 209n.
Imperial Oil, Ltd.: 295, 298
Indianapolis, Ind.: 102
Iniskin Peninsula, Alaska: 283

Izaac Walton League of America: 287

Jackson, Dan M.: 18
Jacobs, J. R.: 85, 119
James, Judge William P.: 169–70
James C. Willson & Company: 149
Jeffers, William M.: 206
Jeske, W. E.: 69
Johnson, Gen. Hugh S.: 208
Johnson, Gerald W.: 295
Joiner, Columbus M. ("Dad"): 143
Jones, Charles Stone: 4ff.; joins Rio Grande Oil Company, 21; visits Obregón, 34–36; secures new Rio Grande financing, 38; becomes Rio Grande president, 63; as catalyst between Sinclair Oil and Cities Service, 168, 199–203; becomes Richfield president, 174; opposes navy acquisition of North Coles Levee, 226–28; promotes smog control, 229–32; opposes Sinclair in withdrawal from Texas, 234–37; promotes overseas exploration, 268–72; leads oil-conservation movement in California, 275–80; and government antitrust action, 302ff.; negotiates merger with Atlantic, 308ff.; last act as Richfield chairman, 325
Jones, W. Alton ("Pete"): 160, 162, 164, 167–69, 171, 174, 199ff., 235, 268, 313, 319
Jorgensen, Kai: 186
Juárez, Mexico: 26

Kaveler, Herman H.: 275–76
Kelley, Albert: 97, 103, 179–80
Kellogg, Fred R.: 30, 81–89, 91, 94, 119, 331
Kellogg Oil Company: 81–85, 87
Kelly, H. H.: 178
Kenai Peninsula (Alaska): 268, 284ff., 293, 328
Kent, Jerre M.: 73, 76, 78, 124
Kernan, Francis: 315

Kern County Land Company: 89–90, 189, 194–97, 261
Kettleman North Dome Field (California): 49
Kiefer Field (Oklahoma): 6
Kilgore, Texas: 143
King, W. G., Jr.: 182, 292, 304
Klondike (Canada): 68
Klose, Gilbert C.: 159n.
Knight, Gov. Goodwin J.: 231
Knight, O. A.: 253
Knox, Frank: 225
Kramer, Victor H.: 324
Kuhn, Loeb & Company: 171

Laredo, Texas: 3
Larry Doheny (tanker): 210, 218–19
Larson, Gordon P.: 230–31
Las Cruces, N.Mex.: 20
Las Vegas, Nev.: 291
Law, Robert: 63
Lawrence, Kans.: 86
Lawrence Radiation Laboratory, University of California: 294
Lea, Tom (mayor of El Paso): 18
Lea, Tom (artist): 18
Lea County, N.Mex.: 30
Leffler, Ross: 287
Leithead, Barry: 38
Le Mans, France: 99
Ligon, C.: 18
Lindbergh, Charles A.: 108, 117
Lloyd, Frank T.: 265
Lloyd, Geoffrey: 209
Lockhart, Arthur Mills: 7, 18, 32, 41, 63
Lockhart, Cecil H.: 20, 63
Lockhart, Charles H.: 4
Lockhart, Henry: 163
Lockhart, Herman L.: 18, 63
Lockhart, Leslie Marion: 18, 20, 54–55, 60, 63
Lockhart, Lloyd Earnest: 4ff., 12ff., 18ff., 27, 30ff., 89, 331
Lockhart, Lynn L.: 20, 30, 63
Lockhart & Company: 37

359

Lockheed Aircraft Corporation: 321
Loeb, Joseph F.: 154
Long Beach, Calif.: 76, 123, 131, 204ff., 275, 280
Long Beach Field (California): 205ff., 274, 279–80
Los Angeles, Calif.: 24, 32–33, 35, 38, 42, 53, 61, 70, 78, 81, 85, 89–91, 93, 116, 137, 165, 205, 211, 229ff., 236
*Los Angeles Examiner*: 160
Los Angeles Field (California): 81
Los Angeles Oil & Refining Company: 85, 87
Los Angeles Stock Exchange: 32, 71
*Los Angeles Times*: 230
Los Mochis, Mexico: 34
Lost Hills Field (California): 151–52
Loving County, Texas: 38
*Lusitania*: 4
Luton, Charles D.: 49
Luton, Mrs. Caroline Bell: 42, 49

McAdoo, Eleanor (Mrs. William C.): 44
McAdoo, William C.: 44&n.
McCabe, Louis: 230
McCollum, L. F.: 286
Macdonald, Alexander: 171
MacDonald, George: 171, 202
McDuffie, William Chester: 139, 142, 154, 156–67, 162, 165, 171
McGraw, Max: 287
McKay, Clarence R.: 180
McKay, Douglas: 284
McKee, R. W.: 154–55
McKeon, John: 157
McKittrick Field (California): 68
McPhillips, Frank: 241
Maddux Air Lines: 117
Marathon Oil Company: 30, 268, 288
Maricopa Field (California): 82
Marketing (petroleum products): 34–36, 85–86, 90ff., 122–24,

142–43, 153–59, 180–82, 186–87, 206, 208–209, 234–38
Martin, Austin O.: 73, 76
Mazatlán, Mexico: 34–35
Mellon, Andrew: 235
Merchants National Bank (Los Angeles): 119
Meyer, Louie: 102
Miami, Fla.: 167
Mid-Continent Airlines, Inc.: 117
Mid-Continent Oil & Gas Association: 285–87
Midland, Texas: 234–35
Midway-Six Oil Company: 69
Midway-Sunset Field (California): 68–69, 72, 85, 196
Millikan, Robert A.: 198
Milton, Tommy: 98–99, 102
Mitsubishi Company: 223
Montgomery, Richard A.: 178, 182, 196, 247
Morgan, Frank A.: 41–43, 46, 49, 178, 182, 190, 240, 243
Morgan, Stanley & Company: 310
Morton, Perry W.: 280
Murphy, Jimmy: 99–100, 102

National Audubon Society: 287
National Petroleum Company: 85, 87
National Petroleum Council: 255
National Railways of Mexico: 35
National Wildlife Federation: 287
Natural gas: 194–98, 257–65, 299–301
Natural Resources Council of America: 287
Nasser, Gamal Abdel: 268, 270
National Industrial Recovery Act: 179
Navojoa, Mexico: 34
Newberger, George W.: 131, 154
Newhall, Calif.: 91
New York City, N.Y.: 38, 142–43, 202, 236, 314; Stock Exchange, 54
Nilson, Svend: 220–22
Nishino, Capt. Kizo: 211, 214, 218

Nogales, Mexico: 34, 36
Norman Wells, Canada: 288
Norris Oil Company: 241
North American Wildlife Foundation: 287
North Coles Levee Field (California): 189–99, 224ff., 299
North Slope (Alaska): 284, 307, 316ff., 327ff.

Oakland, Calif.: 123
Obregón, Gen. Álvaro: 3, 35–36
Ohio Oil Company: 30, 189–90, 268, 286
Oil conservation: 194ff., 273ff., 299–300
Oil exploration: 37ff., 76, 91, 151–52, 189–94, 234–35, 239ff., 283ff., 317ff., 327ff.
Oil production: 47ff., 72, 76, 93, 131, 159, 194ff., 204–206, 236, 288–90
Oil refining: 21, 24–25, 27, 30, 38–39, 81–83, 85, 90, 97, 103–104, 122, 124, 180, 207–209, 229ff., 237
Oil Workers International Union: 179, 251–55
Oklahoma City Field: 49, 158–59, 169
Oldfield, Barney: 95
Olin, John M.: 287
Olinda Field (California): 85
Olin Mathieson Chemical Corporation: 287
O'Neil, P. H.: 154, 171
Orange County, Calif.: 85
Orcutt Field (California): 40
Osaka, Japan: 223

Pacific Lighting Corporation: 257, 260, 299–301
Pacific Oil Institute: 252–53
Pacific States refinery (San Francisco): 93
Pacific Western Oil Company: 51, 139, 142, 153, 156, 159

Pan American Petroleum and Transport Company: 137
Pan American Western Petroleum Company: 133–39, 145, 153, 164–66, 170, 174, 179, 302–303
Panero, Tony: 97
Paolo, Peter de: 102–103
Parco Oil Company: 60
Pasadena, Calif.: 171, 203, 229ff.
*Pat Doheny* (tanker): 210
Pearl Harbor, Hawaii: 209–10
Peattie, Donald Culross: 275
Peattie, Louise Redfield: 275
*Perils of Pauline, The*: 324, 326
Perkins, Mrs. F. K.: 250
Pershing, Brig. Gen. John J.: 13–18, 25
Peterson, Rep. Harden: 227
Petroleum Corporation of America: 171
Petroleum Securities Company: 137, 139, 145
*Petroleum Week*: 279n.
Philadelphia, Pa.: 62–63, 312–14, 323–26
Phillips Petroleum Company: 287, 309
Phoenix, Ariz.: 30
Phoenix refinery (Bakersfield): 90
Pierce Petroleum Corporation: 60, 62, 180
Pipelines: 25, 32, 38, 85, 137, 194, 236, 288, 299–301, 318
Point Barrow, Alaska: 317–18
Pomona, Calif.: 94
Porter, Larry E.: 196
Portland, Oreg.: 205
Port Moresby, New Guinea: 220
Prairie Oil & Gas Company: 60, 62–63, 162–63, 200
Prairie Pipe Line Company: 200
Price-Waterhouse & Company: 312
Pringle, William H.: 287
Procter & Gamble Manufacturing Company: 204–205
Providence, R.I.: 143
Prudhoe Bay, Alaska: 307, 318ff., 328ff.

Prudhoe Bay Field (Alaska) : 328ff.

Quesada, Elwood: 109

Racing, auto: 95–103
Ragland, Reginald W.: 226n., 228, 304
Rainier, Nev.: 294
Ramsey, W. R.: 38
Ramsey brothers (oil explorers) : 39
Rattlesnake Dome Field (New Mexico) : 30
Ravel, Arthur: 9–10
Ravel, Louis: 8–9
Ravel, Sam: 8–9
Redondo Beach, Calif.: 89
Reservoir Hill Gasoline Company: 38
Richards, R. W.: 224–25
*Richfield* (tanker) : 123
Richfield Oil Company: 30, 80ff.; founded, 85; capital expanded, 87; role in auto racing, 97–103; role in aviation, 105–17; merges with United Oil, 118–22
Richfield Oil Company of California: 129ff., 302–303; founded, 129; expands northward to Washington State, 131; purchases Pan American, 133–38; goes into receivership, 154ff.
Richfield Oil Corporation: 171ff.; first directors of, 171–72; first officers of, 178; builds Watson refinery, 180, 186; first annual report, 183; discovers North Coles Levee Field, 189ff.; pioneers unitization, 194ff.; gains stake in Wilmington–Long Beach Field, 204ff.; pioneers manufacture of 100-octane gasoline, 207ff.; contributes tankers in World War II, 210ff.; defends North Coles Levee against navy, 224ff.; leads in smog control, 229ff.; withdraws from Texas, 233ff.; discovers Cuyama fields, 239ff.; applies conservation methods, 256ff.;

leads oil-conservation movement in California, 273ff.; discovers Alaskan oil, 283ff.; researches nuclear oil recovery in Canada, 294ff.; merges with Atlantic, 308ff., 322ff.; explores for oil on Alaska's North Slope, 316ff.
Richfield Oil Corporation of New York: 142–43, 148, 151, 165, 168–69
Richfield Station, Calif.: 85, 89
Rio Bravo Oil Company: 39
Rio Grande (river) : 7, 24, 331
Rio Grande Oil Company: 3ff., 122, 142, 163, 165, 169, 171, 178, 196, 205, 232, 234; founded, 7–8; incorporated, 18; opens first refinery, 21, 24–25; builds first Arizona refinery, 30; enters California, 30ff.; builds Vinvale refinery, 32; attempts marketing in Mexico, 34–36; begins exploration, 37–39; reorganizes under Delaware laws, 38; discovers Elwood Field, 40ff.; merges with Sinclair Consolidated, 58ff.
Rio Grande Oil Corporation: 170–71
Rio Grande Valley Bank & Trust Company: 21, 24, 26, 32
Ritchie, W. T.: 9
Rockdale, Texas: 4–6
Rockefeller, John D.: 235
Rocky Mountain Oil & Gas Association: 286
Rogers, R. I.: 78
Rood, Rodney W.: 323
Roosevelt, Pres. Franklin D.: 44n., 208, 218, 225–26, 284, 287
Roseberg, S. R.: 81, 91
Royal Dutch–Shell group: 143, 147, 156, 163
Russell, Hubbard S.: 241, 245–47

Sabath, Rep. Adolph Joaquim: 170n., 303
Sacramento, Calif.: 241

Sand Springs, Okla.: 180
San Francisco, Calif.: 93, 122, 123, 131, 189, 211, 218–19; Stock Exchange, 78
San Joaquin Valley (California): 68, 83, 85, 118, 257
Santa Barbara, Calif.: 39–41, 44, 49, 211, 214
Santa Barbara County, Calif.: 53
*Santa Barbara News-Press*: 44, 46
Santa Cruz, Calif.: 211
Santa Fe, N.Mex.: 309
Santa Fe Springs Field (California): 31–32, 93
Santa Maria District (California): 40
Sarles, Roscoe: 95–99
Schenck, Joseph M.: 174
Schneider, Louis: 102
Schwarzenbach, Ernest B.: 315
Seaton, Fred A.: 285, 287
Shell Oil Company: 76, 130, 200, 317
Sherman, Richard W.: 42–43
Sherman Antitrust Act: 255
Signal Hill Field (California): 31–32, 76, 79, 93, 118, 156, 196
Signal Oil & Gas Company: 50
Simmonds, Norman: 208–209, 304
Sinclair, Harry F.: acquires Rio Grande, 60–63; acquires interest in Richfield, 163ff.; leads in Richfield reorganization, 167ff.; chairman of Richfield board, 174; increases Richfield holdings, 199ff.; forces Richfield withdrawal from Texas, 233ff.
Sinclair Consolidated Oil Corporation (also Sinclair Oil and Consolidated Oil): 60, 62–63, 151, 171, 180, 200, 202, 234–36, 295, 303–304, 306, 314, 318–19, 323, 328
Smith, Barney & Co.: 315
Smith, S. S. ("Syd"): 256
Smog control: 229ff.
Somervell, Gen. Brehon B.: 209, 288

Sour Lake, Texas: 38
South Coles Levee Field (California): 189–90, 198, 224–25, 227
South Cuyama Field (California): 299
Southern California Edison Company: 300
Southern Pacific Railroad: 27, 30, 35, 41
Southwestern Petroleum Company: 131
Spaatz, Carl: 109
Spalding, Mr. & Mrs. Silsby: 51, 142
Sparrows Point, Md.: 219
Spencer, P. C.: 307, 310, 315
Standard Airlines: 116
Standard Oil Company of California: 30–31, 35–36, 85, 130, 138, 142, 147, 165–66, 189–90, 208, 224–27, 285, 288, 317
Standard Oil Company of Indiana: 62, 137
Standard Oil Company of New Jersey: 62
Standard Trust: 62
Starke, Eric A.: 37–38, 41
Steele, Dudley: 108, 116
Steiniger, E. L.: 313, 315
Stewart, William L.: 231
Storke, Thomas M.: 44, 48
Strader, L. F.: 180
Streeter, Thomas W.: 154
Strutt, Erick: 275
Stuart, Adm. H. A.: 224ff.
Suez Canal: 292ff.
Suman, John R.: 39
Summerland, Calif.: 41, 46
Sunray DX Oil Company: 313
Sunray Mid-Continent Oil Company: 286
Superior Oil Company: 261, 264
Swanson River Field (Alaska): 285, 288, 317
Swearingen, John E.: 309
Sweeney, Stender: 182, 304
Symington, Gilbert J.: 30, 81

Symonds, Gardiner: 313

Taft Anti-Inflation Act: 255
Talbot, James A.: 58, 80, 118, 130ff., 142ff., 155; joins United, 78; arranges United-Richfield merger, 119; becomes Richfield president, 128; arranges purchase of Pan American, 133–38; becomes Richfield chairman, 138–39
Taliaferro, Paul: 313
Tankers: 123, 210ff., 290, 292
Teller, Edward: 295
Tenneco, Inc.: 313
Tetzlaff, Teddie: 95
Texas & Pacific Railroad: 27
Texas Company: 6–7
Thompson, Fred: 119
Tide Water Associated Oil Company: 151, 312
Tide Water Oil Company of New York: 151
Tinker, Ned: 57
Toft, Omar: 97–98
Toms, G. Parker: 174
Toplitzky, Joe: 149–50, 154
Transcontinental Air Transport: 117
Transcontinental & Western Air, Inc.: 117
Travers, W. J.: 304
Treanor, John: 154

Union Oil Company of California: 30, 68, 73, 128–29, 163, 231, 276, 288
Union Pacific Railroad: 180, 205–206
United Oil Company: 63, 67ff., 118–19, 130, 151
Universal Consolidated Oil Company: 149–50
Utah Oil & Refining Company: 90

Van Horn, Texas: 6

Van Horn Trading Company: 6
Vaqueros sand: 41
Ventura, Calif.: 39, 300
Vernon, Calif.: 30, 81
Villa, Francisco ("Pancho"): 3–4, 8–15, 26, 33
Vinson, Rep. Carl: 227–28
Vinvale refinery (California): 46, 180

Walker, Elisha: 57
Washington, D.C.: 225, 227–28, 270–71, 323ff.
Waters-Pierce Oil Company: 6
Watson refinery (California): 180, 194, 207, 231
West, A. J.: 241
West Coast Air Transport: 117
Western Air Express, Inc.: 105, 117
Western Oil & Gas Association: 285
Whaley, W. C.: 285
White, Weld & Company: 315
Whittier, Colon F.: 64, 68–69, 76, 78, 89, 119, 124, 131, 151, 331
Whittier, Mericos: 151
Whittier-Campbell Company: 69–70
Wickes, Forsyth: 163
Wilkins, George Herbert: 105, 108
William H. Daum & Company: 32
Williamson, Harold F.: 159n.
Wilmington, Del.: 322, 325–26
Wilmington Field (California): 203ff., 279–80
Wilson, E. T.: 38
Wilson, Pres. Woodrow: 3–4, 11, 18
Wingo, T. M.: 21, 24
Winter, T. A.: 85, 87, 91
Wintergust, Edward F. ("Big Ed"): 98
World War I: 4, 16, 18, 20–21, 25, 86, 211
World War II: 207ff., 284, 288

Zimmermann, Erich W.: 278